Wemyss

WEMYSS OF IRELAND

Theresa Cleaver (*Weymes*)

ACKNOWLEDGEMENT

My gratitude goes to Michael Weymes for his enthusiasm and dedication to sharing the research for Sir Patrick Wemys and Patrick Joseph Weymes of Westmeath. Michael wrote a novelette at the end of this book on PJ Weymes. It is with great regret to say that Michael died November 2019, may he rest in peace. *Michael Weymes family came from Sligo and have no connection to Sir Patrick Wemyss of Danesfort.*

Also, my gratitude to Brid McGrath for her Members of Commons article. Ruth Illingworth for Mullingar History. Ken Bryant Smith for his input on the Wheeler family. Giles Colchester and the national Trust for information on the Colchester's Wemyss. My thanks to many near and distant cousin who sent information to me over the years.

If I have inadvertently missed to give credit where credit is due to any article or references please contact me via my Website and I shall rectify it in the next edition.

CONTENTS

INTRODUCTION

The return of the Ancestors

Poem by Theresa Cleaver

For 30 years I've chased you across the human race, to unexpected nations to find a little trace.

Your face is now in shadows but I will persevere, until the early morning light shall make it all so clear.

It started as tapestry that didn't look quite right, but then I turned it over to a most amazing sight.

For in this lace there was a face from another time and space, awaiting our embrace, from that hidden place.

You thought you were forgotten but your legacies ascend, you are united in our blood, paternity till the end.

First of all, I'll give you a very short brief on me. I was born in Wicklow, Ireland, the youngest child of Joseph and Gertrude Weymes. During the time I was a nurse in London, I met my husband Dave, and we have three adult children. I was dual registered in Psychiatric and General nursing and worked in Dublin, London, Switzerland, and Canada. I won't include my age for vanity reasons and if you're any good at genealogy you'll soon find it. I am a practicing Roman Catholic.

Alas, I never met my grandfather Patrick Joseph Weymes (PJ), and knew nothing about his existence until the age of eleven when to my astonishment my father went to visit him in the local hospital in Westmeath. I pleaded to meet PJ to no avail as my father insisted, he was very old and blind and he was not in any state to accept visitors and he passed away soon after. Later, my father Joe told me how he had been a very rich man, a magistrate, philanthropist, maverick, and a great singer. He also mentioned that PJ was approached by researchers early 1900 who felt he had a good chance of claiming the title of Baronet of Bogie, which eventually went to an American, Sir John Kessler Wemyss.

In 1990s with three young children, I started to research my family tree with the added incentive to discover why the researchers thought my grandfather PJ Weymes might be entitled to the title Baronet of Wemyss. I knew from the fragments of the prerogative Will index of **Francis William Wemys 1782** that my family were mainly military and that we descended from Sir Patrick Wemyss of Danesfort (b. 1604).

I was indeed fortunate that I lived near London so I started my quest at *National Archives, Kew* and the *Society of Genealogists (SOG) London* that holds many army records going back centuries. Along with sending off many letters to archives in Ireland and Scotland I spent many hours in dusty archives milling through records in the days before everything was online.

While putting this book together in July 2020, I discover who Sir Patrick Wemys father was, and it had been buried for years in the research box, and had been overlooked for various reasons. It was the **Testament Dative of Margaret Melville, Sir Patricks grandmother. It mentioned her sons Patrick and Lodovick.** With this I deduced that his father was the Reverend Patrick Wemyss, who married Elizabeth Preston of Fife Scotland.

There have been high and lows in researching, the highs when a some of the puzzle came together and lows when I had to take the convoluted path to discovery. I have been indeed fortunate to have made the acquaintance albeit via email of many of my cousins and distant cousins, both in England, Ireland and as far as America. I have oceans of research and could fill another few books with them, but the key information is set out here. In this book I have included a lot of history to show where they lived in time and the impact this would have had on their lives and personalities, and possibly open a window to an inner world. Hopefully this data will not tire you too much with facts and figures as can be the case with genealogy, and that you too will see your ancestors on these pages which will inspire you to look closer. Perhaps even say a prayer for them. God Bless

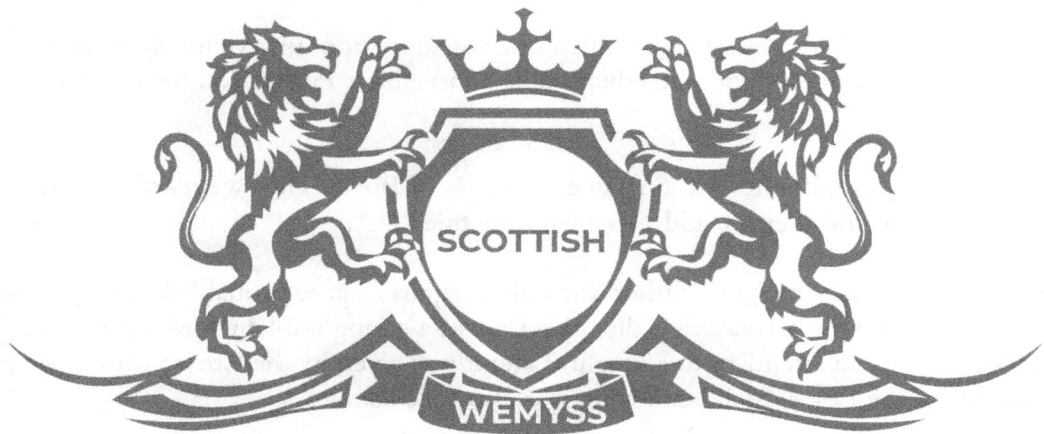

BARONET OF WEMYSS & BOGIE TITLE

& Chieftain of the Clan of Wemyss

In 1900s Patrick Joseph Weymes b. 1879, Westmeath was approached by researchers who considered he had a claim the title of Baronet of Wemyss and Bogie. He was unsuccessful and the title went to Sir John Wemyss Kessler in America. I presume the reason why PJ was unsuccessful was because he did not know who Sir Patrick Wemys b.1604 father was. Fortunately, I found his father this year and he was Patrick Wemys b. abt. 1587 of Raith Fife Scotland.

WEMYSS TITLES

The Wemyss of Ireland were classed as landed gentry and they had a large working estate with tenants in Danesfort Kilkenny. The landed gentry, was a British social class consisting of landowners who could live entirely from rental income, or at least had a country estate. It was distinct from, and socially below, the British peerage.

Knight-Sir Patrick Wemys was a knight which was a military honour, eventually given as a reward for service to the Crown but was not a hereditary title, although Sir Patrick son their son and grandson took the title.

Baronet-Sir Patrick grandfather was Sir James Wemyss of Bogie. They were knights and the title were passed on to his son and they are addressed with the title "Sir".

Esquire-Patrick Weymes my grandfather was called esquire/squire probably because he was a magistrate and owned property. Originally the term was a young nobleman who, in training for knighthood, acted as an attendant to a knight. Later it was given by the Crown for certain positions such as Justice of the Peace. Rich landowner was also called squire.

Gentlemen. In English history, a man entitled to bear arms but not included in the nobility, but also the Church of England clergymen, members of Parliament and army officers.

Wemyss Professions (Gentry four professions: church, law, medicine, military.)

Sir James Wemyss (Baronet) of Bogie was a knight. His children from Margaret Melville - eldest James the heir joined the military. Sir Patrick Wemyss of Danesfort father was the Reverend Patrick Wemyss and his brother Lodovick became a doctor of divinity and vicar.

The Wemyss of Danesfort were all military and ran their estates. The Wemyss of Kildare: Francis Wemyss and Joyce Blundell's children were military. Maurice became a Vicar, James and Patrick were military doctors, James was in the east/west Indies and Patrick was an apothecary in Senegal Africa.

"There is no king who has not had a slave among his ancestors, and no slave who has not had a king among his." Helen Keller

During the Irish Civil War in 1922, the Public Records Office attached to Dublin's Four Courts was burnt down along with hundreds of years of documented history going back to the 14th century, along with grants of land by the crown, and thousands of Wills and title deeds. This made researching my family history in Ireland very difficult. I have had to take a convoluted course with many obstacles to find my ancestors over the past 30 years. This is why I have collected and finished so many different family's trees of Wemys in Ireland some not related to Sir Patrick of Danesfort (b. 1604).

To that end, I have had to rely on other means to get information, for example, newspapers, army records in Key London. Thirty years ago, it was all leg work and dusty archives, but today some are digitalised online, but I had already acquired most of it 20 years ago and a lot has not made it ways onto the internet. It's interesting to note that you can also be fed misinformation online where people just copy the mistakes.

Research for Wemys I started my quest to find the Weymes of Westmeath's ancestors with only an Index to Francis William Wemys prerogative Will index, Offaly 1782. This was all that remained of my Grandfathers Patrick Joseph Weymes research when they tried to link back to Sir Patrick Wemys to acquire the *Title Baronet of Wemyss*. The Weymes of Westmeath is connected to Sir Patrick Wemyss though his grandson Francis Wemyss (1691) who lived only a few miles away from the Westmeath Wemyss at Kill Kildare and had fourteen children with similar names to our own.

FRANCIS WILLIAM WEYMES b.1684 Kildare- *As written* **RefT. 559/41**

Weyms children

Dr Patrick

James

Francis of Toole alias Coolderry Kings Co Will 1782

married Frances Derany

children

Francis

Anne

Mentioned in will of F.W.Lt. Colonel M. Weyms: Jas and Capt. Francis Weyms.

Also, in Will Rev William Weyms and his son William.

All I was given was that our ancestor was either Francis, James or Dr Patrick.

Military records of the above-mentioned family

Army Records: armed forces & conflict on half pay in 1787 English Half-Pay:
Patrick Wemyss 1787 Apothecary Officers of Hospitals- Senegal.
Wemyss 1787 Major Regiment Capt. 20 F.
James Wemyss 1787 1st Lieu Marine Officer Military
Maurice Wemyss 1787 Lt Col Marine Officer Military

Army Records Have the following still on half pay in 1798:
Maurice Wemyss 1798 *Regiment Officers of The Marine Forces*
James Wemyss 1798 *Regiment Officers of The Marine Forces*
Francis Wemyss 1798 *Regiment Officers of The Marine Forces*

Index to Irish Wills Vol 1

Sir Henry Wemys b.1638 Kilkenny, d.1722. **Eliz Butler -**Eliz (Nee Preston ,1st cousin of Sir Patrick Wemys (1604)) Duchess of Ormonde in prerogative WILL 1688 left her estates to Henry Wemyss and Thomas Hume. Same person: Patrick Wemys Probate 1853, Kilkenny, Ireland May-Jun 1853, Patrick Wemys Probate 1853 /Aug-Nov 153, Event Place: Galway, Ireland. **Patrick Wemys 1854 Kilkenny** Probate June 1864 Dublin.

Wemys **James** Residence Danesfort, Co Kilkenny Event Year **1834** Wemys **Patrick** Danesfort, Co Kilkenny **Event Year 1792** Year of Will.

NOTES: PRONI-Original documents confirm that Maurice has two other brother's Dr Patrick and James, Will dated 10 sept 1781 Prerogative 1 March 1782.

*SOURCE: St Thomas Dublin 1750-1791 register. PRONI ** Prerogative WILL index 1782., and Deeds from Dublin Archives. Ireland Landed Estate Court Files, 1850-1885. Probate June- july1864 Dublin-doc no 025 vol 073 -Patrick Wemys, Jan – march 1854 Kilkenny. Doc 060, No 026. Familysearch.com*

SIR PATRICK WEMYSS FATHER

PATRICK WEMYSS *b.abt 1587 Rumgally and Craighall Fife Scotland.*

Patricks residence, was Raith, Fife where his mother Melville's family came from. He was the son of Sir James Wemyss b. abt. 1558 Bogie, Kirkcaldy, Fifeshire, and Margaret Melville of Raith b.1568, d Oct 1598, her father was Lord William Ruthven. Patricks was the grandson of Sir David Wemyss and Cecilia Ruthven.

Patrick married abt 1603 Elizabeth Preston b. abt 1586, Craigmillar Fife Scotland. Her father was Richard Preston of Craigmillar and her brother was Richard Preston who became Baron Dingwall and whose child Elizabeth married James Butler, Earl of Ormond Kilkenny in 1629. So, Patricks mother was Elizabeth who was Elizabeth's Butlers Aunt. See *chapter*

*Patrick was a curate or possibly Vicar at the Church at Hemingbrough, where Abigail was born and later Vicar at St Stephens church Acomb, near York. Patrick died young possibly shortly after 1610.

Patrick Wemyss & Elizabeth Preston's children

Patrick Wemys b. 1604

Abigail Wemyss b. 10 Feb 1610, of Hemingbrough, York. She who married Mr Griffith

NOTE: I cannot prove this Vicar is Patrick, however Sir Patrick had a sister Abigail born about this time and Patricks brother Dr Lodovick became a Vicar which was common for the gentry. Abigail b 1610 is stated as Patrick Weems daughter Hemingbrough, York. In Sir Patrick Will index Abigale is married to Mr Griffith.

SOURCE: THE HISTORY OF HEMINGBROUGH. 1610-11, Feb. 5. Abigail, dau. Patrick Weemes 14 of Hemingbrough, bp. 14 Patrick Weemes was vicar of Acomb, near York. Was he at this time one of the curates at Hemingbrough ? https://archive.org/stream/historyantiquiti00burt/historyantiquiti00burt_djvu.txt Elizabeth married a second time Richard Christy by whom she had a son Richard Christy who was Sir Patricks half-brother.

REVERAND PATRICK WEMYSS

SIR PATRICK WEMYS father

Finding Sir Patricks father only came to light when I was finally laying the script ready for publication in June 2020.

Nineteenth Century researchers on Sir Patrick, father.

According to James Graves 1874 (see picture) who saw the papers of the Danesfort Wemyss had in their possessions Sir Patrick's father was another Sir Patrick Wemyss of Rumgally and Craig Hall.

Fife Grandson of:

Sir David Wemyss of Wemyss, married Cecilia Ruthven.

Sir David's Wemyss sons

John, Henry. Andrew, David and:

Patrick Wemyss b. 1565 d. 1625 was Laird of Rumgally and Craig Hall Fife. He married Elizabeth Sandilands abt. 1590 and his sons were David, William and John.

Sir James Wemyss of Bogie married **Margaret Melville** and secondly Elizabeth Dune Durie.

JAMES WEMYSS of Bogie & MARGARET MELVILLE b. abt 1568. d. 1598 married 1686

Their children:

Sir James Wemyss of bogie HEIR, b. abt 1586

Patrick Wemyss b. abt 1586 d. abt1615

Dr Lodovick Wemyss b. abt 1587 d.1659 London

Second marriage: James Wemyss married to Elizabeth Durie and their children **were** David, George, Henry, Andrew.

MARGARET MELVILLE WILL

Margaret Melville left an inheritance to her other 2 sons, Dr Lodovick and Patrick. The Melville's were from Raith and there is an entre for a Patrick Wemyss of Raith relative of Alexander Melville, hence why he is called Patrick Wemyss of Raith.

TESTEMENT Margaret (Melville) Wemyss - *Patrick Wemyss & Dr Lodovick Wemyss Bogie*

CC8/8/34 - recorded 10 November **1599 - Testament Dative of Margaret Melville sometime spouse to James Wemyss of Bogie** within the parish of Kirkcaldy who died in October 1598 **given** up by James, Wemyss, her husband as father and administrator to their children Lodovick **and Patrick Wemyss.**

H.M.C. Ormond, N.S.11, P355: Sir Patrick Wemyss has rented land of Danesfort from Elizabeth Preston Butler and James Viscount Thurles.

*...**Patrick Weymes and Richard Christy** gentlemen, the said Richard late Earl of Desmond his **sisters soones** and couzin germen to the said Lady Elizabeth Preston and their assigns for the tearme of one and twenty years, one paire of gloves of gloves price xxs onto the said Lady Elizabeth Preston and the heirs males of her begotten, at the feast of Michas yearly, if the same be lawfully demanded, shall be enjoyed by the said Patrick Weymes and Richard Christy and their assigns for and during the said tearme of one and twenty years any thinge herain contained to the contrary thereof in any notwithstanding.*

SOURCE: **Scottish Archives.** *https://archive.org/stream/heraldgenealogis08nich/heraldgenealogis08nich_djvu.txt.*

SIR PATRICK WEMYS MOTHER

ELIZABETH PRESTON of Craighall Fife Scotland

Sir Patrick Wemyss b.1604 Ireland mother Elizabeth was the only sister of Sir Richard Preston Earl of Desmond.

Elizabeth Preston's marriages

Elizabeth first marriage was to Patrick Wemyss of Raith about 1603. On a prerogative Will index for Sir Patrick there was an Abigail also written as his sister. Elizabeth's second marriage was to a gentleman called Richard **Christy** by whom she had a son Richard Christy (half-brother to Sir Patrick). This is documented in Elizabeth Preston Butler (Patrick first cousin) lease of the land of Danesfort for both brothers in 1629 the year of her marriage to the Earl of Ormond.

NOTE TC: *James & Margaret son **Patrick** could not be from Rumgally and Craig Hall Fife because that was his Uncles Patrick estate see above. So, the reply to Reverend James Graves was correct.*

There is among the same records a long list of Lawrences whose property was confiscated at the same period. This may account for the sudden termination of some of the branches of the family.

R. GWYNNE LAWRENCE.

Tong.

The WEMYSS BARONETCY.—Your correspondent S * * * (p. 62 *supra*) seems to be in error as to the son of Sir James Wemyss of Bogie, who married the sister of Lord Dingwall. Papers in the possession of the Wemyss family of Danesfort, co. Kilkenny, *seem* to show that the father of Sir Patrick Wemyss who settled in Ireland was another Sir Patrick, who married Lord Dingwall's sister, and not Sir John. I append a tentative sketch of the pedigree:

Sir David Wemyss, of Wemyss,=Cecilia, dau. of William
ob. 1591.   Lord Ruthven.

Sir John Wemyss.   Sir James Wemyss, of Bogie.

John We-   James   Sir Patrick Wemyss,=A sister of Sir Richard Preston,
myss, Earl   Wemyss,   of Rumgally and Craig   created Lord Dingwall and Earl
of Wemyss.   died s.p.   hall in Fifeshire.   of Desmond by James I.

Sir Patrick Wemyss, knt. settled in Ireland. His
seal of arms, Quarterly, four lions rampant, a
crescent for difference.

Sir James Wemyss, of Danesfort, co. Kilkenny.

If any of the readers of *The Herald and Genealogist* could give the names of Sir Richard Preston's sisters, and their matches, it would settle the question.

Inistog, Stonyford, March 26, 1873.   JAMES GRAVES.

In his previous communication, vol. vii. p. 479, Mr. GRAVES puts Sir Patrick Wemyss, first of Danesfort, as son of — Wemyss, a native of Scotland, and — Preston his wife, and asks for information as to Sir Patrick's Scotch ancestry. He now calls Sir Patrick son of another *Sir* Patrick, whom he styles of Rumgally and Craighall. According to Douglas's *Peerage*, the founder of the Rumgally or Rumgay family was Patrick, fifth son of Sir David Wemyss of Wemyss, and younger brother, *not son*, of Sir James of Bogie. The dates of the marriages of the brothers and sisters of this Patrick range from 1574 to 1598, so that as far as time is concerned he might have been father of Danesfort, who died in 1661, but is there proof that he was?

Lamont says that in 1658 Wemyss of Rumgay, then a young man, sold the estate for 16,000 merks to Mr. James McGill, minister at Largo: he adds that Rumgay held of the laird of Craighall.

Craighall did not belong to the Wemyss; it was purchased by Sir Thomas Hope, Lord Advocate, from the old family of Kynynmond, and is still in the possession of his descendants.

S * * *

*The Wemyss Baronetcy. — Your correspondent S * * * (p- 62 supra) seems to be in error as to the son of Sir James Wemyss of Bogie, who married the sister of Lord Dingwall. Papers in the possession of the Wemyss family of Danesfort, co. Kilkenny, seem to show that the father of Sir Patrick Wemyss who settled in Ireland was another Sir Patrick, who married Lord Dingwall's sister, and not Sir John. I append a tentative sketch of the pedigree:*

Sir David Wemyss, of \Verayss,=Cecilia, dau. of William ob. 1591. I Lord Ruthven.

Sir John Wemyss. Sir James Wemyss, of Bogie.

John We- James Sir Patrick Wemyss, =pA sister of Sir Richard Preston,

Wemyss, Earl Wemyss, of Rumgally and Craig

of Wemyss. died v. p. hall in Fifeshire. 4s created Lord Dingwall and Earl

of Desmond by James I. _i

Sir Patrick Wemyss, knt. settled in Ireland. His seal of arms, Quarterly, four lions rampant, a crescent for difference.

Sir James Wemyss, of Danesfort, co. Kilkenny.

If any of the readers of The Herald and Genealogist could give the names of Sir Richard Preston's sisters, and their matches, it would settle the question.

Inisnag Stonyford Maixh 26, 1873. James Graves.

In his previous communication, vol.vii. p.479, Mr. Graves puts Sir Patrick Wemyss, first of Danesfort, as son of— Wemyss, a native of Scotland, and — Preston his wife, and asks for information as to Sir Patrick's Scotch ancestry. He now calls Sir Patrick son of another Sir Patrick, whom he styles of Eumgally and Craighall.

According to Douglas's Peerage^ the founder of the Rumgally or Rumgay family was Patrick, fifth son of Sir David Wemyss of Wemyss, and younger brother, not son, of Sir James of

Bogie. The dates of the marriages of the brothers and sisters of this Patrick range from 1574 to 1598, so that as far as time is concerned, he might have been father of Danesfort, who died in 1661, but is there proof that he was?

*Lamont says that in 1658 Wemyss of Rumgay, then a young man, sold the estate for 16,000 merks to Mr. James McGill, minister at Largo: he adds that Rumgay held of the laird of Craighall. Craighall did not belong to the Wemyss; it was purchased by Sir Thomas Hope, Lord Advocate, from the old family of Kynynmond, and is still in the possession of his descendants. t^ * * * 62*

NOTES AND QUERIES. The Wemyss Baronetcy (Yol. VI. p. 479) Is your correspondent in re Wemyss following up the descent from a son of Sir James of Bogie, which may be suggested as not improbable? If that descent ould be proved, it appears that Wemyss of Danesfort may be heir male of the family, and perhaps as such entitled to a Baronetcy.

The Herald and Genealogist 1874.

VOLUME THE EIGHTH. LONDON: ' ' R. C. NICHOLS AND J. B. NICHOLS, PRINTERS TO THE SOCIETY OF ANTIQUARIES, 25, PARLIAMENT STREET, WESTMINSTLft.

1) The Wemyss Baronetcy (Yol. VI. p. 479) Is your correspondent in re Wemyss following up the descent from a son of Sir James of Bogie, which may be suggested as not improbable? If that descent could be proved, it appears that Wemyss of Danesfort may be heir male of the family, and perhaps as such entitled to a Baronetcy.

Sir David Wemyss of Wemyss. Sir John. Sir James of Bogie.

2)John Earl of James, died John an officer in the army, went to Ireland and Wemyss. v. p. left issue.? married sister of Lord Dingwall.

David Earl Sir John David, Henry, Mr. George, of Wemyss, of Bogie, of Bal- of East Principal of

died s. p.m. died s, p, farg. Cou- St. Leonard's 1679. land. College.

Sir James of Bogie, created Ludovick, Margaret, wife a Baronet 1705; male de- died s. p. of Archbishop seendants extinct. Paterson.

3)Danesfort.

It is stated that the title is destined to heir's male whatsoever, which may be the case, although very unusual at so late a date. It is at present assumed by a John Wemyss resident in India, cousin and heir of a gentle-

4)man who assumed it some 40 years ago. They state themselves to descend from a brother of Mrs. Paterson who had been disinherited by his father. There is, however, I think distinct evidence that Margaret Wemyss was an only child. In 1659 she was served Heir general, not heir of provision, of her father. Lamont in his invaluable Diary gives details as to her marriage and sale of East Couland, — nothing of a brother.

*S * * **

ORIGINS OF THE NAME WEMYSS

My family wrote their name as in Gaelic as Uaimeas (derived from Scottish Gaelic) whereas Michael Weymes wrote his name in Gaelic as Debhuimh (which is of course derived from the Irish Gaelic).

The name Wemyss is said, to derive from the (Scottish) Gaelic word "Uiam" meaning "cave". This Gaelic word, when used by people speaking in Old English became "Weim" or "Weem". It then evolved over time into the villages present name "Wemyss". Some Linguists scholars have said that Wemyss is derived from the Gaelic word "Uiam" meaning cave. It later became "uamh"[oo-arv or oorv], which later evolved into Weim and Weem. If "-ais" is added onto the end of the word (eg "Uiam" becomes "Uiamais") the meaning changes to "at the cave". This variant of the word evolved over time into Wemyss. A third view we have found is that a cave in the old Gaelic or Celtic (Scottish variant), was called vumhs or wamh; from that these lands received the name of Vumhs-shire-- Wemys-shire.

Variant speeling of the name Wemyss

De Bhuimh is the Irish (Gaelic)Wemyss Wemys Wyms Wymes Weymes Wimbs Wymbs Weems, Wames Weims Wymess Weimis, Weimys Weyms Weymis Wemes, Wems Weemyss Wemise Wemyes, Weeme Waymus Waymes Wymbly,Wims Wimsey Wymsey Wheims,Wheims Wymie Wyme Whyms Wyme Veims Vemyss Veymis Van Weymes.

Wemyss Caves

There are several major caves at Wemyss, each with its own name. They are all at the base of the cliff, and they look out across the Firth of Forth estuary to the North Sea. Wemyss Bay on the West coast of Scotland is sometimes assumed to be the place of origin of the Wemyss - but this is in fact wrong. In local legend it is thought that Wemyss Bay is named after a well-known local character/resident who had the name Wemyss.

For the purpose of this genealogy book and to avoid confusion, we will be concentrating on the family of the Baronetcy of Wemyss and Bogie which eventually passed to a Sir John Wemyss Kessler in America. However below is a short summary on the Earl of Wemyss and March.

SIR JOHN WEMYSS -Mary Queen of Scots and the Wemyss Castle

The Scottish Wemyss family had possessed the lands of Wemyss in Fife since the 12th century.

My father Joe often told me the folklore that when Mary Queen of Scots was staying in the Wemyss castle one of the young male Wemyss's stayed hidden under her bed for the night. Luckily, he was not detected or it might have been off with his head and perhaps I would not be telling this story.

SIR JOHN WEMYSS. b.1513 d. abt. 1572 Son of David Wemyss and Catherine (Sinclair) Wemyss. Sir John Wemyss was a great supporter of Mary, Queen of Scots, and it was at the newly enlarged Wemyss Castle that she first met her future husband c1564, Henry Stuart, Lord Darnley. Sir John was made lieutenant of Fife, Kinross and Clackmannan in 1559. He led his men in the queen's army at the Battle of Langside in 1568. He fought the English fleet during its attempt to land near Wemyss Castle. Fought in Battle of Pinkie in 1547, was captured, but later released. Sir John Wemyss married twice and had twelve children. First wife Margaret and he divorced her in 1556 and second wife Janet Trail.

EARL OF WEMYSS AND MARCH

SIR JOHN WEMYSS- 1ST EARL OF WEMYSS
Earl of Wemyss and March and the the Baronets of Wemyss and Bogie share a common ancestry, Sir David Wemyss of Wemyss and Cecilia Ruthven. Also, Sir David was Sir Patrick Wemyss of Danesfort great grandfather.

Earl of Wemyss and Earl of March are two titles in the Peerage of Scotland, created in 1633 and 1697 respectively, that have been held by a joint holder since 1826. John was b.abt 1586 d.1649 in Wemyss, Fifeshire, Scotland. He was the son of John Wemyss and Mary (Stewart) Wemyss and grandson of: Sir David Wemyss of Wemyss and Cecilia Ruthven. John Wemyss died in 1649 and was succeeded by his only son, David Wemyss, 2nd Earl of Wemyss.In 1625 John Wemyss was created a Baronet, of Wemyss in the County of Fife, in the Baronetage of Nova Scotia. In 1628 he was raised to the Peerage of Scotland as Lord Wemyss of Elcho, and in 1633 he was further honoured when he was made Lord Elcho and Methel and Earl of Wemyss. He later supported the Scottish parliament against Charles I, and died in 1649. He was succeeded by his son David, the second Earl who spent a lifetime nurturing the resources of his estate, in particular his salt and coal mines. In 1672 David resigned his peerages to the Crown in return for a new patent with original precedence and extending the limitation to his daughters. Lord Wemyss had no male issue and on his death in 1679 the baronetcy became extinct. He was succeeded in the peerages according to the new patent by his daughter Margaret, the third Countess of Wemyss. She married as her first husband, her third cousin twice removed Sir James Wemyss, Lord Burntisland. He was the son of General Sir James Wemyss of Caskieberry, grandson of James Wemyss, younger brother of Sir John Wemyss, Great-grandfather of the first Earl of Wemyss. She was succeeded by her son from her first marriage, David, the fourth Earl. ____ The present Earl of Wemyss and March James lives with his wife Amanda Feilding in their Gloucestershire home Stanway.

SOURCES: en.wikipedia.org/wiki/Earl of Wemyss and March. Sir William Frazer's 'Memorials of Wemyss of Wemyss which are available at www.internet archives.org. en.wikipedia.org/wiki/Clan Wemyss

DAVID WEMYSS OF WEMYSS

David was b abt 1535 d. 22 Feb 1597 in Wemyss, Fife, Scotland.

His father was: Sir John Wemyss b.11 July 1513 d.1571 in Perth, Perthshire, mother was Margaret Otterburn b.1515, d. bef 1567 in Redhall, Scotland. They were divorced in 1556. He second wife was, Janet Trail.

Sir John Wemyss of Wemyss and Margaret Otterburn children

John Wemyss d. abt. 1571- 1st EARL OF WEMYSS

Sir David Wemyss of Wemyss *see below*

Margaret Wemyss d. Sep 1608

Agnes Wemyss

Elizabeth Wemyss

Eupheme Wemyss **d**. 16 Nov 1593

Sir John Wemyss of Wemyss and Janet Trail Children

Gavin Wemyss

Patrick Wemyss d. a 1596

SIR DAVID WEMYSS OF WEMYSS *1572-1597*

Sir David Wemyss- ancestor of the families of Bogie, baronets, and of some families of the name in Ireland.

In 1557 he took his father place to lead his men in battle and continued to do so. He succeeded his father in the barony of Wemyss on 14 May 1572. He won the young King James VI.'s favour by lending money to him on more than one occasion. During the festivities in May 1590, ensuing on the King's marriage with Anna of Denmark, Wemyss was honoured by a royal request that he should for one-night give hospitality to certain distinguished Danish visitors. King James himself was a guest in the castle in the following June. David married Cecilia on the 7 May 1556, daughter of William, Lord Ruthven and sister of Patrick, 3 rd. Lord Ruthven.

David Wemyss and Cecilia Ruthven children:

Sir John Wemyss of Wemyss HEIR d. Jun 1622. *He succeeded* his father David in Feb 1597 He married in 1574, Margaret, daughter of Sir William Douglas of Lochleve.

Sir James Wemyss of Bogie d. c 1640 2. Married Margaret daughter of John Melville of Raith in 1585

Andrew Wemyss b.*1583 d 1583. he* received half-lands of Newton Markinch, Fife, on 3d January 1577.

Patrick Wemyss of Rumgay b1560 abt. d.1625 obtained the lands of Rumgay. He married Elizabeth Sandilands.

David Wemyss, forebear of the Wemys of Fingask

Henry Wemyss d.1652, forebear of the Wemys of Foodie

Margaret Wemyss d. Sep 1636 she married James Bethune of Creich.

Jean Wemyss, she married to James Macgill of Ran|keillor, in 1578.

Cecilia Wemyss she married to—Kinnynmonth of that ilk, anno 1585.

Elizabeth Wemyss, she married to Alexander Wood of Lamyletham, in 1597.

Isobel Wemyss, she married to John Auchmoutie of that ilk.

SOURCE *The Peerage of Scotland By Robert Douglas, Esq;.1767 , XXII. Sir DAVID, ____He married Cecilia, * daughter of William second lord Ruthven, ancestor of the earls of Gowrie, by whom he had five sons, and five daughters. _____ *Sir David Wemyss, was ancestor of the families of Bogie, baronets, and of some families of the name in Ireland. Douglas' Baronage, p, 561, and the Scots Peerage, vol 8, p.493ff, Sir William Fraser r (1888 Category Birth, Marriage, Death & Parish Records 1577, in Wemyss Charter-chest. * Register of the Commissariat or Edinburgh. The peerage of Scotland: collected from the public records, and ancient chartularies of this nation, ... Illustrated with copper-plates. By Robert Douglas, Esq; Douglas, Robert, Sir, 1694-1770. https://www.thepeerage.com/p1256.htm., The peerage of Scotland.*

PATRICK WEMYSS & ELIZABETH SANDILANDS

While researching Sir Patrick Wemyss father -eliminated this Patrick.

Testament dative of -Elizabeth Sandilands, wife of Patrick Wemys b abt 1560 d.1625 of Rumgay.

Their son: **Patrick Wemyss** b. abt **1591 of** Rumgay, Fife, Scotland.

Elizabeth Sandilands. d.2 February 1606 and her executor were her husband, Patrick Wemys as father and lawful administrator for David, John and William Weyms, their lawful children. **James Wemys of Bogie** was cautioner (Edinburgh Commissary Court - CC8/8/42/1 - 13 June 1606).

Rumgay also known as Rumgallie

Testament dative of **Patrick Wemys of Rumgallie.** He died June **1625** and his inventory was given up by his son, David Wemys 'now of Rumgallie'. The cautioner was Mr William Wemys, student at the University of St Andrews (who is more than likely his son mentioned in Elizabeth Sandilands' testament dative) (St Andrews Commissary Court CC20/4/8 - 9 February 1626)

Ancestor of Wemyss of Craigshall Fife

The Commissariat Record of Edinburgh, 1600-1700. List of Burials excerpted from Register in possession of the Registrar of the Canongate. The Commissariat Record of Edinburgh. Register of Testaments. Second Section--1601-1700.

Wemyss, Patrik, of Rumgay. See Sandilands, Elizabeth.

Owner of Rumgay: Rumgay appears to have belonged to George Douglas brother of William Douglas of Lochleven in the 1580s. The Fife Sasines record David Wemys being served heir to his father, 28 August 1625 in the lands of Rumgay. The feudal superior was Mr Thomas Hope of Craighall (Lord Advocate) (RS31/5 f.438)

JAMES WEMYSS BARONET OF WEMYSS

First Baronet of Wemyss

Wemys of Danesfort Kilkenny Ireland are descendent from this line

SIR JAMES OF BOGIE b abt.1558. d.1640, fife Scotland was the second son of Sir David Wemyss b. 1535 d.1597 and Cecilia Ruthven.

He married in 1585, MARGARET MELVILLE d.1598, daughter of John Melville of Raith. He married secondly, ELIZABETH DURIE, on 22 May 1599 sister of Robert Durie of that ilk

Sir James Wemyss & Margaret's Melville's children

James Wemyss-HEIR*. b abt 1585 d.1640, Kirkcaldy Bogie Fife. Married Margaret Kininmonth had three children, the eldest, who was named John and who followed his grandfather as Sir James Wemyss of Bogie because James predeceased his father Sir James Wemyss. James named as a witness at a baptism for the James son of David his brother on January 1641.

Patrick Wemyss b. abt 1586, d abt 1615. Fife, Scotland, (still living in 1599-see testament Margaret Melville). *Irish Wemyss ancestor.*

Dr Lodovick Wemyss b. abt, 1587d abt 1640. Lodovick Wemyss, Doctor of Divinity, is named on 20th August 1631 in connection with an assignation by Sir James Wemyss of Bogie, his father. He is also referred to in a writ of 6th October 1658, where his son James is nominated.

PATRICK WEMYSS & DR LODOVICK WEMYSS BOGIE

*Testament **Margaret (Melville) Wemyss**: CC8/8/34 - recorded 10 November 1599 - testament dative of Margaret Melville sometime spouse to James Wemyss of Bogie within the parish of Kirkcaldy who died in October 1598 given up by James, Wemyss, her husband as father and administrator to their children Lodovick and Patrick Wemyss. He was appointed executor dative by decree of the Commissary Clerk on the 25 July 1599.*

*SOURCE: Scottish Archives * Scots Peerage -vol VIII, pp.493-496 - National Library of Scotland.*

Second wife -Elizabeth Durie b. abt 1562 d. aft.1653. at Bogie, Kirkcaldy, Fifeshire, Scotland. Marriage contract dated 22nd of May 1599, and she survived her husband and died in April 1653.

Sir James Wemyss of Bogie & Elizabeth Durie Children

John Wemyss Esq, an officer in the army, who having acquired a considerable fortune settled in Ireland, married a sister of Lord Dingwall and is the ancestor of Wemyss of Danesfort. *(We never found any documents to this effect)*

*Henry Wemyss. b. abt 1599, d. abt 1645. Purchased land at Easter Conland from his sister Janet about 1643. His grandson carried on the line of the Baronet of Bogie. He married 1st 1639 Isabel, daughter of Sir John of Kirkcarldy of the Grange, by whom he had 5 children. He married secondly, in 1653 Margaret, daughter of Robert Durie of East Newton and Margaret Durie, his wife but by her hand no issue.

*David Wemyss b. 1600 Bogie, Kirkcaldy, Fifeshire, Scotland. d. bef 1653. David by his wife Margaret Orrock, left two sons and two daughters, James baptized 1st January 1641; John baptized 23rd of October 1646, Elizabeth, baptized June 1st 1642; all three named in the Will of their Aunt Janet Wemyss on April 1st 1653, and another daughter Janet, baptized 25th June 1643.

George Wemyss b. abt. 1605 d. unk. Principal of Saint Leonard's College, Saint Andrews, appears as a son of *Sir James Wemyss of Bogie, and Elizabeth Durie* in various writs, beginning 15th January 1631. He was admitted Provost of the Old College there on 1st November 1664. He married Magdalene Lundie with whom he had a charter of Wester Pitcaple on 1st March 1648.

Andrew Wemyss d. 1649. of Glennistoun is named, in 1653, as a brother of Janet Wemyss, referred to below. He had a daughter, Elizabeth named in her aunt's will, and an inventory of his effects was given up on 4th January 1673 by James Wemyss of Glennistoun, perhaps his son.

Elizabeth Wemyss. b. abt 1608 Bogie, Kirkcaldy, Fifeshire, Scotland. Married first John Boswell of Pittedy 1628, secondly, 1638 James Arnott of Wester Fernie.

Janet Wemyss d.1640 married John Lunie son of Robert Lunie of Baigonie he was Laird of Easter Conland. She sold Easter Conland to her brother *Henry* a short time before his death. She made her will in April 1643, and in it she named her brothers, ***James, David, and Andrew*** with their children, and appointed her nephew *Sir John Wemyss of Bogie* her executor. She died on the 20 April 1653 without issue.

SOURCE: *Scots Peerage Documents from the Dublin archive. www.thepeerage.com/p1371.htm#i13706* ***Bond of provision by their father Sir James Wemyss, David Wemyss, named with his brother Henry in a bond of provision by their father Sir James Wemyss of Bogie, of date 11 October 1622. They were sons of Elizabeth Durie.** SOURCE: *Children of Sir James and Eliz Durie taken from: The House of Wemyss: A Thousand Year History by Sir John Wemyss Kessler*

Other references to Sir James Wemyss of Bogie

Baronage of Scotland -(1798) page 561 -documents from the archives

'Sir James Wemyss, 2nd son of Sir David Wemyss of Wemyss obtained from his father the patrimony of the lands of Bogie and others. He received a charter under the Great Seal on 2 February 1519. He married Margaret, daughter of John Melville of Raith and had several children, **but only one reached maturity**, a son James who married Elizabeth, daughter of David Durie.

NOTE: It is not true that "**but only one reached maturity** "because their son Rev Dr Lodovick Wemyss died in 1640 and Patrick his brother died after 1610.

Lodge's peerage of Ireland v. III. p. 307 *

Sir James Wemyss of Bogie, of whom the present Sir James Wemyss of Bogie is lineally descended; also, some considerable families of the name of Wemyss in Ireland.

Source details/peerageofscotlan00lond/page/286/mode/2up/search/Wemyss Burke's Peerage, Baronetage & Knightage

NOTE: Michael Weymes and I did extensive research to find this John but found no proof of him. I believe this John is in fact Patrick b.1586 Margaret Melville son mentioned in testament 1599. See chapter on who was the Sir Patrick father. In Burks peerage there is no mention of the second marriage to Eliz Durie but this marriage is well documented elsewhere.

Earlier connections to the Melvilles: *The Melvilles Earls of Melvilles and the Leslies Earls of Leven* By Sir William Fraser K.C.B. Indenture between Sir John Wemyss of that Ilk and John Melville of Raith, relative to the water privilege of the Mill of Pitconmark,2th June 1427, (Page245). Bond of Manrent by John Melville, heir-apparent of Raith, to Sir John Wemyss of that Ilk,6th August 1487.

SOURCE: * www.peerageofscotlan00lond/page/286/mode/2up/search/wemyss. Burke's Peerage, Baronetage & Knightage. Scotland, Fife Death Index, 1549-1877 Record set Scotland, Fife Death Index, 1549-1877 * Sir David Wemyss, second son Sir James Wemys http://tei.it.ox.ac.uk/tcp/Texts-HTML/free/K11/K113361.000.html, https://archive.org/. *James Wemyss the eldest taken from Scots Peerage-vol VIII, pp.493-496 - National Library of Scotland.

Other references to Patrick of Raith: *Patrick Wemyss- of Raith*, Fife, Scotland, Relative -Alexander MELVILLE

JAMES WEMYSS of Bogie *b.1590 d. 1634*

James father was Sir James Wemyss of Bogie and his mother was Margaret Melville. James did not become his father's heir, because he pre-deceased his father who died in 1640. James son, became Sir John of Bogie and was educated by the elder Sir James, their grandfather.

Margaret Kinninmonth Wife- James, the eldest son and apparent heir of Sir James of Bogie married Margaret 1612, (b. 1589 d.1640 Wemyss castle) daughter of Andrew Kinninmonth of that ilk, by Helen his wife, daughter of Henry lord Sinclair, and by her he had three sons and one daughter.

Sir James Wemys b. 1590 and Margaret's Kinninmonth Children

Sir John Wemyss b. aft 1612, d.aft 1689, who became his grandfather's heir.

David Wemyss of Balfarg b. abt 1615 m. Mary Wemyss (dau of David Wemyss of Fingask). His son became Sir James Wemyss of Bogie after Sir John died in about 1672.

Henry Wemyss who got from his grandfather, the lands of Contine, etc. and married Isabel, daughter of Sir John Kirkcaldy of Grange

Elizabeth Wemyss, who married Alexander Orrock

SIR JOHN WEMYSS OF BOGIE

Second Baronet of Wemyss

John was b. aft 1612, d before 02.1679. John was the eldest son of James Wemyss and Margaret Kinninmonth. *Sir John Wemyss of Bogie married 08.1635 to Margaret Elizabeth Aytoun daughter of Sir John Aytoun. James second marriage 20.08.1675 to Margaret Johnston d bef 16.08.1707, daughter of Sir Archibald Johnston of Wariston. Sir John lived in great extravagance leaving the estate overwhelmed in debt, he died without issue and was succeeded by his nephew James Wemys the son of his brother David Wemyss.

*John succeeded his grandfather Sir James Wemyss of Bogie in 1640. He was knighted by King Charles I while still a young man. "He was put in possession of the lands and barony of Bogie, also the coal and salt works about Kirkcaldy, by his grandfather Sir James, many years before his death." He got a Crown Charter under the seal of King Charles II dated 26 Jan 1666.

NOTE: Margaret was the daughter of Andrew Kinninmonth by his second wife Cecilia Wemyss, daughter of David Wemyss and sister of Sir James Wemyss of Bogie.

*SOURCE: The Baronage of Scotland, Containing an Historical and Genealogical Account of the Gentry of that Kingdom by Sir Robert Douglas of Glenbervie, Edinburgh, 1798, page 561 *Douglas, Robert, Sir, The Baronage of Scotland, Vol. I, Edinburgh, 1798. Pages 561f. Paul, James Balfour, Sir, The Scots peerage; founded on Wood's edition of Sir Robert Douglas's peerage of Scotland; containing an historical and genealogical account of the nobility of that kingdom, Vol. VIII, Edinburgh, 1911. Pages 495f.*

Legislation- Act appointing Sir John Wemyss [of Bogie] to be commissary-general

The estates of parliament, having taken into their consideration the report of the grand committee concerning the great obstruction found by them in their procedure and taking course for providing of magazines of victual by the want of a commissary-general, and finding [Sir Adam Hepburn of] Humbie altogether unwilling to accept that charge, and herewith also considering and having real proof and experience of the affection and fidelity of Sir John Wemyss of Bogie and of his abilities to exercise and discharge the office and place of treasurer of the army and commissary-general of the kingdom, the said estates of parliament did therefore unanimously, after voicing, nominate, elect and choose the said Sir John Wemyss of Bogie, knight, to the aforesaid place and office to be treasurer of the army and to be commissary-general of the whole kingdom and of all the forces, armies, regiments and companies levied or to be levied and employed within the same, with all privileges, honours, fees and casualties belonging thereto, with power to him to nominate and constitute deputes, one or more, to serve in the said place. And ordain [Sir Alexander Gibson of Durie], clerk register, to draw up a commission in favour of the said Sir John Wemyss to the aforesaid place and office.

SOURCE: NAS. PA2/23, f.428v.

DAVID OF BALFARGE SHERIFF OF FIFE & LAIRD OF WEMYSS

David Wemyss of Balfrage b. 1615, d. 1647, at Fife Scotland. He was the second son of James Wemyss of Bogie, and Margaret Kinninmonth.

He obtained from his grandfather Sir James of Bogie the land of Balfarge in the parish of Markinch.

"David, or Mr. David of Balfarg, referred to in writs of 1672 and others, as brother of Sir John Wemyss of Bogie. In September 1653 he obtained the office of Sheriff of Fife.

He is said to have married Mary, daughter of David Wemyss of Fingask and had issue:

Sir James Wemyss, who succeeded his uncle Sir John in Bogie.

Ludovick Wemyss, said to be drowned at sea with his only child.

Margaret Wemyss, was married to David Boswell of Devon

SOURCE: The Records of the Parliaments of Scotland to 1707, K.M. Brown et al eds (St Andrews, 2007-2018), date accessed: 20 October 2018 • Charles I: Translation • > 1646, 3 November, Edinburgh, Parliament • > Parliamentary Register • > 16 February 1647 [1646/11/244]1 https://www.rps.ac.uk/search.php?action=print&id=22762&filename=charlesi_trans&type=trans.http://thepeerage.com/p47340.htm#c473392.1 .↑ The Scots peerage; founded on Wood's edition of Sir Robert Douglas's peerage of Scotland... by Paul, James Balfour, Sir, 1846-1931, page 494 digitized here: https://archive.org/details/scotspeeragefoun08paul/page/494/mode/1up/search/James+wemyss .↑ The Baronage of Scotland, Containing an Historical and Genealogical Account of the Gentry of that Kingdom by Sir Robert Douglas of Glenbervie, Edinburgh, 1798, page 562

SIR JAMES WEMYSS OF BOGIE

1St Baronet of Bogie (1705) and Third Baronet of Wemyss

James was born 1634, Wemyss, Fife, Scotland and died 1705 Lancashire, England. His father was *David Wemyss of Balfarg* and Mary Wemyss. James was educated by his uncle, Sir John Wemyss, to whom he succeeded. James was a great loyalist and invariably attached to the interest of the royal family.

Baronetcy of Nova Scotia: In 1703, baronetcy was conferred by Queen Anne on Sir James Wemyss of Bogie, Fifeshire. Sir James Wemyss of Bogie, was also: hereditary chief and laird of Clan MacDuff. Held Nova Scotia (Canada) Baronetcy. Lived in Fife, Scotland.

Sir James married *Anne Ayton on 11 Jan 1670 Anne, daughter of Sir John Ayton of that ilk, by Lady Elizabeth Wemyss, his wife, daughter of John, Earl of Wemyss, by Janet his wife, daughter of Andrew third Lord Gray.

Sir James Wemyss and Ann Ayton Children

Sir John Wemyss, HEIR, married Lockhart

Thomas Wemyss d.1716, who married Annabella, daughter of------Maxwell, Esq.

David Wemyss b.1679, who married Catharine, daughter of Mr. John Baillie, second son of Billie of Hardington. Had a son who went to Jamaica.

Margaret Wemyss b.1675, married 1) John Bethune of Blebo Craigs. 2) Philip Hamilton of Kilbrackmont.

SOURCE: *The Scots Peerage, Vol. VIII, page 496. The Baronage of Scotland, Containing an Historical and Genealogical Account of the Gentry of that Kingdom by Sir Robert Douglas of Glenbervie, Edinburgh, 1798, page 562. The Scots peerage, Vol. VIII, page 496*

"James Wemyss of Bogie, son of Mr. David Wemyss of Balfarg, succeeded sometime between 1672 and 1679. He greatly encumbered his family estate. For various services he was created a Baronet on 12 October 1704, with remainder to ' his heirs-male.' He married, on 11 January 1670, Anna, second daughter of Sir John Aytoun of that Ilk and Elizabeth, fourth daughter of John, first Earl of Wemyss. They and their heirs-male were included in the entail of the Wemyss estates in 1671.

*David Earl of Wemyss

Upon the death of David , Earl of Wemyss 1680 without male issue, Sir James became the male representative, and by the old investitures, would have succeeded to the estate and honours of Wemyss, but Earl David having altered their destination, and having resigned them into the hands of the crown, obtained a new grant of the estate and honours to himself and life rent and to his youngest daughter and her heirs male fees. Sir James in consequences, as the male heir and his posterity, ever after carried the arms of Wemyss simply, without any mark of cadence.

American Weems see chapter

Sir John Kessler Wemyss has based his claim for the title of Baronet of Wemyss of Bogie on Sir James Wemyss of Bogie (d.1705) marrying Elizabeth Loch about 1700. I have researched in several Scottish Peerage and I could find no documentation anywhere for these claims.

From Sir John Kessler book: Elizabeth Loch (? d.1720) was *the sister of Doctor William Loch who was a large land holder in the American colony Maryland at that time.* Her children were *Williamina Wemyss b. 1704 settled and married in Pennsylvania* was the only sibling to claim to be the daughter of the Baronet Sir James Wemyss which there is no record of. *David Wemyss b. 1706. Doctor James Wemyss b.1707 d.1781 Lived in Maryland. Married twice had issue.*

*SOURCE: The Scots peerage, Vol. VIII, page 496 *A genealogical and heraldic dictionary of the peerage and baronetage Burks Complete baronetage by Cokayne, George E. (George Edward), 1825-1911. https://archive.org/details/completebaroneta04coka/page/429/mode/1up. Baronets are a step below a baron. They never have sat in the house of Lords and they're the hereditary equivalent of a knighthood i.e. "Sir So-and-so".*

SIR JOHN WEMYSS *b.1670 d. abt 1740*

2nd Bart of Bogie, 4th Bart of Wemyss s.1705

*John married **Anne Lockhart**, daughter of Sir William Lockhart, Advocate by Marie Carmichael, 17 Apr 1699, Abbots hall, Fifeshire, Scotland. She survived him and d. 20 June in 1766. They had several children most died before 1740 of whom only one survived James (just a few listed below).

Sir John Wemyss & Anne Lockhart Children

Sir James Wemyss b. abt 1712??

George Wemyss b.1714 in Edinburgh d 17.12.1747. He was a merchant of Edinburgh and partner with John Hope.

Barbara Wemyss m. Sir Henry Seton, 3rd Bart of Abercorn (d 1751)

SIR JAMES WEMYSS *b.1712. d.aft 1766 Died unmarried.*

3nd Bart of Bogie, 5th Bart of Wemyss s. abt 1740

**He was left with great debts and sold the estate and lived in Kirkaldy and died unmarried a few years later, when the Baronetcy became dormant. Sir James Wemyss, 3rd Baronet, of Bogie, died c 1770, and his papers passed into the hands of his sister, Barbara, wife of Sir Henry Seton, Baronet, of Abercorn. He died unmarried.

The title passed to the descendants of Henry Wemyss 3rd son of James Wemyss (& Melville).

BARONETCY OF NOVA SCOTIA

A baronetcy of Nova Scotia was, in 1703, conferred by Queen Anne on Sir James Wemyss of Bogie, Fifeshire, descended from the 2d son of Sir David de Wemyss, progenitor of the earls of Wemyss, by patent, to him and his heir's male whomsoever. On the death of Sir James, 3d baronet, without issue, the representation in the male line devolved on the descendant of the 1st baronet's next brother, Henry, Sir James Wemyss, writer to the signet, Edinburgh, son of the Rev. James Wemyss, minister of Burntisland, who died in 1821. On the death of this gentleman, 4th baronet, unmarried, Dec. 31, 1849, the title devolved on his kinsman, Sir John Wemyss, born Aug. 1, 1830, a merchant of Berhampore, Bengal, eldest son of John Wemyss, Esq., writer in Kirkcaldy, cousin-german of Sir James Wemyss, 4th baronet. Sir John, 5th baronet, was served heir to the baronetcy in the court of the sheriff of chancery at Edinburgh, Oct. 1, 1858.

SOURCE: **Complete baronetage By Cokayne, George E. (George Edward), 1825-1911. Burke's Peerage and Baronetage Genealogical and Heraldic Dictionary *To see the rest of Sir John and Ann Lockhart children: https://www.stirnet.com/genie/data/british/ww/wemyss02.php *https://manuscripts.nls.uk/repositories/2/resources/182 https://electricscotland.com/history/nation/wemyss.htm

This passed to the descendants of Henry Wemyss 3rd son of James Wemyss (& Melville).

HENRY WEMYSS b.abt 1600. d.1654 of Botine.

Son of James Wemyss & Melville.

Henry Wemyss bought land at Easter Conland from his sister Janet about 1643. His grandson carried on the line of the Baronet of Bogie. Henry got from his Grandfather Sir James, a considerable inheritance. He married 1st 1639 Isabel, daughter of Sir John of Kirkcaldy grange, by whom he had 5 children. He married secondly, in 1653 Margaret daughter of Robert Durie of East Newton and Margaret Durie, his wife but by her hand no issue.

Henry Wemyss & Isabel Kirkcaldy Children:

*****John Wemyss** b.1645, d.1714 Maine Bogie (some also call James)

After displeasing his father by marrying contrary to his wishes he was left by him at his death with very slender means, having banqueted most to his daughter. Having be taken himself to an agricultural life, he obtained from his uncle Sir John, an advantageous lease of the mains of Bogie. Which his descendants in a direct line continued to possess till toward the end of the last century.

He was succeeded in the farm by his son,

John Wemyss, b.1686: who had several children and upon his death was s. by his son,

John Wemyss b.1714 d.1794(age 80). He continued on the farm as his ancestors.

He married Cecil daughter of Robert Durie Esq, a near cadet of the ancient family of Durie of that ilk in Fife, of whom he had 4 sons:

John Wemys and Cecil Durie children

Sir David Wemyss. b.1735 d. 1818, 4th baronet of Bogie Brewer.

Sir James Wemyss b.1747 d. 02. February 1822, minister of Burntisland 5th baronet of Bogie

John Wemyss b.1752 d. 1850

Robert Wemyss b.1862

NOTE This family line married into the Durie family many times.

*SOURCE: *Burks peerage, John is written as James - *Burke's Peerage, Baronetage & Knightage, Complete baronetage By Cokayne, George E. (George Edward), 1825-1911.*
https://www.stirnet.com/genie/data/british/ww/wemyss02.php

SIR DAVID WEMYSS *b.1736 d.1818*

4th Bart of Bogie, 6th Bart. of Wemyss s. 1794

David's father was John Wemyss and mother was Cecil Durie and he was a brewer in Kirkcaldy Fife. Died without issue.

SIR REV JAMES WEMYSS *b. 1747 d.1821*

5th Bart of Bogie, 7th Bart. of Wemyss s.1818

James was second son of John Wemyss and brother of Sir David Wemyss. Reverend James Wemyss was minister of Burntisland, Fifeshire, married Christian the daughter of Samuel Charteris, Esq, solicitor of customs for Scotland.

Reverend James Wemyss never took up the Baronetcy, but his son James did, when his father died in 1821 and he became Sir James Wemyss.

A baronetcy of Nova Scotia was, in 1703, conferred by Queen Anne on Sir James Wemyss of Bogie, Fifeshire, descended from the 2d son of Sir David de Wemyss, progenitor of the earls of Wemyss, by patent, to him and his heir's male whomsoever. On the death of Sir James, 3d baronet, without issue, the representation in the male line devolved on the descendant of the 1st baronet's next brother, Henry, _____Sir James Wemyss, writer to the signet, Edinburgh, son of the Rev. James Wemyss, minister of Burntisland, who died in 1821. On the death of this gentleman, 4th baronet, unmarried, Dec. 31, 1849, _____the title devolved on his kinsman, Sir John Wemyss, born Aug. 1, 1830, a merchant of Berhampore, Bengal, eldest son of John Wemyss, Esq, writer in Kirkcaldy, cousin-german of Sir James Wemyss, 4th baronet. **Sir John, 5th baronet,** *was served heir to the baronetcy in the court of the sheriff of chancery at Edinburgh, Oct. 1, 1858.*

Wemyss and farming- Mains of Bogie, Kirkcaldy

Sir James Wemyss of Bogie's, 1st Earl of Bogie. great grandson James Wemyss took a lease on "Mains of Bogie" from his Uncle Sir John and became a farmer. This farming tradition was carried on through the Wemyss's family. One of James Wemyss's (farmer of Bogie) great grandsons were Rev James Wemyss of Burntisland who inherited the title of baronet of Bogie.

SOURCE: *The house of Wemyss Sir Thomas Kessler Wemyss* The Scots peerage, Vol. VIII, page 496-497 *The Baronage of Scotland, Containing an Historical and Genealogical Account ... By Sir Robert Douglas (of Glenbervie).* https://archive.org/details/completebaroneta04coka/page/429/mode/1up *Journal Article -A Seventeenth Century Deal in Corn Bruce Seton. The Scottish Historical Review Vol. 18, No. 72 (Jul., 1921), pp. 253-257 https://www.jstor.org/stable/25519354?seq=1*

SIR JAMES WEMYSS b.1796, d.1849

6th Bart of Bogie, 8th Bart. of Wemyss s.1821

Sir James Wemyss**, son of the Rev James Wemyss minister of Burntisland, Fifeshire, by the daughter of Samuel Charteris, Esq, solicitor of customs for Scotland. Succeeded on the death of his father, but does not assume the title; is a writer to his majesty's signet in Edinburgh. Resided at 5 great Stuart Street Edinburg d. unmarried 1849.

SIR JOHN WEMYSS b. June 25th 1830 d. 1878

7th Bart of Bogie, 9th Bart. of Wemyss s. 1849

John father was John Wemyss and mother was Ester Ferrier married in 1828, died unmarried

John Wemyss and was Ester Ferrier children

Sir John Wemyss

Sir David Wemyss

*Sir John Wemyss

Wemyss, late (Sir) John, of Bogie, co, Fife, a merchant of Berhampore, Bengal, (son of John Wemyss of Kirkcaldy ,writer); b. 1830: died at Allyghur, N.W.P. India, having been served heir to the former (Sir) James Wemyss, in the court of the Sheriff of chancery, Edinburg, Oct, 1858, and is now (1879) succeeded, according to the Lodge, by his brother (Sir) David, of Mirzapur Merchant.

Sir John, 5th baronet, was served heir to the baronetcy in the court of the sheriff of chancery at Edinburgh, Oct. 1, 1858. He died of a fever, in Allychur, North West Provence India.

SIR DAVID WEMYSS b.1837 d. 1913

8th Bart of Bogie, 10th Bart. of Wemyss s. 1849

David's father was John Wemyss and mother: Ester Ferrier. He died unmarried.

Sir David Wemyss** of Toronto Canada, grandson and Heir, been s. and h of John Wemyss of Kirkcaldy, writer, succeeded, to Baronetcy, 8th March 1878. He was the brother of Sir John Wemyss.

FROM HERE THERE ARE NO ARCHIVES DOCUMENTS OF THE EARL OF BOGIE OF FAMILY

*SOURCE: *The baronetage and knightage By Joseph Foster. Burke's Peerage and Baronetage Genealogical and Heraldic Dictionary*
*https://www.stirnet.com/genie/data/british/ww/wemyss02.php **Complete baronetage By Cokayne, George E. (George Edward), 1825-1911*
https://archive.org/details/completebaroneta04coka/page/430/mode/1up

THE MANSE OF BURNTISLAND

MRS JANET LEVENS REMINISCENCES

Janet daughter of the Rev James Wemyss of Burntisland

Born in 1800 and the daughter of the Rev James Wemyss of Burntisland - told by her in 1891 to her daughter, Christine Charters Leven. Mrs Leven was a cousin of Mary Somerville.

Extracts:

My father called us one day to look at a "ship on fire" coming up the Forth near Inchkeith. This turned out to be the first Steamer seen on the Forth.

My father, the Rev James Wemyss, was the first who wore a gown in Burntisland Church. It was presented to him in 1779 by the Magistrates, but some people objected to it strongly and said "it was just a rag of popery". One old woman, Alice Thrift, who always came to church with a plaid over her head, got a bonnet, a large poke one, that the front of it might prevent her seeing minister with his gown on in the pulpit.

*My father never took up the Baronetcy, thinking a poor minister was as well without it, but my brother **James did, and he became Sir James Wemyss.** He was a Writer to the Signet and died at the age of 55 from bronchitis. He went to Russia at one time and visited Admiral Sir Samuel Greig at the Palace given by the Empress to his father, Sir Samuel Greig. It was called "Sans Ennui". When the latter came to this country to visit his mother and relatives, the Empress Catherine sent a Fleet with him. Lady Greig went about Edinburgh as she was accustomed to at St. Petersburg, with pages carrying her train, which attracted so much attention the Magistrates begged her to go out incognito.*

At the manse the servants used to spin all the evening as, with the early dinners, we dined at three o'clock they had plenty of time, and often there were two spinning wheels going. It was common for the servants to take a child on their knee and give them a "spinning ride".

The flax was grown on the Glebe, at the Kirkton and when spun the yarn was sent to a weaver at the Kirkton and made into table cloths and sheets and then sent to Luncarty Bleach Fields to be bleached. The sheets I am still using are some of those grown on my father's Glebe and are quite strong yet.

Some of the table cloths marked 1790 are getting rather frail however, and no wonder. These are Mr Leven's.

The manse originally belonged to my father, but he sold it to the Heritor's, but retained a garden across the road, in which, on his death my mother-built Hill House and removed there with her four daughters. The Rev Charles Watson, my father's assistant and successor, went into the manse.

When the Railway came it was converted into an hotel and a new manse was built on Cromwell Road.

My father always kept the Glebe in his own hands and sometimes rented a grass field in addition as he kept a horse and a cow and sometimes two.

Wemyss Weems of America

Sir John Kessler Wemyss has based his claim for the title of Baronet of Wemyss of Bogie on Sir James Wemyss of Bogie (d.1705) marrying Elizabeth Loch about 1700. Nothing found in Peerage on this marriage.

In his book -Sir John Kessler Wemyss claims Elizabeth Loch (? d.1720) was the sister of Doctor William Loch who was a large land holder in the American colony Maryland at that time.

Elizabeth Loch children. Williamina b.1704 married in Pennsylvania was the only sibling to claim to be the daughter of the Baronet of Wemyss which there is no record of. David Wemyss b. 1706, Doctor James Wemyss b.1707, d.1781 Lived in Maryland. Married twice had issue.

Weems of Maryland* *The Weems family is one of the oldest families in Maryland, originally settling in Anne Arundel County in the eighteenth century. The family originated in Scotland, being descended from the noble Wemyss line, although there is disagreement among genealogists concerning how the American and Scottish lines are connected. Family tradition suggests that William Wemyss, killed in 1715 at the Battle of Preston, was the father of the American immigrants. More recently, researchers have suggested that a James Wemyss fathered the American line.* SOURCE: **https://www.geni.com/people/James-Wemyss/6000000014597585819*

The Fife Family History Society Journal: *This work also deals with the family of Wemyss of Wemyss, but also gives a history of the cadet branches of the family, including the Wemyss of Bogie Three children of Sir James Wemyss, 1st Baronet of Bogie and 3rd Baronet of Wemyss, by his second wife,* **Elizabeth Loch,** *were early emigrants to the USA. They were James, Williamina, and David Wemyss, and left for America between 1715 and 1721. James, who was born in about 1700, was the first to go, being taken by his elderly cousin, Dr William Loch, a widower, as his heir and successor. He studied medicine under his instruction, and after his death moved to Maryland, where he occupied the plantation of Loch Eden in Calvert County. He died 13 August 1781. He was twice married: firstly (1734) to Sarah Parker; and then (February 1744) to Wheeler Crompton. He left issue by both wives, and from him is descended the present Wemyss-Kessler baronets of Nova Scotia in Canada. Williamina Wemyss (1706 -1784), who was named in honour of King William III, came to America in 1721, probably to marry William Moore of Moore Hall, which she did the following year at Chester, Pennsylvania. They had 12 children. She died 6 December 1784, and she and her husband are buried at St David`s, or Radnor, Episcopal Church, Chester, Pennsylvania. Little is known of the 3rd child, David Wemyss, apart from the fact that he was born in about 1703, and probably accompanied his sister, Williamina, to Chester, Pennsylvania, in 1721.*

NOTE TC: *I have researched in several Scottish Peerage's and found no documentation anywhere to the claims that Sir James married Elizabeth Loch or if she had the children out of wedlock and I could not find her parents. All three of Elizabeth's children were living in America by 1720 with their Uncle Dr Loch in Maryland. Williamina Weems called herself honourable throughout her married life. There is no mention of her brothers ever refereeing to the Earldom?*

Complete baronetage by *George Edward Cokayne (1825-1911): Wemys c 1704 dormant abt 1770 but assumed 1825_____ He married Ann daughter of sir John Ayton of Ayton, by Elizabeth, daughter of John (Wemyss) Earl of Wemyss. He died soon after 1705.* NOTE: *Cokayne makes no mention of any second marriage with Elizabeth Loch.*

SOURCE: The Fife Family History Society Journal https://fifefhs.org/wp-content/uploads/2018/01/Published-family history.pdf. The House of Wemyss: A Thousand Year History. By Sir Thomas Wemyss-Kessler. Memorials of the family of Wemyss of Wemyss by Fraser, William, Sir, 1816-1898. https://archive.org/details/memorialsoffami02fras/page/n6/mode/2up/search/ireland.

Sir George Wemyss b.1867 d. 1917 s.1940 Died unmarried *9th Bart of Bogie, 11th Bart. of Wemyss*

Eldest son of Reverend Thomas L.B. Weems and Laura Rosecrans born in Illinois, America. He lived in Montrose, Colorado and never married. He was a business man in banking ranching and mining. *George Weems who, after doing genealogy and corresponding with Sir David Wemyss of Toronto, Canada, found that he was the heir of the Baronets of Bogie and Wemyss. In 1913 he inherited the titles. His nephew, the present Baronet, inherited the titles in 1926.

*Mary Weems: Mary Weems was the sister of George and only living relative so she inherited his estate and title in 1917. When Mary inherited the estate of Sir George Wemyss of Montrose it was with the understanding that under the entail of the original title granted to Sir James Wemyss the 1st Baronet by Queen Ann in 1704, which said that the remaining could only go to the male Heir of Sir James Wemyss, the first Baronet, so Mary Weems could inherit the title but as a woman could not use it. She could however, hand it on to her nearest direct Heir-male on her death. In this case she passed it on to the son of her oldest daughter, Laura Camille (husband Charles Gump), who was born in November 1926, a few months before she died on 26th February 1926. The main stipulation that Mary Weems made in her will when she passed the title on to the new born son as her Heir designated was that she required that he add the name Wemyss to his surname when he reaches twenty-one. Mary Weems and her husband had two daughters Laura and Georgia.

SOURCE: *The House of Wemyss: A Thousand Year History Sir John Wemyss-Kessler. The Wemyss family is said to come from Clan MacDuff and settled in Wemyss in Scotland. They eventually became known as Wemyss of Wemyss. When members of the Wemyss family immigrated to America a large number of them changed their surname to Weems.*

Sir John Kessler Wemyss *b. nov 26th 1926, 10th Baronet of Bogie and 12th Baronet of Wemyss and 33rd Laird and Chieftain of the clan of MacDuff*

He inherited the name at birth in 26th November 1926. He lived at Montrose state of Colorado. His parents were Charles Ernest Gump and Laura Camille Hawkyard. Charles Gump died in 1936 and his wife Laura Hawkyard married a second time George Kessler in 1940. John Wemyss Kessler changed his name from Gump to Kessler at the suggestion of his step-father, George Keller, when he took the additional name Wemyss on his twenty first birthday. He served in the navy in the second world war____He worked as a chemist for Bell telephone laboratory until he retires in 1980. He married Theresa Conocchioli in 1950. They had one daughter Lisa Camille born 1958 and a son Thomas. He wrote the book The House of Wemyss: A Thousand Year History.

Sir Thomas Kessler Wemyss *b. abt 1953 (Present day 2020)* 11th Baronet of Bogie and 13th Baronet of Wemyss. Thomas was the son of Sir John Wemyss-Kessler.

Note *TC: I am unable to find any information on Sir Thomas Kessler Wemyss it stops on his sister Lisa Camille on P 117, in Kessler book.*

PRESTON OF PRESTON & CRAIGMILLER SCOTLAND

Elizabeth Preston was first cousin to Sir Patrick Wemyss of Danesfort Ireland.

Earl of Musgrave married Edmund Sheffield his only daughter Elizabeth married Thomas Butler 10 the Earl of Ormond and Ossory she had an only daughter Elizabeth Butler who married Richard Preston Earl of Desmond whose only child Elizabeth Preston married James Butler 12th Earl of Ormond. **Memoirs of Oliver Grace MP (Page 58 A)**

RICHARD PRESTON *b.1569 d.1628 1st Earl of Desmond*

Sir Patrick Wemys b.1604 Danesfort Ireland Uncle

Richard Preston born Perthshire, Scotland 1st Earl of Desmond was the brother of Elizabeth Preston mother of Sir Patrick Wemys b.1604, Wemys of Danesfort. Richards daughter Elizabeth Preston who married the Duke of Ormonde Kilkenny was Sir Patrick Wemys first cousin.

Title of the Earl of Desmond*

Richard Preston d.28 October 1628, 1st Earl of Desmond already created Lord Dingwall in 1609, was created Earl of Desmond, Kilkenny, Ireland, by Scottish King James I of England and Ireland in 1619. He was also created Viscount Cullen and Baron Dunmore in Ireland. He was a favourite of the king and was appointed one of the gentlemen of his bedchamber.

Richard married *(the match being brought about by the king)* **Lady Elizabeth Butler**, daughter and heiress of the 10th Earl of Ormonde Thomas Butler by his second wife Elizabeth Sheffield, and widow of Theobald Butler, 1st Viscount Butler of Tulleophelim. On the Earl's death in 1614, he took possession of his landed property, in prejudice of the rights of the heir male, Walter Butler, eleventh Earl of Ormond, in whose favour a settlement had been made by the late Earl and Walter was imprisoned by the king for not submitting his estate. Richard and Elizabeth had one daughter, Elizabeth, whom the duke of Buckingham intended for the wife of his nephew, George Fielding, second son of William first earl of Denbigh. *The match never happened because of the assassination of the duke of Buckingham and the death of Lord Dingwall (Earl of Desmond), the latter being drowned on the passage between Dublin and Holyhead, 28th October 1628. The barony of Dingwall devolved on his daughter, and the earldom of Desmond on Lord Fielding, in whose family it still remains. Lady Elizabeth Preston married James Butler, 1st Duke of Ormond.

Attained Noblemen of Scotland - *James Preston, Lord Dingwall, 2nd Duke of Dingwall. In 1711 was declared commander in chief of all the British forces at home and abroad. But he supported the Stewart cause in the rebellion and was attained. Escaped to France where he died at age 71, in 1745.*

*Note TC: *James Butler and Elizabeth Preston got married 1629 one year after her father's Richard who drowned on a passage between Dublin and Holyhead in 1628. Ironically, Richard was transporting furniture and other items from there Ormond estate to England.* **NOTE: There was a Roger Preston.** *Ensign in Henry Hazzard's company in* **James Wemyss's** *regiment of foot at the time of its disbandment in Apr. 1645.References: Spring, Waller's army, 155.Armies: Waller (Southern Association) https://www.british-history.ac.uk/no-series/cromwell-army-officers/surnames-p.* **SOURCE:** *Wikipedia. National Library of Scotland-https://deriv.nls.uk/dcn23/9508/95088345.23.pdf.*

LADY ELIZABETH PRESTON BUTLER

Child of Richard Preston, 1st Earl of Desmond

Elizabeth Preston, Baroness Dingwall was born on 25 July 1615. She was the daughter of Richard Preston, 1st Earl of Desmond and Lady Elizabeth Butler. She was engaged in 1622 to George Feilding, 1st Earl of Desmond. But she married at the tender age of 14 years James Butler, 1st Duke of Ormond, son of Thomas Butler, Viscount Thurles and Elizabeth Poyntz, in September 1629. She succeeded in 1609 as the 2nd Baroness Dingwall. After her marriage, Elizabeth Preston Butler, was styled as Countess of Ormond on 24 February 1633. She died on 21 July 1684 at 68 years.

WALTER BUTLER 11th EARL OF ORMOND

The Butler dynasty were all Catholic up until Sir James who was removed from Walter and brought up by a protestant clergy.

Walter served as a Member of the Irish House of Commons for Tipperary. Consistently a devout Catholic, he was known as "Walter of the Beads". His claim to the family estates was thwarted by King James I of England who engineered the marriage of Black Tom's (Thomas Butler) daughter and heiress, Elizabeth with one of his own Scottish favourites, Richard Preston. He made Preston Earl of Desmond and awarded most of the Ormond estates to Elizabeth instead of Walter. Walter spent much time and money in litigation in opposing the King's scheme. His persistence in refusing to resulted in him being committed to the Fleet prison in 1617. He remained incarcerated for eight years in great want with no rents reaching him from his estate. Earl Walter was set at liberty in 1625 and a large part of his estates restored to him. For some while he lived in a house in Drury Lane, London, with his grandson James, afterwards Duke of Ormond in 1629, then fifteen lived with him and I believe this was when he courted Lady Elizabeth Preston who resided in London with the help of Sir Patrick Wemyss who was also in London at this time.

Earl Walter from 1630 lived in Carrick until he died at the age of seventy-four, a big and corpulent man valiant and of high stomach as appeared by what he suffered rather than submit, he was accounted in his time as the strongest man in the kingdom, as all of his ancestors were also been remarkable for bodily strength.

Daughter of Elizabeth and James Butler Lady Elizabeth Butler-Elizabeth Stanhope, Countess of Chesterfield.

his cousin the lady Elizabeth Preston as might give him an opportunity of conversing or corresponding with her. Whilst he was under these difficulties and discouragements, and tormented with the apprehensions that delay would ruin his hopes and expectations by those opportunities and advantages which his corrival the Earl of Desmond had to accomplish his aims, it fell out very happily that Mr. Patrick Weymes, a near kinsman of the Lady Elizabeth Preston, and one who was chiefly intrusted with the management of her estate in Ireland, arrived at London; which the Earl of Ormond understanding he soon found means to be acquainted with him, and so far insinuated himself into his friendship as to prevail upon him to be an instrument of endeavouring an happy union between him and his cousin the Lady Elizabeth.

The first step Mr. Weymes made towards this was to give his lordship an opportunity for a view of the lady at Church next Sunday in the City of London (which was a good omen) without the privity of the lady; and whether designedly or by good fortune his lordship had the satisfaction of sitting with her ladyship in the same seat. The next step after this interview his lordship made himself by going in disguise (as a romantic lover) unto Kensington with a pedlar's pack upon his back; where first encountering the young ladies, daughters to the Earl of Holland, his lordship so charmed them with his civil deportment that they run into the house to the Lady Elizabeth, and told her there was at the back door one of the handsomest pedlars they had ever seen, and represented him so advantageously to her that they obliged her to come to take a view of him and the wares in his pack. It is not improbable that notwithstanding the Earl's disguise the young lady had some impression and idea of the person who had sat with her in the seat the Sunday before; for on opening his pack he presented to her a pair of gloves, into one of which he had before conveyed a letter, which she, in his drawing on of the glove perceiving, pretended to have no money in her pocket to pay for the gloves; and notwithstanding the young ladies offered to lend her money, yet she retired to her chamber to fetch money, and being there, perused the letter, and soon after returned with the gloves again (into which she as cunningly conveyed an answer) which she returned to the amorous pedlar, pretending they had an ill smell. What were the contents of either of these letters can be no otherwise possibly guessed at (because they were so secretly contrived, as all amorous intrigues are) than by the success. For within a small space after the young couple liked each other so well that notwithstanding all the circumspections and strict guards of the Countess of Holland they were happily married, to the great surprise and displeasure of the Court, the Duke of Buckingham and the Earl of Holland. But they being both the king's wards and under age, the Earl of Ormond as an atonement and peace offering was necessitated to enter into bonds to pay the Earl of Holland £30,000, which for several years before it was paid lay as an heavy load upon the Earl of Ormond. And yet notwithstanding

James Butler, 1st Duke of Ormond, and several members of his family, are buried in a large vault (22 feet long) at the east end of Henry VII's chapel in Westminster Abbey. James was the eldest son of Thomas, Viscount Thurles and his wife Elizabeth (Poyntz) and was born in London on 19th October 1610. He succeeded his grandfather as 12th Earl of Ormond in the Irish peerage. At the Restoration of Charles II, he was made Lord Steward of the Household and held the crown in the coronation procession. Created Duke of Ormond in 1661 he was also a Knight of the Order of the Garter and Lord Lieutenant of Ireland.

He concluded peace with the Roman Catholic Irish on behalf of the King and left Ireland and served as a colonel under the Duke of York in Spain. He was buried on 4th August 1688. When his father Thomas died in a shipwreck in 1619, he became Viscount Thurles. The year following that disaster, age 9 years his mother brought him back to England, and placed him, at school with a Catholic gentleman at Finchley — this doubtless through the influence of his grandfather Walter the 10th Earl. It was not long before *James I of England*, anxious that the heir of the Butlers should be brought up a Protestant, under the care of George Abbot, archbishop of Canterbury. The Ormond estates being under sequestration the young Lord had but £40 a year for his own and his servant's clothing and expenses.

Elizabeth Preston Butler: His wife was his cousin Elizabeth b. 25th July 1615, was the daughter of **Sir Richard Preston** and his wife Lady Elizabeth (daughter of Thomas Butler, 10th Earl of Ormond). In 1642 she had to flee with her children from Kilkenny Castle to Dublin during the Catholic uprising. They had sons Thomas, Richard and John, Earl of Gowran. Their daughter Mary, Duchess of Devonshire was buried with them on 6th August 1710.

James Butler, 1st Duke of Ormond Elizabeth Preston, Baroness Dingwall

Children

Thomas Butler, Viscount Thurles b. c 1632, d. 1633

Thomas Butler, Earl of Ossory+ b. 8 Jul 1634, d. 30 Jul 1680

Lord John Butler, 1st and last Earl of Gowran1 b. a 1639, d. b 1686

Richard Butler, 1st Earl of Arran+1 b. 15 Jun 1639, d. 25 Jan 1685/86

Lady Elizabeth Butler+3 b. 29 Jun 1640, d. Jul 1665

SOURCE: Elizabeth Preston, Baroness Dingwall Taken from thepeerage.com/F, #10209, b. 25 July 1615, d. 21 July 1684

James Butler* spent a lot of his time between Dublin and London, befriending his fellow protestants ____One of his earliest letters written by him penned in Dublin, is addressed to his wife's kinsman **Patrick Wemyss**, one of the new ruling cliques in Kilkenny, in whom he was engaged in covert financial schemes, involving another local protestant official, Sir Cyprian Horsfall. (1630)

LETTER DATE 1929: *"There have been several things of tokens of love delivered between mutually between the Lord Thurles and the young ladye, the Countess of Desmond, within less than ten days after, took those that the Lord had and sent back those that the young lady had". The last paragraph of 1629 gives very interesting information as to the close relationship between* **Patrick Wemys** *and (ancestor of Otway O'Connor Wemys, esq, of Danesfort county Kilkenny) and the lady Elizabeth Preston afterwards Duchesses of Ormond.*

H.M.C. Ormond. N.S.11, P355: **Sir Patrick Wemyss is rented land of Danesfort from Elizabeth Preston Butler and James Viscount Thurles.**

... Patrick Weymes and Richard Christy** gentlemen, the said Richard late Earl of Desmond his **sisters soones** and couzin germen to the said Lady Elizabeth Preston and their assigns for the tearme of one and twenty years, one paire of gloves of gloves price xxs onto the said Lady Elizabeth Preston and the heirs males of her begotten, at the feast of Michas yearly, if the same be lawfully demanded, shall be enjoyed by the said Patrick Weymes and Richard Christy and their assigns for and during the said tearme of one and twenty years any thinge herain contained to the contrary thereof in any notwithstanding.*

Sir Patrick Wemys in charge of collecting rents for Elizabeth Preston in Kilkenny Ireland. Elizabeth Preston (Ormonde) Lands Ireland - *[17.] Charles I. to Lord Deputy and Council of Ireland, 1629.*

Sir Patricks mother Elizabeth Preston

Sir Patrick Wemyss mother, Elizabeth Preston married first Patrick Wemyss of Raith, Fife and secondly a man named Christy. In Elizabeth Preston Butler her niece above manuscript mentioned her aunt and her sons, Sir Patrick and Richard Christy, in views to land leased to both of them in Danesfort Kilkenny.

NOTES TC: H.M.C. Ormond, N.S.,11, P355. Edward Sheffield was Elizabeth Preston's Butler Uncle.SOURCE: *edited by Toby Barnard, Toby Christopher Barnard, Jane Fenlon.*

IRELAND

WEMYS

ORIGINS OF THE IRISH WEMYS *

The following Wemyss is sometimes put forward as their sole origins:

1. General migration: Sligo has the biggest concentration of Weymes possibly starting from medieval times and is in easy reach of Scotland.

2. Robert Bruce's followers: Some fled to Ireland in the mid-1300. Wemyss family were loyal to Bruce.

3. Scottish settlers: These came to Ulster during the plantation - Wims

4. Sir John Wemyss of Logie and Glenawley: Became high sheriff of Fermanagh and some consider being the original Irish Wemyss. He was murdered by a servant of the Bishop of Clogher in 1628.

5. Sir Patrick Wemyss b.1604 d.1666 Fife, Scotland, settled in Easter 1631 at Danesfort, Kilkenny. This direct line died out with John Wemys of Danesfort 1892.

We have documented several family trees that can be traced back to Sir Patrick.

6. John Wemyss of Bogie: He was the grandson of Sir James Wemyss of Bogie who some say had an only son named James.

Baronage of Scotland by Sir Robert Douglas (1798) page 561: *Sir James Wemyss, 2nd son of Sir David Wemyss of Wemyss obtained from his father the patrimony of the lands of Bogie and others. He received a charter under the Great Seal on 2 February 1519. He married Margaret, daughter of John Melville of Raith and had several children, but only one reached maturity, a son James who married Margaret, daughter of David Durie). They had one only surviving son. John who became an officer in the army and ' having acquired a considerable fortune settled in Ireland where his posterity still remains and makes a good figure'.*

Sir John Wemyss Kessler put forward the theory that the Irish Wemyss descended from John son of Sir James and Durie. **Extract:** Sir James Wemys of Bogie married Margaret Melville then Elizabeth Dure. His sons
_____ *John Wemyss Esq, an officer in the army, who having acquired a considerable fortune settled in Ireland, married a sister of Lord Dingwall and is the ancestor of Wemyss of Danesfort.*

Wemyss Earl of Wemyss by Douglas, Robert, Sir, 1694-1770: *Sir DAVID*,*

_____*He married Cecilia, * daughter of William second lord Ruthven, ancestor of the earls of Gowrie, by whom he had five sons, and five daughters. Sir John, his heir. Died 1649 (Scotland, Fife Death Index, 1549-1877), Sir James Wemyss of Bogie, * of whom the present: Sir James Wemyss of Bogie is lineally descended; also, some considerable families of the name of Wemyss in Ireland.*

SOURCE: The House of Wemyss: A Thousand Year History Sir John Wemyss-Kessler. Page 106.
*https://quod.lib.umich.edu/e/ecco/004896980.0001.000/1:251?rgn=div1;view=fulltext, *Sir William Frazer's 'Memorials of Wemyss of Wemyss, which are available at www.internet archives.org

In a letter from the King to Lord Deputy (6/6/1627) the King states; it has now been proved that Sir John Weymes; High Sheriff of county Fermanagh was murdered by chaplains and servants of the Bishop of Clogher. The King formerly stayed all proceedings in the matter, being unwilling to cause a scandal in the Church. There was no love lost between Lord Balfour, (Sir John's father in law) and the Bishop of Clogher and it was a consequence of this that Sir John lost his life. Some of the Bishops servants went to Lisnaskea, where they found three or four horses of Sir Johns, which they took away and sold in Enniskillen. Later in the same week they went out again and took some mares belong to Lord Balfour who were pasturing on the Bishops land, for which Balfour refused to pay rent for. At Enniskillen when they were overtaken by Sir John and some of Balfours tenants. Sir John who was incensed with the indignity done to him thrust a pike through the shoulder of one of the servants, William Galbraith. In the course of the fight that followed, **Williams's brother Humphrey killed Sir John.** The Galbraiths were later tried for murder, but escaped the doom that Balfour had hoped for, but the Bishop had to pay a heavy fine for the wrongdoing of his servants.

In Pynnars Survey page 536 entry (237) it states that:

Sir John Wemyss had the following children; **James,** Elizabeth and Anne. Pynnars

Survey pages 511/512 have a complete account of the ongoing conflict between Lord Balfour and the Bishop of Clogher, and also a thorough description of the circumstances that lead to the death of Sir John Wemyss.

Available records indicate that Sir John Wemyss of Logie the male line died out.

Francis was the son of Maurice Wemyss and Elizabeth. He married (1) Joyce Blundell and (2) Mary McCulloch. He had the following family; Maurice, Rev William, Francis, Patrick, James MD, Henry, Elizabeth, Anne, Sarah, Martha, Joyce, Catherine, Mary, Antionette with Joyce Blundell and Henrietta with Mary McCulloch. He was High Sheriff of Kings County in 1694 and a Captain in the Duke of Norfolk's regiment of foot in 1689. He was a professional soldier, and in 1706 he wrote to Ormond seeking preferment in any new English regiment or the Irish Guards. He mentioned how poor Irish rents were and that he had twelve children.

Sir Henry Wemyss MP for Callan 1692/3, 1695/9; Co. Kilkenny 1703/13/14, Estate: Danesfort, Co. Kilkenny. Sir Henry was born abt. 1643 Died 1722 and was the son of Sir Patrick Wemyss and Mary Wheeler. He married Elizabeth Blundell eldest daughter of Sir George Blundell. They had the following children: Patrick, George, Henry, Mary, Sarah, and Elizabeth. He was Sheriff of County Kilkenny in 1695. He was knighted in 1677.

Henry Wemyss b 1703 d. 1750 **MP for Callan** Estates: Danesfort. Co. Kilkenny: St James Palace, London. Henry was the firstborn son of Patrick Wemyss and Anne Hancock. Henry was unmarried and was a Captain in the army. He died suddenly in London on 12th October 1750.

James Wemyss b.abt 1709 **MP for Callan 1751/60** & 1762/65. Estates: Ballyreddyn, Kilkenny. Son of Patrick Wemyss and Ann Handcock, he married Jane Stratford and they had the following children: Catherine, Maria, and Harriet. He was a 2nd Lieutenant in Dunbar's Regiment.

Patrick Wemyss b.1707 d.20 January 1762. **MP for Kilkenny** 1747/60; **Callan** 2-20 Jan 1762. Estates Dollville, Kilkenny. Son of Patrick Wemyss and Ann Handcock, he married Catherine Bermingham 1750, no issue. Catherine married within a month of Patricks death to Capt. John Cullen Leitrim.

Patrick Wemyss b.1679 d.25 September 1747. **MP for Gowran** 1703-13-14, Kilkenny 1721-7-47. Estates: Danesfort, Kilkenny. Eldest son of Sir Henry Wemyss and Elizabeth Blundell. On 14 May 1702 he married Anne Handcock, they had the following children: Henry, Patrick, James, Elizabeth, Mary, Jane, Sarah, Hannah, Abigail and Harriet.

James Wemyss b. abt 1755 d.8 august 1820. **MP for Kilkenny City** 1793. Estates: Danesfort, Kilkenny. Only son of James Wemyss and Jane Stratford he married Martha Blundell in May 1773 and they had the following children: Henry, Lucy, Emma, Janel, Martha, and Charlotte. He entered the army as an Ensign in 1766 and in 1789 he was a Lieutenant Colonel.

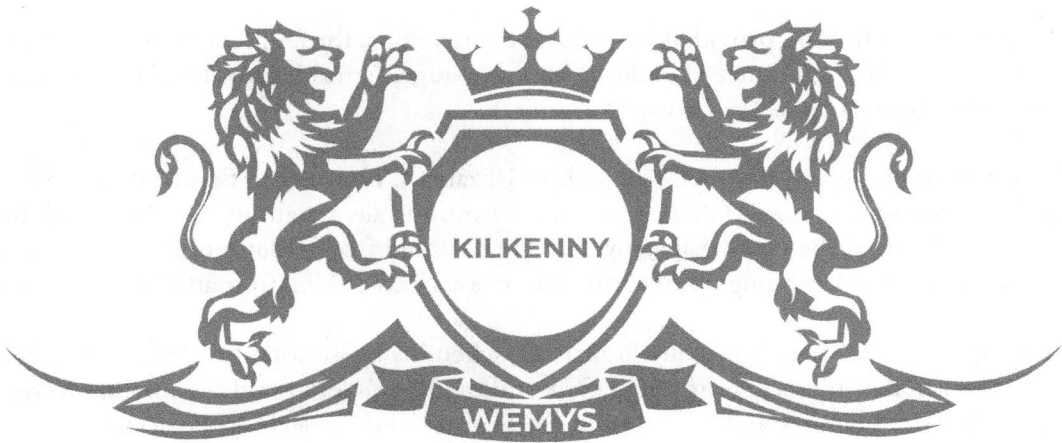

Wemys was a Scotsman, a cousin of Elizabeth Preston, Lady Ormond, and a very close associate of her husband from 1620, when both men lived in London; he was credited with having introduced the couple and, with Smyth*, witnessed their marriage settlement. He came to Ireland with Ormond (Walter Ormond granted him lands at Danesfort and Bennett bridge in 1929, and he was a commissioner to sell and lease for Elizabeth Preston; William Smyth* and Comerford* were witnesses to the deed). They had many land deals in Kilkenny, Tipperary and Carlow, and he was a frequent party to or witness of Ormond's deeds. He was made a freeman of Waterford in 1633 and was a member of the 1634 Kilkenny commission of the peace and sheriff from 1631 -5, which explains his absence from the 1634 parliament.

He lived at Danesfort. His wife provided other local connections; through her he was connected to archbishop Barlow of Tuam, Francis Hamilton* and the judge, James Donnellan. He is also described as Maule's cousin and thus linked to Crowe*.

His son Henry married George Blundell's* daughter Elizabeth. He went to Scotland in 1639, acting as a messenger between Ormond and Charles, and was Ormond's lieutenant in 1640, although he also held the rank of captain in the new Irish army. 520 He returned from Edinburg in November 1641and fought at Julianstown, commanding 50 of Ormond's troops and at Mellifont and Drogheda 1641-2.

He commanded Ormond's troops at Kilrush in 1642, when his horse was shot from under him. In the following year he acted as messenger to bring Ormond the King's letter authorising him to negotiate a cessation with the Confederates and he fought with Birrone* and Borlace* at Porlester.

His foot company, still part of Ormond's regiment, was quartered in High Street, Dublin, between October and December 1643 at least. In December 1644 and January 1645, he was involved with Henry Moor's* mother and others in a plot to capture Drogheda and hand it over to the Scots, for which he was imprisoned; it is at this time that he seems to have had a break with Ormond. He wrote to the King* and Francis Hamilton* from prison, appealing for their help and indicating that he had Charles's support for his actions; in letters to his cousin Col. Wemys in London and Major Crawford he stressed his Scottish origins, which he blamed for his victimisation.521 By August 1645 it was reported that " Sir P.W. is out upon bond to procure Sir Henry Tichbourne within 3 months to the exchange for him" 522 In August 1646 he was with his regiment in Ulster, where, with Montgomery*, he received saddles from John Davies*;during the same month he receive4d an order to raise and transport a troop of horses from England to Ireland for parliamentary service, and a commission as captain of the troop.

Five months later he was in Belfast and in the following year was colonel of a regiment of horses in Ireland, where he received a letter from Sterling soliciting support for a remonstrance from the Irish army to the Westminster Parliament; with Phillips* and the Hamiltons* and Montgomeries*he was stationed with his troops in Ulster in May 1647.

He fought in the parliamentary side at Dunganstown. In March 1651 he was in Kilkenny, where he had contact with the imprisoned Hugh Montgomery*. He remains in Ireland during the 1650s, giving evidence on behalf of Thomas Arthur in 1652, witnessing a deed for Francis Bolton of Queen's County in April 1654 and certifying George Peppers good conduct in July 1655. He was commissioner to raise the assessment for Ireland for the last quarter of 1654 and the second half of 1657 in Kilkenny, where he was an alderman. He was commissioner for the poll money ordnance in Kilkenny in 1660-1. He held no military commission in 1650s, but gained his command on the restoration and held it at his death.

519 Patricks father's name is unknown; the identity of his mother is taken from H.M.C Ormond, N.S.,11, 355; Sir W Frazer, Memorials of the family of Wemyss of Wemyss. 3 vols., (Edinburgh, 1888) includes information on many Patricks, but none who can be identified with this m.p., nor who married Elizabeth Preston. Douglas, Peerage of Scotland,1, pp 413-7, (Dingwall) provides no clues to this mystery.

520 N.L.I. MS. 2306.p.295 notes that he was owed £25 for 6 months wages as captain at Easter 1641.

*521*_____, A Declaration set forth by the Lord Lieutenant and council... (Dublin, 1645), pp 6-8.

522 N.L.I. MS. 2541, f.143; Carr* to Cadogan*, 28 August 1645.

523 This, and his other activities suggests that he was motivated by a strong Presbyterianism.

* Given by kind permission of Dr Brid McGrath Department of History Trinity College Dublin 2.

Land and People 1600 R.A. Butlin

Ireland* at the beginning of the seventeenth century was still perceived by Englishmen as a colony on the western periphery of Europe- and island lying, as Campion had described it thirty years before," aloof in the western ocean". Notwithstanding the rapid decline and transformation of the authority of the Gaelic chiefs, large areas of the country were still characterised by a way of life totally alien to the experience of English observers, which had much more in common with the pastoralist regions of the Atlantic periphery of the northern- western Europe then with the essentially lowland cultures of south and south- eastern England and the great basins and plains of continental western Europe. The cultural, social, economic, and religious mores of Ireland were so far removed from those of the English that they were partially used as justification for the policy of attempted civilisation and anglicisation aimed at decreasing political instability and negativing the use of Ireland as a strategic base for an attack on England, notably by Spain.

History of Ireland (1536–1691): Ireland during the period 1536–1691 saw the first full conquest of the island by England and its colonization with Protestant settlers from Great Britain. This established two central themes in future Irish history: subordination of the country to London-based governments and sectarian animosity between Catholics and Protestants. The period saw Irish society transform from a locally driven, intertribal, clan-based Gaelic structure to a centralised, monarchical, state-governed society, similar to those found elsewhere in Europe. The period is bounded by the dates 1536, when King Henry VIII deposed the FitzGerald dynasty as Lords Deputies of Ireland (the new Kingdom of Ireland was declared by Henry VIII in 1541), and 1691, when the Irish Catholic Jacobite's surrendered at Limerick, thus confirming British Protestant dominance in Ireland. This is sometimes called the early modern period. * **R A Butlin**

Bishops War 1640: **Bishops' Wars 1639-From 1638 to 1640 Scotland rose in a revolt known as the Bishops' Wars against the Charles I's attempt to impose Church of England prayers there, believing them to be too close to Catholicism. Charles tried and failed to coerce Scotland by military means, but also refused to obtain funding by recalling Parliament, instead relying on his own resources.

Irish Rebellion of 1641: **The Irish Rebellion of 1641 came about because of the resentment felt by the Catholic Irish, both Gael and Old English, in regards to the loss of their lands to Protestant settlers from England and Scotland. The Catholic Irish were frightened by reports that the Covenanter Army in Scotland was considering an invasion of Ireland in order to eradicate the Catholic religion. At the same time there was also a threat of invasion by Cromwell's Puritans who were at war against King Charles1. It was hoped that the King would redress the complaints of the Catholics and halt or even reverse the policy of plantation.

The Irish Confederate 1642: The Irish Confederate, War of 1642-In 1642 the Old English formed an alliance with the Gaelic Lords at the Assembly of Kilkenny. This alliance caused the rebellion to escalate into the Confederate war, which would continue until Cromwell's invasion and subjugation of Ireland 1649-1653. *NOTE TC: Bishops' Wars 1639-From 1638 to 1640 -The Irish Rebellion of 1641. SOURCE: *A new History of Ireland By Moody, Martin, Byrne. ** Wikipedia-History of Ireland (1536–1691)*

Patrick Wemyss (Wemys, Weames, Weemes, Waymes) was a close associate of the Earl of Ormond from the 1620's. He was a cousin of Elizabeth Preston, Lady Ormond and indeed it is believed that it was Sir Patrick who introduced the couple. He came to Ireland in about 1629 and Walter Ormond granted him lands at Danesfort and Bennettsbridge. They had land deals in the counties of Kilkenny, Tipperary and Carlow. He was made a freeman of Waterford in 1633 and sheriff of Kilkenny from 1631 to 1635. Through his marriage to Mary Wheeler who was a daughter of Jonah Wheeler, the Bishop of Ossory; and through her he established many powerful local connections.

In 1639 he went to Scotland acting as messenger Between Ormond and Charles. As a member of Ormond's army, he fought at Julianstown, Mellifont and Drogheda in 1641/2. He also fought at Kilrush in 1642 when it is reputed that his horse was shot from under him. In 1643 he acted as messenger to bring Ormond the Kings letter authorising him to negotiate a cessation with the Confederates. In December 1644 and January 1645, he was involved with Henry Moore's mother and others in a plot to capture Drogheda and hand it to the Scots. He was imprisoned for his actions and Ormond broke with him. From his prison he wrote to the King and Francis Hamilton. He claimed he had the support of Charles for his actions. In his letters to Col. Wemys and to Major Crawford he stressed his Scottish origins. He was exchanged for Sir Henry Tichbourne in late 1645. In 1646 he was based in Ulster and in the following year he was Colonel of a regiment of horse. It was during this period that he was knighted. In 1654 he was a commissioner to raise assessments for Ireland and he was also an alderman of Kilkenny He was M.P for Kilkenny in 1661 the year in which he died.

NOTE: Patrick's father's name is unknown. Sir W. Frazer the author of Memorials of the Family of Wemyss of Wemyss has references to many Patrick's, but none could be identified with him or any that married Elizabeth Preston who is recorded as Patrick's mother.

SIR PATRICK WEMYS DANESFORT KILKENNY

Patrick Wemys b.1604 in Fife Scotland. Patrick father was the Reverend Patrick Wemyss from Raith Fife who married Elizabeth Preston. Sir Patrick was the Grandson of the Sir David Wemyss of Wemyss who married Cecilia Ruthven. Sir David's sons were John, James, **Patrick**, Andrew, David. Sir David's son, Sir James married Margaret Melville and secondly Elizabeth Durie. By Margaret he had three sons James, **Patrick** and Dr Lodovick. With Elizabeth they had David, George, Andrew, Henry. Patrick was the nephew of Sir Richard Preston.

Patrick married Mary Wheeler about 1634 at Queens County, Audoen's Church, Dublin, Ireland. Mary was a daughter of Jonah Wheeler the Bishop of Ossory, Kilkenny and through her he established many powerful local connections. They had five sons. She was buried: May 31,1660, at St Canice Dublin.

SIR PATRICK LIEUTENANT - *Messenger between King Charles 1 & Lord Ormond*

Sir Patrick Wemys went to Scotland in 1639 acting as messenger between Ormond and King Charles 1. He returned to Ireland from Edinburgh in 1641. Again In 1643 he acted as messenger to bring Ormond the Kings letter authorising him to negotiate a cessation with the confederation and he fought with Birrone and Borlace at Portlester.

Conflicts: Sir Patrick was a lieutenant of Ormond's army and fought at Julian town, Mellifont and On November 22, 1641, he entered Drogheda with 50 horses for its defence. He held the title of Captain in the new Irish army. He also fought at Kilrush in 1642 when it is reputed that his horse was shot from under him.

*Letters from P.W. to Ormond, begins "My Lord and patron", delivering letters from Ormond to the King via Sir Henry Vane, giving O the low-down on what was happening with the King in Scotland. **"Sir Patrick Wemys, I presume, hath brought you your commission long ere this."**

James Butler and the Royalist cause in Ireland 1641-1650.** 1640. Troop of horse of the Earl of Ormond: James, Earl of Ormond and Ossory, Captain; **Patrick Wemys,** ___

Ormond to Sir H. Vane, Carrick, 19 October 1641, Ormond petition to Charles: `for his justice in a business that has received many trials and confirmations to my ancestors" asks V to read his petition, which **Wemys** will show him, & asks for his support.

Protestants became a majority in Dublin in the 1640s, when thousands of them fled there to escape the Irish Rebellion of 1641. When the city was subsequently threatened by Irish Catholic forces, the Catholic Dubliners were expelled from the city by its English garrison.

SOURCE: * Ormond's biographer, Thomas Carte Bodl. Carte MS. 63, ff 421 r-v, Ormond to Sir Robert King & Col.? Beale, Neale? 9 April 1646. ** Ormond's biographer, Thomas Carte Carte 65, f. 11,

The manuscripts of the Marquis of Ormonde *1641*

_____*Therefore, my Lord, I and Sir Robert are of this opinion: if your Marquis* p Lordship would be pleased to send* **Sir Patrick Weinbs [Wemys]** *to "Ormonde. Lisnegarvy as upon an oceasionall journie, (to whom Sir Robert*

1641 hath wrote (o that purpose,) I and Sir Robert would take an occasion to meet him, and there to understand what your Lordship would have donne, and in what readinesse your affiure3 are, and with him to send a letter to Lieutenant-Colonel Sanderson, expressing the report 3 r ou have heard of his abilities, and that you impute his former carriage [to] somme discontents and wants, and lo assure him of your recommendations to his Majestie, and with the first opportunitie that he shall have experiment of your good opinion of him, and to promise him a standing companie, and moreover, to intrust **Sir Patrick Wembs** *with one 80 peices as a guift from your Lordship unto him, this, and the letter not to be delivered but by Sir Robert's advice and mine, to which if we assent, we will oblige ourselves to return your Lordship such satisfaction that you shall not repent.*

High St Dublin Residence: Sir Patricks foot company under Ormond were stationed in High St, Dublin in October December 1643. Protestants became a majority in Dublin in the 1640s, when thousands of them fled there to escape the Irish Rebellion of 1641. When the city was threatened by Irish Catholic forces, the Catholic Dubliners were expelled from the city by its English garrison.

Sir John Gilbert's valuable 'History of Dublin": *He supplies a long list of notables who had residences in the City. Liberties. Lord Meath, whose name and that of his son Lord Brabazon are still to be seen in two of the wide, spacious streets, lived in Thomas Street (his house has long since sunk to the degraded position of a tenement-house_____the Earl of Kildare in Thomas Street (The Earl removed there from the Carbric) the Earl of Roscommon in High Street, where also lived* **Sir Patrick Wemyss** *and the Plunket's; High Street and Thomas Street, like Meath Street, are spacious, and some of the houses have the air of having seen better days. In 1647, the Countess of Roscommon,* **Sir Patrick Wemyss, founder of the family of Danesfort,** *and Sir Thady Duff, were resident in* **High-street,** *and copper tokens are extant issued by the following inhabitants of this locality: - The High Street - Mac Gillamocholmog's Street - The Ram Lane - Bertram's Court - Rochel Street.*

SOURCE: *T. Carte, A Collection of original letters and papers concerning the affairs of England from the year 1641 to 1660 found among the Duke of Ormond's Papers. (London, 1739). 25 September 1641, from Edinburgh, pp 1-5; pp 5-9, October 1641. p. 27 Arthur Trevor to Ormond, Oxford, 10 December 1643, pp 27-8.

Calendar of the State Papers Relating to Ireland, 1633 - 1647 *Further draft order of the Same. Eighty "bowes" [bowls] of meal to be given by Commissary Norris to* **Sir Patrick Wemyss** *for his troop. P. End. S.P. Ireland 203, 48. One hundred pounds*

Calendar of the State Papers Relating to Ireland, 1633 - 1647 _____ *3 May. Same to the Lord Lieutenant and Lords Justice for* **Sir Patrick Wemyss.** *Ordering that he be granted a custodian of all the houses, cur-telages, &c., in the city of Dublin belonging to. James Bath, of Athcarne. Philip Hoare, of Kilsachlane Kilsallaghan], Thomas Couran, of "Wanton, Edward Allen, of Bishop court. Robert Arthur, of Dublin. Alderman, and Christopher Chamberlain, of Dublin, whereof these men were sized at the time of their committing high treason; and of all subsequent rents. Sic, without giving any account of them.*

Commission for **Sir Patrick "Wemyss,** *Kt., to be captain of a troop of horse, consisting of 60 harquebusiers and officers.*

A letter to be sent to the Ulster Commissioners, taking notice of what they consider as a great miscarriage towards them on the part of some Scottish officers. Let them send particulars. Nothing to their discredit will be believed here.

Sir Patrick "Wemyss *to be recommended to the* **Lord Lieutenant of Ireland.** *Other details. Articles to be drawn up for Lieut.-Col. William Wetton to raise 300-foot soldiers in this kingdom and take them to London-Derry. Usual terms. Same for* **Sir Patrick Wemyss** *to raise and transport a troop of horse to Ireland. Same terms as Colonel Temple.*

CARLOW CASTLE

Carlow Castle formerly an estate of the Dukes of Ormond, and gave the title of baron in the Irish peerage to the Earls of Arran. The castle was taken by Sir Peter Carew, in 1568, from Sir E. Butler, who was then in rebellion: in 1642 it was besieged by the Irish, but was relieved by **Col: Sir P. Wemys;** and here the Marquess of Ormond mustered his forces prior to the battle of Rathmines.

Siege of Carlow Castle Ireland in 1641 In 1641, the whole county was overrun by the insurgents, and the castle of Carlow was invested by a strong party and reduced to great extremity; a number of Protestants had taken refuge within its walls, and the garrison was about to surrender, when it was relieved by a detachment of the Earl of Ormond's forces under the command of **Sir Patrick Wemys.** On his approach the insurgents raised the siege, and, after burning the town, took flight, but 50 of them were killed in the pursuit.

THE SIEGE* 1641-1642. With the eruption of the Irish rebellion of **1641**, many English settlers along the southern Pale sought refuge in Carlow Castle. At this time, the castle belonged to Barnabas O'Brien, 6th Earl of Thomond, who, as Lord Lieutenant of County Clare, was in that Atlantic county when the rebellion broke out. He subsequently fled to England, abandoning Bunratty Castle to the rebels.

Catholic Confederates. The rebels were Catholic Confederates, an alliance of disillusioned Catholics, Irish and Old English alike, hoping to recoup the money and lands they had lost since the plantations began. Many amongst them also hoped to re-establish Catholicism at the preeminent religion. By now there was a substantial English Protestant settlement across County Carlow, primarily in Carlow Town, Hackettstown and in the north.

Bunratty Castle Siege. Shortly before Christmas **1641**, a musket-wielding rebel force commanded by Sir Walter Bagenal and Sir Morgan Kavanagh besieged Carlow town. They may have offered fair quarter and safe passage to the sea if the castle surrendered but, in any event, such an offer was rejected. For the 400 or so trapped in the castle, life became a nightmare. A flood further hampered efforts to break the siege. Some women slipped out to forage for food; they were captured by the rebels and hanged in full view of their families in the castle. A servant girl who was sent to fetch water was likewise shot. Within the castle, the besieged began to starve; Edward Briscoe and his wife watched seven of their nine children die 'by want of necessaries'. It is thought most people in the castle slept in the bailey.

NOTE: *Walter Bagenal* (1614-52), was a leading figure in the Catholic Confederation during the wars of the 1640s.

SOURCE: *Given by kind permission from:* **Turtle Bunbury** *website.* **http://www.turtlebunbury.com/history/history_wai/Leinster/history_wai_carlow.htm*

James Butler Marquess of Ormond. James Butler, Marquess of Ormond**, was commander of the Crown forces in Ireland who took on the Confederates. Shortly before Easter **1642**, he sent a force under **Sir Patrick Wemys** (and possibly Thomas Preston) to relieve the town. As Wemys approached, the rebels burned Carlow and fled. By July 1643, the Leinster countryside was so scorched by war that nothing was growing and starvation was rife.

THE SIEGE OF 1647. The **1642** siege had been an old-fashioned medieval siege. In the spring of 1647, things became considerably tougher when Carlow Castle underwent its first ever artillery siege. General Thomas Preston and the Confederates of Leinster surrounded the castle so effectively that when Lord Ormond sent fifty men to bolster the defence, the reinforcements were unable to get through. On 10th April 1647, Major Harman, commander of the King's garrison, surrendered the castle. It was to remain a Confederate stronghold for the next three years.

SOURCE: *Given by kind permission from: Turtle Bunbury website.* **http://www.turtlebunbury.com/history/history_wai/Leinster/history_wai_carlow.htm*

BATTLE OF JULIANSTOWN

The Battle of Julian town was fought during the Irish Rebellion of 1641, at Julian town near Drogheda in eastern Ireland, in November 1641. The Officer in charge of the battle of Julian town was **Sir Patrick Wemyss.** His account of the battle can be read in his letter to the Earl Ormond, recorded in the *Calendar of State Papers* relating to Ireland, 1641.

The prelude to the planned Siege of Drogheda 1641 by northern counties insurgents led by Sir Phelim O'Neil and supporters from Cavan and Monaghan to lay siege to the strategic garrison, grain store and seaport. Insurgents during their plan to unsettle English rule in Ireland, had already attacked several towns and villages within the Pale including the palace of the Protestant Bishop of Meath and the burning of Navan and Athboy.

Either by chance or otherwise the insurgents came upon an untrained and hastily raised force of Government soldiers, largely composed of planter refugees from the northern counties sent against them. The two sides met at the bridge at Juliantown. The British commander gave the order to counter march, which the half-trained recruits misinterpreted as a march to the rear. The British army began slowly edging backwards. However, the rebel force believed that the British had shouted contúirt bháis! (danger of death). The Irish, up on hearing this and seeing the panic and confusion amongst the British force let loose with a war cry and charged with unyielding ferocity.

What followed was a simple rout. The soldiers attempted to hold them off by firing in volleys, but were unable to co-ordinate their actions and panicked when they saw the rebels bearing down on them. Many threw down their muskets and ran away, the remainder being either killed or captured.

One disputed source tells that the rebels spared the Irish in the soldier's ranks, but killed the English and Scots. It is noted from the Cavan depositions that several of those men killed at Juliantown were in fact refugees who had joined the ranks of the army, having previously been robbed and turfed out of their homes by the insurgents.

NOTES: The River Nanny at Julianstown, Co Meath. The consequences of the Julianstown skirmish were far more disproportionate to its military significance. The victory by the insurgents made them seem much more formidable than they actually were and helped to spread the rebellion to the rest of Ireland. This also was a rude wake up call to the marquis of Ormond's crown forces and showed the determination and support in Ireland for the insurgents supported by old English palesmen. This indirectly helped to trigger the English Civil War and Confederate Ireland, a short-lived independent Irish state.

SIR PATRICK WEMYS LETTER TO EARL OF ORMOND

Duleek Barony, County of Meath

Only known letter from Sir Patrick Wemyss

Letter from **Sir Patrick Wemyss** to Earl of Ormond 29th November 1641. *

Calendar of State Papers Relating to Ireland 1641

Battle of Julianstown, Duleek Barony, County of Meath

I will now tell you of our misfortune. We lodged last night at Balrederie (Balrothery,), as my officers could not make the men march to Drogheda. We were informed that the enemy were upon us, but they did not fall on us.

Next day on the march, we sent out scouts and saw a few rebels, but after crossing the Julianstown bridge, I saw them advancing towards us in as good order as ever I saw any men. I viewed them all, and to my conjecture they were not less than 3,000 men. They had three troops of launciers, two troops that had pistols and two field pieces. I advised the foot captains to draw their men within the field just opposite where they were, for when we first did see them, we were marching in a dirty lane, and a high ditch on every side of us. So that my persuasion prevailed with them, they drew up themselves handsomely. I drew up the troops on their front, and told the captains that we were engaged in honour to charge them, and that I would charge them first with those horses I had.

They promised faithfully to second me. But when I made the trumpet sound, the rebels advanced towards us in five great bodies of foot; the horse, being on both wings, a little advance before the foot; but just as I was going to charge, the troop cried unto me and told me the foot had left their officers, thrown down their arms, and took themselves to running. It was useless to fight, so I withdrew as best I could and escaped with a loyal remnant to Drogheda.

Two of my troop whose horses went lame were left behind. I hear however that they are safe, except for their clothes, which were taken from them, not by the rebels, but by natives as they passed through the village. All our arms and ammunition are in the rebel's hands. We can get no food here for man or horse.

P.S- There march upon every division of the rebels a friar or a priest. I do perceive here they do too much undervalue the rebels: for believe me, they will find them no such contemptible men.

SOURCE: *House of Commons Journal Volume 4: 30 September 1645

Several Castles relieved

Wednesday, the Sixth

The *Army* rested at *Athy*, and the *Lieutenant General* sent four Troops of Horse to relieve the Castles of *Catherlagh* and *Cloughgrement* (viz.) his *Lordship's* Troop, commanded by **Sir Patrick Wymes;** Sir George Wentworth's Troop, commanded by Captain Thomas Harman, Captain Thomas Armstrong's Troop, commanded by himself; and part of Sir Charles Coote's. When they came within sight of the Town, the Rebels observing their approach, set the Town on fire and fled; whereupon Captain Harman, best knowing that Country, and which way they would take, did with his Troop of Horse pursue them, and killed 50 of them, (the rest escaping into a Bog) brought in good Store; of Cattle, and relieved the Castle, where there were 500 Persons who were exceedingly distressed, having been a long time besieged by the Rebels.

The Troops returned that Night to their Quarters, having relieved both the Castles. The same Day Sir Charles Coote was sent; forth with a Party of Horse and Foot, and relieved Captain George Graham's Castle, called Ballilenon, wherein there were 300 Persons Castle Rebon was reliev'd the same day by the Lord Lieutenant's and Sir Tho. Lucas's Troops; and a Castle near it, called Bert, taken in, and eight Rebels found in it, who were immediately hanged.

Monday, the Eleventh of April 1642

The Troops, in their return back, marched thorow O-Dunn's Country, and burnt all the Country until they came to Castle-Cuff; from thence marching to portnehinch, thorow Woods and Bogs, the Rebels fell upon them, and Captain Yarner was shot in the Forehead, of which shot he is well recovered. Some of the Troops were hurt, and divers of their Horses killed; and the Passage of Portnehinch was possessed by the Rebels, so that the Troops were forced to swim the River of theBarrow.

The Lieutenant-General knowing that the Troops were to return that way, and considering that it is a dangerous Passage, (he being himself indisposed by reason of Sickness all Saturday and Sunday) sent thither 500 Foot commanded by Colonel Monk and the Lord Lisle's Troop of Horse, commanded by Captain Tersvell, who burnt all the Country, and kept the Rebels so busy in fight, who had intrench'd themselves upon that Passage, as gave our Troops opportunity to get safe over another Passage, but were so ill guided in the Night thorow the Bogs, that they were constrained to stay all that Night in the Bogs until Morning; and in this hard Journey there were lost, and made unserviceable above 100 Horse; the Horsemen having sat eight and forty Hours on Horse-back, before they came back to the Fort at Mary-Borough; also the Lieutenant-Genaral upon Easter-day sent his own Troop of Horse, commanded by **Sir Patrick Wymes** to Ballynekill, to relieve the English that were there, who were in great distress for want of Victuals; where the Troop quartered that Night.

Monday Morning, the Eleventh

Sir Patrick gave directions, that all the Cars and Horses that could be found there, should be made ready to bring in Cornfor the relief of the Castle, and with his Troop brought in unto them 80 Barrels of Wheat and Beer, belonging to one Dempsie, a notorious Rebel which they took within Musket shot of his Castle. About five of the Clock in the Afternoon there were 1000 of the Rebels, and a Troops of Horse, that shew'd themselves upon a Hill called Ballioskill within two Musket's shot, and did not advance.

Sir Patrick Wymes burnt all the Villages belonging to Dempsie, and returned back that Night with the Troop to the Fort of Mary-Borough. That Night the Lieutenant-General received intelligence, by Letters from Colonel Crawford, that the Rebels with about 40 Colours were encamped on both sides of the River of Barrow, and were there making up the Bridge of Magainy, which had been in the Beginning of the Rebellion broken by order from the State_____

SOURCE: British historical collections *Containing the Principal Matters Which happened from the Meeting of the Parliament, November the 3d, 1640. To the End of the Year 1644. Wherein is a particular Account of the Rise and Progress of the Civil War to that Period: 4.5-Publisher Browne, 1721*

Thursday, the Fourteenth

The Army continued Athy, the Rebels quartering on both sides the River at the Bridge of Magainy, within four Miles of Athy, with about 7000 Foot, and 200 Horse; amongst whom were (as we understood by some Prisoners taken in the fight) the Lord Viscount Montgarrat, the Lord Viscount Ikerin, the Lord Baron Dunbonie the Baron of Lughmoe, and most of the principal Rebels of the Counties; of Wickloe, Wexford, Catharlagh, Kildare, Kilknny, and Queens-County, who drew up a part of their Forces to a place called Tankarstown, near Grange Mellon, a Castle defended by Mrs. Borroughs and some Warders, which had been long besieged by the Rebels, where the Lieutenant's Troop of Horse, commanded by **Sir Patrick Wymes** *and Captain Armstrongs Troop, were quartered; from which Castle in the Morning, by directions from the Lieutenant-General, Corner Butler, and Cornet Magragh, were sent to discover the Rebels; but they observing that part of the Troops were a foraging, sent overall Troop of Horse, each Horseman carrying behind him a Musquete who cross'd the River, thinking to cut off both the Cornets what* **Sir Patrick Wymes** *and Captain Armstrong, being upon the top of Castle, observing, did in prevention thereof get together so many the Horsemen as were in the Quarter, and charged the Rebels there, skirmish with the two Cornets, and forced them back over the River, kill'd one of their Horsemen, hurt divers of the rest, kill'd all the Foot, and some were drowned in swimming back again. In this Service* **Sir Patrick Wymes** *had his Horse kill'd under him, and two of the Lieutenant-General's Troop were then shot. The same day in the Forenoon, the Lieutenant-General, accompanied with Sir Charles Coote, Sir Thomas Lucas, Colonel Crauford, Colonel Monk, and other Commanders, and Volunteers, with 200 Horse, went to view the strength of the Rebels, and in what manner they lay_____*

THE SIEGE OF TREDAGH

Seven hundred Rebels slain

In which order we advanced toward the Rebels, till by the interposition of a Hedge and hollow Way, some of the Troops were forced to go about, and then drew up again in the same order on the other side of the Hedge, within almost Musket shot of the Rebels; then were sent out Parties of Firelocks and Musqueteers to begin the sight. After they had given Fire for a good space upon the Rebels, and the Rebels upon them, Sir Thomas Lucas with all the Troops on the Left Wing, viz. his own Troop, Captain Armstrong's, and the Earl of Ormond's (which last was commanded by **Sir Patrick Wymes,** *and led by Sir Thomas Lucas) followed by the other Division; wherein Sir George Wentworth's, commanded by Captain Harman, Sir Charles Coote's by Lieutenant Devalier, and the Lord Lieutenant's by Captain Yarner, who commanded that Division, marched up in order towards two Bodies of the Rebels, consisting of 3000, with a Troop of Horse on each Wing of the Rebels Divisions, they in the meantime giving Fire in his Face; and the other two Bodies that were on the right Wing, consisting of 5000, doing the like on his left Flank_____*

A Letter written from **Isidore's College in Rome** *1642 1643*

The Holy Father and his two Nephews, Cardinal Anthony Barbarinus, Protector of Ireland, and Cardinal Francis Barbarinus, who hath all the Power here in such matters as concern the Pope, have heard of the War and Consederation, which you make for your Religion and Liberty; and truly I cannot express the greatness of the Joy (no wonder) which they conceive here; in such manner, that if they had received Letters, or if you had sent an Agent unto them, to express your Will or Designs, you should want no help, for your better proceeding; wherefore I would have you to send some able Man, with a Declaration of your Grievances, inform of Law.

Be sure you have a great Heart; make some chief Head among you; but reserve the Crown for Gen O Nexts. Remember the old Slavery, wherein you have lived of long time, and the Destruction which will generally come upon you, except you get the upper Hand. You will prevail, if you join together as you ought; God send it. I would advise every chief Officer among you, to have a Secretary along with him, to write a Diurnal of your Passages, and Overthrows which your Enemies receive, will redound much to your, Glory. Spoil not the Country, for fear of Famine. I will not fail to write according as I shall hear from you. We would send unto you a Bull, after the Form of the Bull which Hugh Mac-Baron got, if we had received your Letters. If the Church do well, they will turn over the Election of Prelates there to the Nobility, and will give them Authority in that point.

SOURCE: CHAP. XIV. Transactions in Ireland, Passages relating there unto, in the Years 1642, and 1643. until the Cessation concluded the 15th of Sept. 1643. A Letter written from Isidore's College in Rome, by Bonaventure O-Conney, to Phelim Roe O Neal in Ireland, dated Jan. 4. 1641/2.

In 1644 December and January **1645 Sir Patrick** was involved with Henry Moore's mother and others in a plot to capture Drogheda and hand it to the Scots. He was imprisoned for his actions in 1645 and Ormond broke with him. From his prison he wrote to the King and **Francis Hamilton**. He claimed he had the support of **King Charles** for his actions. He contacted *Colonel James Wemyss* based in London for help. In his letters to Colonel Wemys and to Major Crawford he stressed his Scottish origins and how he was been victimised for having Scottish origins. He was exchanged for Sir Henry Tichbourne in late 1645. He was praised by the King for his services to crown in Ireland.

Sir Patrick Exchanged for Sir Henry Titchbourne
1644_____* in Drogheda, where a "lady of quality" Lady Moore, was in communication with Monroe, and had keys made to let him into the town, and **"Sir Patrick Weams,** *to whom the king had done many favours and (Ormond) many good offices, was considered faulty in that contrivement, at least, as far as the concealing of it."*

Sir Henry Titchborne**: When the Irish Rebellion of 1641 broke out, he was living at Finglas near Dublin. Despite the hostility of the townspeople of Drogheda, who favoured the rebels, he showed great courage and determination in the task of defending the town, and refused to contemplate surrender even when the situation was desperate. When the garrison was reduced to eating their own horses, he said that "he would stay till the last bit of horseflesh was eaten, then fight his way out". Despite repeated onslaughts from the rebels, and some suspicion of treachery on his own side, he managed to hold out from November 1641 until March 1642 when he received reinforcements from James Butler, 1st Duke of Ormond. This was "for the English, the first good news out of Ireland in five appalling months". [3] He then joined forces with Charles, 2nd Lord Moore to prevent the rebels from regaining control of Leinster. They marched on Dundalk, which they took on 26 March: Tichborne became Governor of the town.

The Moore family: Lady Alice (Loftus) Moore, b.1607 d.1649. Charles was married to Alice Loftus, a reputedly unpleasant woman who, in April 1645, was imprisoned for her attempts to betray the garrisons of Dundalk and Drogheda to Cromwell's army. She was a widow at the time and Charles Moore had been former governor of the town of Drogheda she played a leading part in the plot, taking waxed impressions of the keys to help the plotters seize control. She died on 13 June 1649, from gangrene, after breaking her leg falling off her horse.

Charles Moore*** became, the second Viscount in 1628 and was killed at the Battle of Portlester while fighting for Charles I in the English Civil War in 1643. Moore was a Protestant, unlike many of his relatives who remained Catholic. Charles was succeeded by his son **Henry**, the third Viscount, who was raised to an Earldom, as Earl of Drogheda, in 1661. **Charles's mother was Mary Colley,** daughter of **Sir Henry Colley of Castle Carbury:** her brother Henry Colley d. 1584 junior was an Irish soldier and landowner and was the direct ancestor of the *Duke of Wellington. Also 11th Great Grandparents of* **Princess Dianna** *(Spencer) Windsor & 12th Greats to Dana Neil Wellesley & Prince William & Prince Henry (Harry) Windsor.*

It is documented that Sir Patrick had "a close relative, Colonel Wemyss, who lived in London".

Colonel James Wemyss* (1610? –1667), master-gunner of England and general of the artillery in Scotland, belonged to the Fifeshire family of this name, which is now represented by the Earl of Wemyss. He was descended from **James Wemyss,** second son of **Sir David Wemyss of Wemyss** (1513–1544). His mother was **Janet Durie**, lady of Cardan in the parish of Auchtenderran in Fife. He came to London in the **winter of 1629–30** with his uncle, Colonel Robert Scott, and devoted himself to gunnery and all that appertained thereto.

Notes on Colonel James Wemyss: At the time Patrick was in contact with Col Wemyss, the Colonel was on the Royalist side, he changed to the Parliament side during the English civil war, probably to ensure that whatever way it went there would be a Wemyss on the winning side so as to protect their property and influence. It was actually after the battle of the Cropredy bridge (June **1644)** that Col. Wemyss deflected to the Parliament side. He was promoted to the rank of General and he is recorded as being in charge of Cromwell's Artillery at the battle of Dunbar in Sept 1650. When Royalty was restored, he was pardoned and eventually he was Knighted.

NOTE: Sir David's second son was Sir James Wemyss Baronet of Wemys who was Sir Patrick grandfather, so Colonel James Wemyss and Sir Patrick were the same line and were cousins.

SOURCE: * Belling's, Fragmenta, in Des. Cur. Hib., II, p. 265. **https://en.wikisource.org/wiki/Wemyss,_James_(DNB00) Source Historical Society. ***Upon Colonel Moore's Report from the Committee for Irish Affairs, 'House of Commons Journal Volume 4: 30 September 1645', Journal of the House of Commons: volume 4: 1644-1646 (1802), pp. 293-95. **Wikipedia Upon Colonel Moore's Report, from the Committee for Irish Affairs, 'House of Commons Journal Volume 4: 30 September 1645', Journal of the House of Commons: volume 4: 1644-1646 (1802), pp. 293-95.

The manuscripts of the Marquis of Ormonde

Prison Exchange *Sir Henry Tichburne:* 95_____ *Since [first wrote this letter, wo understand **Sir Patrick Wembs**] and diverse others are committed. If it should prove so, which 1 believe not, we had been in a good condition when he had knowne all our minds. Sir Thomas Lucas in his place were the onely man, or whomsoever your Lordship confides in most. I have dischardged my heart and my conscience. Whatsoever your Lordship hears of my actions or words, believe the ends are to render visible my loyaltie to my kinge, and to witnesse that none more faithfully honors your Lordship then doth your Excellencies most obliged and devoted servant. _____ In the next place we are all waiting upon the returne of **Sir Henry Tichburne**. Your Lordship hath a hard game to play as ever was dealt, a wolfe's eares are but a ticklish hold. I pray God direct your Lordship in a matter of that great importance in which your Lordship and our posterities are concerned. Pardon my devotion if I humbly offer my opinion.*

Prison Exchange Sir Patricks: *Resolved, &c. ** That this House doth approve of the Exchange of Sir Robert Meredith, the Lady Moore, **Sir Patrick Weymes,** Sir Robert Hannay, Captain Ponsonby, Captain Wentworth, Lieutenant Draper, Mr. Batten, Mr. Towneley, Lieutenant Towneley, and Quartermaster Hatch, now Prisoners, or at Liberty upon Bail, in England and Ireland, to the Enemy, to be exchanged for the Lord Brabason, Sir Henry Titchborne, and Sir James Ware, now Prisoners to the Parliament, in the Tower of London: And that the said Sir Robert Meredith shall be at his Liberty to remain free from Restraint in Ireland, or to come into this Kingdom, which he pleaseth: And that, the said Lord Brabason, Sir Hen. Titchborne, and Sir James Ware, giving Security to the Lieutenant of the Tower for Performance of this Exchange, they be thereupon freed from Imprisonment.*

SOURCE: The manuscripts of the Marquis of Ormonde preserved at the castle, Kilkenny Castle. (3 vol. WW X) MSS. ob MARQUIS OP Ormonde. 1644-5. 93 https://archive.org/stream/manuscriptsofmar01greauoft/manuscriptsofmar01greauoft_djvu.txt

On June 19, 1647 Ireland's Lord Lieutenant, the Marquis of Ormond, unconditionally surrendered the city of Dublin to the parliament of England. Ormond's biographer, Thomas Carte, records that in January of this year the Marquis received a private dispatch clearly indicating Charles I's pleasure --if it were impossib1'e to hold Dublin and the other royalist garrisons in his name they were to be surrendered to the English rather than the Irish. The loss of the major royalist stronghold in Ireland proved, in effect, to be the turning point of the war in that Kingdom: it has given Ormond's political character its most ugly stain. In the opinion of his unsympathetic contemporaries, Ormond had traitorously betrayed Ireland; he surrendered Dublin to the parliamentarians in overt opposition to the kings wish that he ally with the Confederate Irish. The fact, however, remains; Dublin could not be held for the king. Ormond chose what he considered the lesser of two evils.

Ormond's biographer, Thomas Carte *1646*: Received letter from R.K. & Beale / Neale suggesting treaty, if Ormond was not engaged to the Irish, & requesting safe passage for **Sir Patrick Wemys***, who would act as intermediary. Ormond replied? March that he would receive any propositions that would preserve the English under his command, by a hand other than **Wemys** "who's coming hither I might not for the present admit of." Which letter I find by or from Major Rawdon* to Sir Maurice Eustace* he received or sent to you, Mr. Annesley, c. 1 March. O had no reply, so he is writing to nudge them to bring propositions. *Sir Pat was just released from prison for treason hence Ormond reaction to him..*

IRISH GENEALOGIST ON THE DANESFORT WEMYS

No 75 Tuesday 19th to Sat 3rd October 1746: Death a few days ago on his way to Bath: *Patrick Wemyss* Knt. For Kilkenny

The Irish Genealogist Vol. 10 No 2 quoting from Faulkner's Dublin Journal of 1762 No 3620: Tuesday 19th to Sat 23 January 1762: Death of *Patrick Wemys* at Danesfort on 20th January

The Irish Genealogist Vol. 10 No 1; Burgesses of Inistoge, Kilkenny c. 1757 *Henry Wemyss*

The Irish Genealogist Vol. 9 No 2 quoting Pue's Occurrences 1765 No 3955: Tuesday 19th to Sat 23rd March 1765: Death on Temple Bar descendant of a noble family Lieut. *Henry Wemyss* and a near relation of Rt. Hon. Countess of Brandon.

The Irish Genealogist Vol.9 No 2 quoting Faulkner's Dublin Journal 1765 No 3997: Tues. 13th to St 17th August 1765: at Bath *James Wemys* MP for Kilkenny

The Irish Genealogist Vol.4 No 6 quoting from Ramsey's Waterford Chronicle 1771 No 207.8: Tuesday 8th to Sat 12th April 1771: Died a few days ago at the house of her brother-in-law, Count. James Staunton at Waterville Galway, *Abigail Wemyss* an unmarried lady.

Marriages from Irish Genealogy records Vol. 8 No.2 for Dioceses of Ossory 1739-1804: 12th December 1772 *Mary Wemys*/ James McRoberts. 1st May 1773 *James Wemys*/Margaret Blundell. 8th November 1781 *Harriet Wemys*/Thomas Pope

Patrick was a nobleman a native of Raith, Fife Scotland b.1604, d. 30 May 1661, buried the next day in St Auden's Dublin. His father was Reverend Patrick Wemyss Vicar of Acombe, near York. (whose father was Sir James Wemyss of Bogie) and Mother was Elizabeth Preston.

Sir Patrick married Mary Wheeler abt.1634 in Queens County. Mary was b.abt.1606 at Grenan, Laois, Ireland, Mary d. May 31, 1660 buried at St Canice Dublin. Mary was a daughter of Jonah Wheeler the Bishop of Ossory; Kilkenny and through her Sir Patrick established many powerful local connections.

Sir Patrick Wemys Mary Wheeler Children

They had five sons of which two died as bachelors. Little is known about the third son Jonah as no records have been found in which his name appears. Only *Maurice* and *Henry* had children.

JAMES WEYMES (Sir) Heir. abt, 1635 Drogheda, Louth Ireland. He died 11 November 1674 and was buried at St Andrews Kilkenny. Married 5 February 1665 Judith, daughter of Sir William Usher, Knight. Clerk of the Council. By whom he had two daughters.

THOMAS WEMYS b. abt,1641, Drogheda, Louth, d.1672, Kilkenny, a Bachelor.

MAURICE WEMYS b.abt, 1639, Drogheda, Louth Ireland d.1670, Danesfort Kilkenny.

Maurice who had a son - Francis Wemys who moved to Kill Kildare and gave rise to the Kildare and Offaly lines covered in different sections.

SIR HENRY WEMYS Knight. abt,1638, Drogheda, Louth Ireland; d.1722, Danesfort Kilkenny. Devisee of half his brother, Sir James' estate. Henry married Elizabeth, daughter of Sir George Blundell, Bart. and had six sons whose heir Patrick, was the ancestor of Wemyss of Danesfort.

JONAS WEMYS b. about 1643, of Drogheda, Ireland died unknown.

Notes TC: Sir Henry Wemys direct descendants stayed in Kilkenny until Major John Otway Wemys the last of this line left for England in 1871 with no issue. Major John Wemys died in Kensington London in 1891 and is buried in Fife Scotland. He was married to Julia Sophia Browne who died with no heir; she sold the Danesfort estate in 1892. Major John was said to have had several illegitimate children but one son was called Otway-Wemys born 08 Dec 1844, Black Mill, St Kilkenny Ireland, born to Sara Courtney. Unfortunately, I was unable to find any other information on her. The name was brought forward by Mary Nolan that states on the birth cert Robert son of John Wemyss gentlemen who had a son-by-son Robert Wemys b 1847 Thomastown Kilkenny. He carried the family name forward.

SOURCE: The history of Hemingbrough, Baptism01610-11, Feb. 5. Abigail, dau. Patrick Weemes 14 of Hemingbrough, bp. 14 Patrick Weemes was vicar of Acombe, near York. Was he at this time one of the curates at Hemingbrough ? https://archive.org/stream/historyantiquiti00burt/historyantiquiti00burt_djvu.txt. Rev James Graves - 1629 Mentioned in marriage agreement between his cousin Elizabeth Preston James Butler (Ormond) and Richard Christy. Dublin Library Archives- Sir pat 1929 appointed commissioner for selling and letting lady Preston's lands: Henry Staines and Pat Wemyss collected rents and payed half yearly £550 to Lord Middlesex and surp

184 Weymond
2&3 Talbot

Wheeler

see Vol 14
Page 43

Wheeler

Martha TUCKER _____

Family 1: Jonas WHEELER

1.+Oliver WHEELER

2. Elizabeth WHEELER

3. Frances WHEELER

4. Grizell WHEELER

5. Sarah WHEELER

6. Martha WHEELER

7. Mary WHEELER

Mary WHEELER _____

Father: Jonas WHEELER

Mother: Martha TUCKER

Family 1: Sir Patrick WEMYSS

Jonas WHEELER

Mary WHEELER

WHEELER FAMILY TREE

Jonas Wheelers daughter married Sir Patrick Wemys.

Mary Wheeler b.1606 in Grenan, d. May 31, 1660 in Of Danesfort, Kilkenny, Ireland. Mary Wheeler was left £10 by her father Jonas.

Her father was Jonas Wheeler (1543–1640) who was Bishop of Ossory from 1613 until his death in 1640 age 97 years which was a great age for that time. Jonas was educated at the puritan seminary of Brasenose College, Oxford and held the office of Dean of Christ Church Cathedral, Dublin from 1595 until 1618 (the last five years in commendam).

"Wheeler, educated at the puritan seminary of Brasenose, was accused of a typically godly aversion to 'all orders and organs'. He had been brought over to Ireland by another Oxford graduate on Hammer's list, the Lord Deputy, Sir William Russell, one of a succession of chief governors, ranging from Grey to Chichester, who had radical protestant associations or inclinations"

Jonas as Queen Elizabeth chaplain

Jonas Wheeler was chaplain to Queen Elizabeth and also chaplain to James I (refer Ossory Clergy and Parishes, Rev. James B. Leslie 1933). Jonas Wheeler was also Dean of Christ Church Cathedral, Dublin (1595 - 1618) and Bishop of Ossory, Ireland (1613 - 1640).

Legal papers relating to lands, 1561-1711 (Records of the Cathedral of the Holy Trinity commonly called Christ Church, Dublin 12th-20th Cent.)

A lease from Jonas Wheeler, Dean, & the Chapter to Richard Roth of the common garden in Rochel Lane, 3 Dec. 1607.

Jonas Wheeler married Martha Tucker b.1646.d.1646: May.

Through his son Oliver*, Jonas was the ancestor of the Wheeler-Cuffe Baronets. He died on 19 April 1640, aged 97. His widow died in 1646. He was described as a prelate who was "esteemed for his hospitable and obliging temper", and for his genuine piety.

SOURCE: https://epdf.tips/james-ussher-theology-history-and-politics-in-early-modern-ireland-and-england.html, *https://en.wikipedia.org/wiki/Jonas_Wheeler_(bishop

Rev Jonah Wheeler & Martha's Children

Mary Wheeler who married Sir Patrick. Oliver Wheeler **b.**1600, d.1673, of Grenan, Grenan, County Laois. **Married** Catherine Weldon (1605-80) daughter of Walter (-1634). Born in County Kent England.

Oliver Wheeler & Catherine Weldon Children

Jonah (1630-97) High Sheriff of Kilkenny in 1673 married Dorcas Perceval (1636-90) daughter of Philip (1603-47).

Elizabeth (1637) married William Hooey (1634-99) son of John (1606-64)." William Hooey whose daughter Elizabeth _____Philip Wheeler (1661)".

Francis (1644-1712) High Sheriff of Kilkenny in 1698. Married Mary Tighe (1652) daughter of Richard (-1674) Mayor of Dublin 1651 & 1655. Residence Lyrath House Kilkenny. They had an only son Richard who married Rose daughter of George Brabrazon. They had Jonah and Oliver.

Francis Wheeler (1644) His Grandson

Jonah Wheeler (1714-76) married Elizabeth Denny Cuffe (1719-89) daughter of Denny Cuffe (1685-1763).

*Wheeler-Cuffe: The Family became known as Wheeler-Cuffe when son Richard Denny Wheeler-Cuffe (1748-97) inherited the Cuffe estates in 1763. His son Sir Jonah Denny Wheeler-Cuffe (1770-1853) was the last Baronet of Ireland in 1799. Jonah only brother William Oliver Wheeler-Cuffe (1779-1863) changed his name to Wheeler and is Kens Bryant's ancestor.

Cuffe Family: Family of Maurice Cuffe (1581-1638) settled in Ireland who was great grandson of Sir John Cuffe (-1552) friend & hunting partner of King Henry 8th.

Denny: Family of Thomas Denny (1595) settled in Ireland who was son of Sir Edward Denny (1547-1600) member of Queen Elizabeth 1st Private Chamber who was son of Sir Anthony Denny (1501-49) Privy Councillor to King Henry 8th. Lease by Lord Ormonde -Lease by Visct. Thurles (aft. Duke of Ormonde) to Jonas (Wheeler) Bishop of Ossory, of the manor and tythes of Dromore and Ballyraghton, Co. Kilkenny, Oct. 20, 1631.

NOTE PICTURE: Sixteenth century standing cup, presented by Queen Elizabeth to her then chaplain Rev. Jonas Wheeler, when he was promoted to the See of Ossory.

"Her Majesty Queen Elizabeth of Glorious Memory gave this cup to the Right Revd. Dr. Jonas Wheeler, when he was promoted to the See of Ossory. Mrs. Sarah Wheeler, Relict of a Descendant from him, Daughter to Arch Bishop Vesey and Sister of Bishop Vesey, presented it to Dr. Richard Pococke Lord Bishop of Ossory, who leaves it to his Successors Bishops of Ossory"

SOURCE: National Library of Ireland on The Commons Queen Elizabeth's Cup, Kilkenny Cathedral. Silver., by Graves, James Rev. **Kenneth Bryant-Smith** **descendent -Australia**, *Burke's Peerage, Baronetage & Knightage

THE WEMYS OF DANESFERT KILKENNY

Extract from A Topographical Dictionary of Ireland (1837)

-------------*This parish, which is also called Dunfert and Dunsert, comprises 5832 statute acres, as applotted under the tithe act: the land is principally under tillage. Danesfort, the seat of* **Major Henry Wemys,** *is pleasantly situated; in the demesne are the ruins of an ancient church. It is a vicarage, in the diocese of Ossory, and is part of the union of Burnchurch; the rectory is impropriate in the mayor, aldermen, and burgesses of the city of Kilkenny.*

The Wemyss of Danesfort were originally Scottish but were classed as Anglo Irish and were in Danesfort for 200 years. Sir Patrick Wemys a nobleman of Fife, Scotland, settled in Danesfort in 1630 after being given the medieval castle, manor in Danesfort from James, Earl of Ormond.

Sir Patrick Wemys was land commissioner to his first cousin Lady Elizabeth Preston.

On the day of their marriage Lady Elizabeth Preston and Lord James Butler leased the lands of Danesfort to Sir Patrick Wemys with the understanding that they give a pair of gloves each Christmas as rent. This was possibly done because Sir Patrick Wemyss contrived that his first cousin Elizabeth Preston and James Butler (Ormond) should first meet at Church in London and sit together in the same pew. Then Lord James Butler still a teenager at the time went to the Lady Elizabeth house in London pretending to be a glove pedlar and managed to get Lady Elizabeth to the back door, knowing there was a message in the gloves she went upstairs read the letter from James then gave the gloves back saying they were not suitable but she had hidden a reply in the gloves.

Direct Descendants

Sir Patrick Wemys & Mary Wheeler

Henry Wemys & Elizabeth Blundell

Patrick Wemys & Lydia Anna Hancock

James Wemys & Jane Stratford

James Wemys & Martha Blunden

Henry Wemys & Elizabeth Cuffe

John Otway Wemys & Julia Sophia Browne

No Male Heir last of this direct family tree

SOURCE: *From IRISH BUILDERS OF CIVILIZATION- National Archives Dublin. Weymes (Patrick)-D3729-30, Lease and counterpart by Earl od Osmond and his feofesse to Patrick Weymes and Richard Christie of Danesfort and Bennet bridge Kilkenny August 3rd 1629.*

The Wemys family were substantial landlords in the townlands of Rathclough, Ballyda, Croan, Knock and Annamult. They built their palatial house beside the principal main road for trade purposes and a cottage on the side of the road as a bakery for food and drink for travellers.

The entrance was approached by a wide Avenue, which was surrounded on both sides by lime trees. The Wemyss carried out a great farming business, with many farm hands and large number of household staff.

Patrick Wemys son Henry Wemys developed the manor in 1690 and it was redeveloped in the eighteen hundred. *It was Georgian in style with a large, handsome columned portico. They also added a bathing pool in the 18th century. A cooper stature of *Charles 1* was in front of the house given as a mark of gratitude from the king for the loyalty of the Wemyss during the civil war.

The lease of land had been renewed from Ormonde in 1711 and 1790, which were fee- farm grants which basically made the Wemys owners. In 1790 Sir John Blunden Baronet, of castle Blunden was granted land from the Wemys.

Sir Johns daughter was married to Lucy Susanna Cuffe and their daughter Martha married James Wemys (b. 1743) of Danesfort. Martha's son Henry Wemys (b. 1785) Danesfort, married Lady Elizabeth Mary Cuffe and were related.

Deer park -They had a large Deer park and built an octagonal Turret about 1730 on an ancient prehistoric site as a hunting den. It was set back from the road and shared with Danesfort House on an elevated site. In the Turret they held parties and deer hunting.

On the ground floor, the women were entertained while the men went upstairs to shoot deer. The poor servants in tribulation of their lives as the gentlemen were drinking had to herd the deer to outside the Turret.

Locally, at Danesfort cross there is a Rath -A ringfort built sometime between the Iron Age and the Viking Age. Nearby are the ruins of the fifteenth century St Michael the Archangels Roman Catholic Church.

SOURCE: House Danesfort Kilkenny: Archaeology and Cultural Heritage, Sites of Architectural Importance

FAMILY LIFE AT DANESFORT HOUSE

Through Mary Wheeler, Sir Patrick made good connections and marriages with the: Agar, Blunden's, Blundell's, Cuffs.

The Wemys educated their children at Kilkenny college and Trinity College Dublin. Maurice Wemys was the youngest to enter trinity at age 14 years. Although they were mainly Military, they also held important post as MPs, and heads of the estates.

Another statue in a field opposite the house was a large bronze statue of **James 2nd** dressed in roman toga. At the Hell Fire club Dublin 1700, *there was an argument about the statues in Dublin Squares and Parks between the Wemys, Langrishes, Blakes and possibly a Butler. They wagered they could steel a statue and convey it to England without it been missed. However, they were pursued by the Watch(police), and Mr Blake shot and killed the pursuers horse causing the cart to tumble and the Watch to fall to his death. When they passed Danesfort Cross they threw the statue into the Wemys field, but were soon caught. Apparently, the law was difficult to enforce at that time and because they came from powerful family's they were released.

This is probably the statue that Folklore says that the Wemyss erected on their estate called by various names "the Scotchman", the "Metal man". It stood on a solid stone and his height was about twelve feet. It was alleged that the statue was pointing with his right hand towards Scotland the country of the Wemyss origin. The statue remained there until 1936, and then sold to Major Loftus.

The last of the Wemyss family were Colonel Henry and Elizabeth (Cuffe) Wemys and son John. Henry and his wife lived uneventful frugal lives, farming and making Jam. In 1826 Lady Elizabeth and Major Henry were described in a letter by Marie Edgeworth at a dinner party with her in-law's Dr and Mrs Butler. She claimed that Major Wemys spoke of little that wasn't farming and Lady Elizabeth was very kind in nature, very fragile, tall and thin, and not very intelligent.

Their son John Otway Wemys was very extravagant and known for fast living. He married at 45 years to Julia Sophia Browne, she was first cousin to his mother lady Elizabeth both them were grandchildren to 2nd Earl of Altamont. They had no legitimate Heir so this was the end of the Wemyss of Danesfort however he was known to have had several illegitimate children from his youth.

Sometime after 1885 he fled his debtors in the middle of the night borrowing carts from neighbours to get his possession to the port. He died May 1891, at 30 Ovington sq. London. The estate went to auction in 1896 and the house eventually fell into decay and ruin.

NOTE: -Hellfire Club was a name for several exclusive clubs for high-society gentlemen in the 18th century.

SOURCES: In the shadow of the Steeple. The old Kilkenny review Night Ride 1970. Kilkenny in the days of the Dukes by Hubert Butler the Wemyss family of Danesfort county Kilkenny by Francis McEvoy

JAMES WEMYS *b.1635 Son of Sir Patrick & Mary Wheeler*

JAMES WEMYS b. abt 1635 and was buried 18 Nov 1672 in Danesfort. MP for Knocktopher. Married JUDITH USHER b.abt 1639 Drogheda Eire. Married on 05 Feb 1665 in Danesfort Kilkenny. She was the daughter of Sir William Usher, Knight. Clerk of the Council. By whom he had two daughters.

Sir James Wemys WILL: Dated 18 Nov 1672, following, devised his estates, subject to a jointure for his wife and portions for his daughters, between his younger brother **Henry Wemys** and his nephew **Francis Wemyss.**

Leased Cow Lane Dublin *(Near Temple Bar Dublin City)*. In Mary Copley also Chichester's WILL Ranelagh, left her house to son for rent to Sir James Wemys and Sir John Cole for Cow St Dublin.

James Wemys & Elizabeth Usher -Children

Elizabeth Wemys b 1667 d.19 July 7, 1688 unmarried in her 21st year, was buried at St Andrews.

Judith Mary Wemys b. abt 1668 in Drogheda and d. bef 1671 in Dublin.

MAURICE WEMYS *b.1639 Son of Sir Patrick & Mary Wheeler*

MAURICE WEMYS b. abt 1639 in Drogheda. He married ELIZABETH WEMYS. b. abt 1660, d.aft. 1770 in Kilkenny. **In Kilkenny Member:** As follows: Maurice died *1670* leaving by Elizabeth his wife a son Francis Wemys of Roestown Kildare MP for Harristown 1695-96. **Maurice *Weyms*-**Year **1670,** Residence Dunfert, Kilkenny.

Proni -Francis Wemys is written as born in 1673. Maurice supposedly died 1670!

The napoleon Series by Ron McGuigan -Also spelt **Morris WEMYS**

Ireland Diocesan and **Prerogative Wills** & Administrations indexes 1595-1858.

Maurice Wemys and Elizabeth Wemys Child

FRANCIS WEMYS b.abt. 1670 in Danesfort Kilkenny. Died in 1738 in *Blind Quay,* Cadogan Alley. Dublin City. He married (1) JOYCE BLUNDELL abt.1690. (2) MARY MCCULLOCH abt.1734. She d.aft. 1747 in *Blind Quay Cadogan Alley* Dublin. **See Kildare**

*NOTES for Judith Usher: Ussher Family 1. Catherine Ussher (1608) married Sir Philip Perceval (1603) 2. Judith Ussher (1636) daughter of William (1610) & Elizabeth Parsons married James Wemyss (1635). William Ussher (1610) married as 2nd wife Ursula St Barbe were 8th ggparents of HRH Prince Charles & 9th ggparents of Lady Diana. *Name sometimes written as Weymes. SOURCE: Sir Arthur Vicars, Index to The Prerogative Wills of Ireland ,1536-1810, And Supplement (1914). Elizabeth Weymes Year 1688*

Son of Sir Patrick Wemyss & Mary Wheeler

Henry Wemys b.abt 1641 Drogheda, d.1722 Danesfort Kilkenny.

Henry Wemys MP -Callan 1692/3, 1695/9; Kilkenny 1703/13/14.bet. 1692–1695 in Callan and Gowran, 1639-48 and Knocktopher 1661. He was returned twice to Callen to King William III Parliaments and twice for the county in the reign of Queen Anne.

Sheriff -He was Sheriff of County Kilkenny in 1695. Henry was appointed a JP for the County and received the honour of knighthood in 1677.

Index to Irish Wills Vol 1 -Sir Henry Wemys, Kilkenny, *1722.* Sir Henry on his death left two sons, and three daughters.

James married ELIZABETH **BLUNDELL** b.abt 1645, in 1671, Diocese of Dublin, Ireland.

Elizabeth, was the eldest daughter of:

Baronet Sir George BLUNDELL MP for Dingle and held the office of Sheriff of King's County in 1657 also MP for Philipstown Ireland between 1661 and 1666. Elizabeth's mother Sarah (see Blundell's), only daughter of Sir William Colley, of Edenderry, Kings county MP for Kildare, 1613, who was the grandson of *Sir Henry Colley*, who was MP for Thomastown in 1559.

Henry Wemys & Elizabeth Blundell -*children*

HENRY WEMYS b. about 1674 in Dunfert, Kilkenny, Ireland. Buried 30th September 1753 at Mallards town the burial ground for St Marys Church Kilkenny. No issue.

*Quaker- Henry Weymes Jr, Denomination **Quaker,** Congregation 8 November 1727, Ireland.

PATRICK WEMYS *HEIR b.* 1679 in Danesfort, Kilkenny, Ireland. d. 25 September 1747. Married *Lydia Anna Handcock* -see chapter

GEORGE WEMYS b.abt 1679 in Danesfort, Kilkenny, Ireland. d. bef 1722. (mentioned in some of the Wemyss deeds for property).

SARA WEMYS b. 1678 in Danesfort, Kilkenny, Ireland. **Married** Rev Martin Hartstonge in 1706.

ELIZABETH WEMYSS b.abt 1672, Danesfort, Kilkenny, Ireland; **Married** ARTHUR (ESQ.) WEBB; b. abt 1660, Webbsborough, Kilkenny. NOTE: *In his WILL Sir Henry left two sons so George must have already died.* SOURCE: ***Archive Religious Society of Friends in Ireland Archives,** *Description YM Parliamentary Committee minutes.1698-1730*

SARAH COLLEY

Sir Henry Colley, or Cowley (died 1584) was an Irish soldier and landowner. He is chiefly remembered today as an ancestor of the 1st Duke of Wellington. Sir Henry Colley a soldier in the royal service was given the manor and castle of Edenderry in 1562 along with Drumcooley and other lands. *Edenderry was then known as Colleystown.*

George Colley in 1581 he left Edenderry to his eldest son George who died in 1614 and was succeeded by his son William.

William Colley William had two children **Sarah** who married **Sir George Blundell** and George who married in 1648 but had no family. On his death the Edenderry estate passed to his sister Lady **Sarah.**

THE BLUNDELLS

Sara Colley & George Blundell's children

Baronet Sir Francis BLUNDELL b.30 Jan 1643, Phillipstown Ofally.d.1707 was an Irish politician.

Winword Blundell Unknown

William Blundell. Married Anne Taylor Daughter -

In 1674 the three of them killed *Thomas Preston*, son of a Catholic peer, Lord Tara. They were acquitted of murder and pardoned by Charles II.

ELIZABETH BLUNDELL.b.1645 Married **Henry Wemys** in 1675- See chapter.

The Blundell family probably occupied the castle on the hill until it was sacked in 1690. It was never rebuilt. The last Blundell burials to take place in Edenderry which were recorded in the Monasteroris Church Register, were Sarah Blundell, died in 1701 and Francis, died in 1707.

Note TC: Georges son who married Ann Taylor were the parents of Joyce Blundell b.abt 1684 d.1732 who married Francis Wemys B 1684 D.1738 my ancestor (Westmeath Wemys)

Agar (later Agar-Ellis) of Gowran Castle, Viscounts Clifden. Charles Agar d. 1696, who moved from Yorkshire to Kilkenny and purchased the Gowran Castle estate. His son **James (1672-1733),** rebuilt the castle as a modern house in 1713, and it descended in his family until 1899. **James's heir, Henry Agar** 1705-46 was MP for Gowran in the Irish Parliament from 1727-46. His brother, **James Agar (**1713-69), purchased the Callan estate from the Cuffs, Earls of Dysart, and his son became the 1st and only Baron Callan. On Lord Callan's death in 1815, the Callan estate was added to the Kilkenny estates of the senior branch of the family.

Ellis Agar (1709-89) who married the 7th Earl of Mayo and later the 18th Baron Athenry, and who was reputedly the mistress of King George II, was the daughter of James Agar (d. 1733). She was created Countess Brandon for life in 1758.

JAMES AGAR & MARY WEMYS Children

MARY WEMYS Daughter of Henry Wemys & Elizabeth Blundell. Mary b.1665 in Danesfort, Kilkenny, Ireland. d.15 April 1771 in Gowran, Kilkenny, Ireland. **Marry married James Agar** (son of Charles Agar and Ellis Blanchevilles) about 1702. James Agar b.1670 in Gowran, Kilkenny, Ireland. d.30 Nov 1733 in Gowran, Kilkenny, Ireland.

Waterford Chronicle *1771 16-19th April:* **Died aged 106,** *Mary Agar, daughter of Sir Henry Wemyss of Danesfort.* **Death Notice** Mary died on Monday 15 April 1771 at Ringwood, Kilkenny, Ireland. Mrs. Mary Agar, a widow aged 106 by whose death a jointure of £1,000 per ann. together with a great share of her personal fortune devolves to her grandson James Agar Esq. one of the Knights of the Shire for this county.

Mary Wemys & James Agar Children

Henry Agar *Heir.* b.1700, d.18 Nov 1746 in Gowran, Kilkenny, Ireland. He married (1) ANNE ELLIS on 29 May 1733. She was born on 26 Jul 1707 in Mendip, Somerset, England. She died on 14 Apr 1761. His children were James, Henry, Charles, Wand Lucy Diana.

Charles Agar, married 22 Nov 1776 Dublin Jane Benson d. 25 Oct 1826, had issue. Their children were, Francis, George, Henry and James and Wellbore Ellis.

James Agar (of Ringwood) b. c 1704, d. 1769 in Gowan Kilkenny. He married REBECCA FLOWER DURROW. She was born in 1706 in Ringwood, Kilkenny, Ireland.

MARY AGAR b.1711 in Gowan Kilkenny, d.04 May 1784 in St Thomas Dublin. She married 1742 **James Smyth** d. 1771 MP of Tinny Park (Wicklow), and had issue one son and three daughters.

SOURCE: *http://landedfamilies.blogspot.co.uk/2013/06/52-agar-later-agar-ellis-of-gowran.html*

ELLIS Elizabeth AGAR (COUNTESS) THEOBD. BRANDON was b. 1708, d. 1789, in Gowan Kilkenny. Elder daughter of James Agar (c.1671-1733) and his second wife **Mary, daughter of Sir Henry Wemyss of Danesfort.** First Marriage -She married 7th Viscount Mayo Theobald Bourke, son of 6th Viscount Mayo Theobald Bourke and Mary Browne on 04 Mar 1726. He was born in 1706 in Ballintober Mayo. He died on 07 Jan 1741 in Middlesex London. Second Marriage -In 1742 she married secondly (1745) Francis Birmingham, 14th Baron Athenry (1692–1750), but died without issue. She was reputedly a mistress of King George II, and was described as having 'genuine wit, elegance of taste, dignity of manners, and superior understanding'. She was created Countess of Brandon for life, 15 September 1758 a peerage which is hard to account for except by exceptional royal favour.

The Countess of Brandon in 1758 Ellis Birmingham was granted (for life only) the title "Countess of Brandon, in the County of Kilkenny", a title in the Peerage of Ireland. She died in Dublin, 11 March 1789, aged 80, and the earldom became extinct on her death. A monument designed by Edward Smyth was erected to her memory in Gowran church by her nephew, the 1st Viscount, to whom she bequeathed a legacy, specifying that £300 should be spent on the monument. The Right Reverend Charles Agar, 1st Earl of Normanton, was Lady Brandon's nephew.

Patrick Wemys HEIR b.1679, d. (Probate 06 May 1762) 25th September 1747, Danesfort Kilkenny, Ireland. Educated at Kisby College. Patrick Wemyss MP for Gowran 1703/4; Co. Kilkenny 1721-7-47. Patrick Weymes*-Denomination Quaker, Congregation 10th October 1731, Ireland. Patrick Wemys** (Wems)SC. (Dr Hindon, Kilkenny), Sept 24,1696, aged 17, s. of Henry, Eques auratus; Kilkenny. BA Vern 1700. (MP. Gowen 1703 AND 1713; Kilkenny. 1721 AND 1727) From Kilkenny Members. Patrick Wemys*** Estate: Sale of houses in Dublin for payment of debts and settling lands in Kilkenny and elsewhere to the same uses." Patrick Wemys**** 1753 - Re: Case for opinion, Query title to lands in Kilkenny. Gives family affairs 1697-1753 1754 - Re: Draft Mortgage, Shillogher, Co Kilkenny, 1760 - Re: Assignment of Lands, Co Kilkenny.1750-55 - Re: Transcript List of State Papers. 1760 - Re: Assignment of Lands, Kilkenny. *Ancestors and descendants of Robert Clements Vol 11.*

Patrick married Lydia Anna Handcock on 14 May 1702 in Dunfert, Kilkenny, Ireland.

House of Lords Journal Volume 20 3 April 1717

*Wemys' Pet. referred to Judges. : *Upon reading the Petition of* **Patrick Wemys** *Esquire; praying, "That Leave may be given to bring in a Bill, to enable him to dispose of so many of his Houses and Premises standing in the City and County of the City of Dublin, the Rents whereof do not exceed Two Hundred and Fifty Pounds per Annum, thereby to raise Money, to pay off and discharge several Debts in the Petition mentioned, and for other Purposes therein expressed: "It is Ordered, by the Lords Spiritual and Temporal in Parliament assembled, That the Consideration of the said Petition be, and is hereby, referred to the Lord Chief Baron of the Court of Exchequer and Mr. Baron Price; who are forthwith to summon all Parties concerned in the Bill; and, after hearing them, to report to the House the State of the Case, with their Opinion thereupon, under their Hands, and whether all Parties that may be concerned in the Consequences of the Bill have signed the Petition; and also that the Judges, having perused the Bill, do sign the same.*

Prerogative Will index -*written in T 559/41:* Patrick Wemys of Danesfort Co Kilkenny WILL 1745. *WILL dated 20 April 1745*, PR 6 May 1762. Children mentioned, Henry Eldest, Patrick Wemys Captain OB anti 1765 (His Will), WILL dated 19 Jan 1762 PR 1 Feb 1762 ob. s.p Wife Catherine Bermingham

Below most probably Patrick b. 1779: **Prerogative Will -William Napper Meath 1741 Land left to sister Anne Marie Pollard in Dublin purchased from **Mr Wemys.**

Sir William Handcock was the son of William Handcock and Abigail Stanley. Sir William Handcock matriculated on 16 March 1670/71 at Trinity College, Dublin, William Handcock, pensioner (Mr Thullis), aged about 17; son of William armiger, born co. Westmeath. Sir William Handcock **married** *Elizabeth Coddington on 31 May 1685 at Ireland. Children of Sir William Handcock and Elizabeth Coddington: John Handcock b. 1687, William Handcock b. 26 Nov 1689, Abigail, Anna, Jane. She married secondly James Forth, MP on 14 Oct 1702 at St Michan's Dublin. Sir William Handcock was the Member for Athlone in 1692. Sir William Handcock made a WILL dated 13 September 1701 at Dublin, Ireland. William Handcock, Recorder of the City of Dublin, mentions his wife Elizabeth Handcock, son John, brothers Matthew, Adam, Stephen (Dean of Kilmaduagh), and others, daughters Ann, Abigail & Jane, father William Handcock of Dublin. His WILL was proved in November 1701 at the Prerogative Court of Armagh.*

SOURCE: *From: 'House of Lords Journal Volume 20: 3 April 1717', Journal of the House of Lords: volume 20: 1714-1717, pp. 436-37. URL: http://www.british-history.ac.uk/report.asp?compid=38635. **Irish wills, pleadings and Pedigrees from the Plea Rolls 1569-1909 - Irish wills and pleadings - 57154-12-32.jpg SOURCE: *Description YM Parliamentary Committee minutes. 1731-1778, Note - Quaker 1723/1727/1745. **Alumni Dublineneses by George Dames Burtchaell ***Chronological Tables of the Private and Personal Acts (1539-2000) Part 8 (1714-1721)1716 (3 Geo. 1) ****Found on "Her Majesty's Stationery Office" on-line.

Patrick Wemys **married** on 14 May 1702 Anna b.1676 d. 1740, daughter of Sir William Handcock. **Anna Handcock's Parents** were **Sir William Handcock** (10 September 1655 - September 1701).

Patrick WEMYS & Anna Handcock Children, three son, eight daughters

JAMES WEMYS *HEIR b.abt.* 1709 in Ballyredden Danesfort, Kilkenny, Ireland, d.20 Apr 1765 in Bath. Married JANE STRATFORD, on 03 May 1742 in Church of St Brides Dublin. Jane b.abt.1709 in Chancery Lane Dublin, d. September 1796 in Athy. *See chapter*

HENRY WEMYS b.1703 in Danesfort, Kilkenny, Ireland. He died suddenly in London on 12th October 1750 in St James Palace London, unmarried. Captain in the army. Buried St Marys Church Kilkenny. Henry Wemys MP for Callan 1727/50, Residences: Danesfort. Kilkenny.

ELIZABETH WEMYS b.abt 1709 d.01 Nov 1744 in Danesfort Kilkenny, Ireland.

MARY WEMYS b.1711, d 10 Jan 1791 buried St Thomas Church. Baptised St Peter's, Dublin, Ireland. Mary m*arried* George Hartpole of Shrule in the Queen's County, Esq; and had 3 Sons and 4 Daughters, Robert, Domvile, Henry, Anne, Martha, Elizabeth, and Mary.

JANE WEMYS b.abt 1713 in Danesfort, Kilkenny, Ireland. Jane m*arried Benjamin* Stratford in 30 June 1748 in Corbally Laoghis Counsellor at Law. He was born in Corbally Laois, Father: Eusebius Stratford Mother: Elizabeth Warren. They had a daughter Euseby Stratford.

SARAH WEMYS b.715, d.1748 in Danesfort, Kilkenny. Sarah married George Mangsergh in 1744 an Officer of Foot.

HANNAH WEMYS b.abt 1717 in Danesfort, Kilkenny, Ireland. Hannah married 1748 ISAAC DRURY HIGH SHERIFF b.2dec 1717, d.1786, son of Edward Drury and Mary Baxter.

ALICE WEMYS b.1719 in Of Danesfort, Kilkenny, Ireland.

HARRIET WEMYS b.abt 1721 in Danesfort, Kilkenny, Ireland. Married: James Staunton in 1752.

ABIGAIL WEMYS d,1773, Waterdel, Galway.

The Irish Genealogist: Volume 4. No 6. from Waterford Ramsey's Chronicle of 1771: 8th to 12th APRIL 1771: Died a few days ago at the house of her brother-in-law James Staunton, Abigail Wemyss at Waterville Galway. Ms Wemyss an unmarried lady.

Prerogative Index Abigail Weymes/Year 1772, Residence Waterdale, Co Galway Record set Ireland Diocesan and Prerogative Wills & Administrations Indexes 1595-1858

Patrick Wemys b.1707, d. Feb 1762 in Danesfort, Kilkenny, Ireland. No issue. Patrick was a professional soldier. Captain Patrick Wemys, Company of Foliot's Foot 1744 (Cavan). **MP-**Patrick Wemyss MP for Kilkenny 1747/60; Callan 2-20 Jan 1762. *Patrick Wemys Pen (Mr Little Enniscorthy), March 1724-25 aged 18; s. of Patrick, Armiger; co Kilkenny (MP, Kilkenny 1747).

Married 01 Jul 1750 in Kilkenny, Catherine Bermingham Athenry b.1709, d.1772, daughter of Francis ATHENRY and Countess of Brandon Ellis Athenry on 01 Jul 1750 in Kilkenny. Catherine married Capt. John Cullen of Co. Leitrim one month after his death.

Folklore says she was a drunkard and murdered Patrick and married John Cullen (Captain) one month after Pat died.

Prerogative WILL-Patrick Wemys Captain OB anti 1765.WILL dated 19 Jan 1762 PR 1 Feb 1762 ob. s.p Wife Catherine Bermingham Patrick.

**Weymes, Patrick Title(s): esq Date: 1735 Subscribed to An History of Ireland, from the year 1599 to 1603. With a short narration of the state of the kingdom from the year 1169. To which is added a Description of Ireland (Vol. 1), 1735, MORYSON, Fynes. Dublin

Weims, Patrick Subscribed to A Master-Key to Popery; containing ... a discovery of the most secret practices of the secular and regular Romish Priests in their auricular, 1724, GAVIN, Antonio. Dublin. *GAVIN, ANTONIO (fl. 1726) converted from Catholicism to Protestantism. He obtained the curacy of Gowran, Kilkenny, for a year. The book is well known to have been total fabrication.*

Estates of Patrick Wemys (1707-1762) ***

ALL Persons to whom Henry Wemys, Esq; lately deceased, died indebted, are hereby desired to apply to **Patrick Wemys** *at Danesfort in the County of Kilkenny, Esq; at his House in* **Aungier-street in the City of Dublin,** *that they may be paid their said Debts; and all Persons who are anyways indebted unto the Estate of the said Henry Wemys, are hereby required to pay in the same directly to the said Patrick Wemys of Benjamin Stratford, or they will be sued for the same without further Notice. Dublin, January 8,* **1750.**

*SOURCE: *Alumni Dublineneses by George Dame Burtchaell **U.K. and U.S. Directories and Lists, 1680-1830 ***FAULKNER/The Dublin Journal*

JAMES *Heir* b.1709 in Ballyredden Danesfort, Kilkenny, Ireland. d. 20 Apr 1765 in Bath. **James married-JANE STRATFORD,** daughter of Robert Stratford on 03 May 1742 in Church of St Brides Dublin. She was born about 1709 in Chancery Lane Dublin. She died in September 1796 in Athy. **James Wemyss MP for Callan 1751/60** & **1762/65.** *Wemys, Ja.,* M.P. for Callen, Ireland. 22 Aug 1765. (G.M. 395.) **Army-**He was a 2nd Lieutenant in Dunbar's Regiment.

Death Notice: Tues., 30 July 1765 - Sat. 3 Aug 1765, death at Bath, **James WEMYS,** *Esq, Member of Parliament for CALLAN, in the County of Kilkenny**.*

Proni T/559 -Prerogative **Will** written as **LT James Wemys** 1765. **Proni** Written as mentioned in his fathers WILL 1745 of Danesfort esq WILL dated 9 June 1765 PR 6 September 1765.

Wemys James (Captain) ***Marriage**: 3 May 1742, Marriage Place: St. Bride, Dublin, County Dublin, Ireland Stratford Jane.

JAMES WEMYS & JANE STRATFORD-Children

James Wemys.HEIR.**b.**.1743 08 Aug 1820 Kilkenny. Married Martha Blunden (daughter of Sir John Blunden) 1773. See chapter

Richard Wemys b.abt. 1750. d. after 1820. No records of marriage or children. **Prerogative Will-**Left in Will to nephew James Wemys land. **Freemans Journal - Saturday, April 01, 1820, Page 4.** Kilkenny assizes-Juror **Richard Wemys** esq 1820.

Catherine Wemys b. abt, 1741. Baptised St Bridget's Dublin. Catherine m**arried** William Disney 18 Dec 1770 at Union of Church Burnchurch Kilkenny.

Mary Wemys b.1745. **Married** James Mc Roberts Dioceses of Ossory 12 Dec 1772.

Annie (Harriet)**Wemys.**b.1747.

Harriett Wemys. b. 1753 d. 20 Feb 1830 Danesfort Kilkenny. (see next page)

*Sir John Blunden** of Castle Blunden Baronet (d. 1782). WILL dated 8 June 1782 -proved 14 Feb 1783. He desires that he may not be buried till his body begins to ----- or his head be severed from his body and without ceremony in the round part of the wood where the laurels planed and the ditch of water surrounds it. Children listed - Sir John Blunden, eldest son and heir; William Pitt - 2nd son, Overington Blunden, 3rd son, Charlotte, Araminta, Lucy,* **Martha, wife of Col James Wemys**

*SOURCES: *The Harleian Society. Volume 49.: England ** Faulkner's Dublin Journal Ireland ***Irish Records Extraction Database. D. A. Chart. Marriage Entries from the Registers of the Parishes of St. Andrew, St. Anne, St. Audoen's, & St. Bride (Dublin), 1632-1800. *Burks peerage. ** Taken from Prerogative WILLS of Ireland*

Ossory Marriage Licence Bonds 1739-1804-**Pope Thomas** *Athy Kildare, Wemys Harriot Union of the Burnt Church Spinster. Protestant* **08 Nov. 1781.** *Residence Marion Avenue, Parish, Blackrock, Dublin.*

Thomas Pope and Harriet Wemyss children

James Wemyss Pope b. 1785, Wellington Kilkenny sept. 1846 Dublin.

Thomas Wemyss Pope** *b. abt 1782 Kilkenny*

Harriet Pope b.abt. 1782. see next page

James Wemyss Pope, Lieutenant Colonel

Pope James Wemyss, Esq, 46 Blessington St Dublin.*

James married abt. 1815 Jane Thomasiue Chaloner, b. 1789 d 1885, of Kingsfort Meath, father Richard Chaloner, mother Francis Marie Herbert, grandmother Nicola Sophia Otway Cuffe. Jane died at Barton Regis, Gloucestershire, England. (The Chaloner name was changed from Hamilton in 1700s).

Magistrate: *Letter from William [Moore], Kilkenny, recommending* **James Wemyss Pope** *of Wellington for the position of stipendiary magistrate for Kilkenny. Letter from William [Moore], Kilkenny, to Henry William Paget, Lord Lieutenant, acknowledging the praise of government for his conduct in the proceedings on foot of the [Carrickshock incident]; recommending James Wemyss Pope of Wellington for the position of stipendiary magistrate for Kilkenny; warning that the state of affairs in Knocktopher and Kilmaganny is awful.*

Obituary Daily Times: *POPE, James Wemyss; (1 September 1846) Dublin DUB IRL; Cork Examiner (COR IRL); 1846-1-9; dja.*

HARRIET POPE: Harriet Pope b.abt. 1782. Niece of James Wemys Martha's Blunden. Harriet married William Pitt Blunden on 29 July 1813. William Pitt Blunden*** b. 22 October 1761, d. 17 April 1817 in Castle Blunden, Kilkenny, Ireland. He was the son of Sir John Blunden, 1st Bt. and Hon. Lucy Susanna Cuffe. He was brother of Martha Blunden Wemys.

William Pitt Blunden and Harriet Pope Children

Harriet Blunden, Sir John Blunden, 3rd Bt. b. 21 Dec 1814, d. 27 Jan 1890, William Pitt Blunden b. 15 Nov 1815, d. 1894, Thomas **Wemyss Pope**** b. abt 1782 Kilkenny Married Marie -____. Daughter: Francisca Maria Wemyss Pope b. 03 May 1857, baptism date 12 May 1857, Roman Catholic. Residence Marion Avenue, Parish, Blackrock, Diocese Dublin.

SOURCE: Record 1346 from 'CSO/RP' NAI REFERENCE: CSO/RP/1832/1346 /1832-NAI REFERENCE: CSO/RP/1832/1346. James Wemyss Pope b. 1781 Wellington Kilkenny https://www.ancestry.co.uk/genealogy/records/harriet-wemyss-24-14x8t1h.*Slater's National Commercial Directory of Ireland 1846 **Repository, National Library of Ireland, Roman Catholic Parish Baptisms, Category, Birth, Marriage, Death & Parish Records ***https://www.ancestry.co.uk/genealogy/records/harriet-wemyss-24-14x8t1h

JAMES WEMYS *b.1743* & MARTHA BLUNDEN

Son of James Wemys and Jane Stratford

James* b.1743.d 08 Aug 1820, **Danesfort,** Kilkenny. James** was an **MP** for Kilkenny City 1793-7-1800 and MP city of Kilkenny 1797, Mayor of the city three times, High Sheriff of the city. Army-In the army he became an Ensign Armigers Regiment 1766. Made LT April 1767, made Major Kilkenny rangers 1770, In 1789 he was a Lieutenant Colonel.

James married Martha Blunden b. 1757, d.16 Mar 1816 at St. Patricks on 1 May 1773 Castle Blunden Kilkenny, Danesfort. She was the daughter of Sir John Blunden of Blunden Castle Kilkenny.

James Wemys & Martha Blunden-*Children*

Henry Wemys (Major). HEIR b. Feb 1785, d. 1860, Danesfort, Kilkenny, Ireland. Married Dec 1822 Lady Elizabeth Mary Cuffe. *See chapter.*

John Wemys (LT)b. abt 1787 Danesfort, Kilkenny, Ireland. Died in London May 5th 1806 from a fall from a horse. Lieutenant in the 1st Dragons Guards. Unmarried.

Emma Wemys b 1783. d 25 Nov 1846

Martha Wemys b.1790. d 04 Aug 1838. Married Abraham Ball of Durver.

Charlotte Wemys b abt. 1794. d1858. Married 18 Sep 1825 St Canice's Church George Armstrong d.11 May 1866.

Susannah Lucy Wemys b.1781 Danesfort Kilkenny. *** Married 20 Feb 1802 to Rev Arthur Rolleston of Corgany Cavan.

Jane Wemys b 1788.d. unk. Married 1809, Dublin Abraham Ball b.1785 d. Jan 1819.of Three Castles Kilkenny (Father Richard and Dorothy Margaret Ball). Residence, Three Cutler, Odagh, Kilkenny, Ireland.

Children: Richard Ball b.1810 d.1858. Abraham Ball B.1812, Martha Ball b.1814, Dorothea Margaret Ball b. abt 1816. d 01 Nov 1880.

Frances Wemys b.1792. Married Thomas Hudson, Patrick Ball. Of 1817 of Ball of Bellevue, Middlesex, Ontario Canada. BALL Thomas Hudson Patrick****, Capt. On the 13th at Odagh Glebe, Kilkenny, Capt. Thomas Hudson, Patrick BALL, son of the Rev S BALL to Miss Frances WEYMES sister to Col WEYMES of the Kilkenny Militia.

SOURCES: ***Irish and Anglo-Irish Landed Gentry** Page 681 **End of the Names of the Members of Parliament in Ireland in 1797. 36.--PARLIAMENTARY CONSTITUENCIES IN IRELAND, At the period of the Union. ***Ossory marriage licence ****Faulkner's Dublin Journal FJ 1817, 6, 4 NPM*

A Topographical Dictionary of Ireland (1837) **DANESFORT**

"Danesfort", or Dunfort, a parish, in the barony of Shillelogher, county of Kilkenny, and province of Leinster, 3 miles (S.) from Kilkenny, on the road to Thomastown; with the parish of Annamult, and part of that of Tradingetown or Ballyreddin, 1263 inhabitants. This parish, which is also called Dunfert and Dunsert, comprises 5832 statute acres, as applotted under the tithe act: the land is principally under tillage. Danesfort, the seat of:

Major Henry Wemys, is pleasantly situated; in the demesne are the ruins of an ancient church. It is a vicarage, in the diocese of Ossory, and is part of the union of Burnchurch; the rectory is impropriated in the mayor, aldermen, and burgesses of the city of Kilkenny. In the R. C. divisions, it is the head of a union or district, comprising also the parishes of Ennisnag, Killahane and Grove, Grange Abbey, and Annamult, and parts of the parishes of Ballyreddin, Burnchurch, Kells, and Ballybar: there are five chapels, situated respectively at Danesfort, Lady's-well, Grange, Bennet's-bridge, and Kells-grange. There is a school at Bennet's-bridge under the National Board, in which are about 80 children; and there are two pay schools, in which about 100 are educated. Here was anciently a castle, built by William, Earl Mareschal; and there are several Danish forts in the parish.

From 1 July 1807 the effective strength of the Kilkenny militia, comprised in addition to the officers, not enumerated, 44 sergeants, 18 drummers, 40 corporals and 560 privates.29 The Kilkenny militia were stationed at Wexford during 1809. Such were the experiences of the Kilkenny militia in Bandon. It was May and provisions were scarce and dear.

Major Wemys commanding the garrison was forced to apply to the lord lieutenant for an increased allowance for bread, potatoes and oatmeal. After some procrastination by Dublin Castle increases were allowed provided the price of bread did not exceed. Irish militia units, prior to 1811, actively sought opportunities to serve in Britain and thus, replicate the services provided by the English militia in Ireland during the 1798 Rebellion. An act of parliament of 1811 provided for the interchange of English, Irish and Scottish groups. This legislation allowing interchangeability introduced major changes in the composition of that force in Ireland. Militia numbers in Ireland for the years 1806-10 amounted to 30,000 men, all of whom were Irish. However, for the years 1811-13 over half the number of militias serving in Ireland were English units. It provided Kilkenny girls with a wider selection of prospective marriage partners. That this occurred is evident from the parish records of St. John's Roman Catholic church adjacent to the Kilkenny military barracks. In February, April and July of 1814 soldiers of the Meath militia, based in the barracks, married girls from that parish (see Appendix No. 6, p. 256).

The Sovereigns and Mayors of Kilkenny 1282-2010

1806 Walter, Earl of Ormond

1807 The Hon. Hamilton Cuffe

1808 The Hon. James Butler

1809 John Otway, Earl of Desart

1811 James Wemys

1812 William Bayley

1813 Samuel Matthews

1814 The Hon. James Butler

1820 Nathaniel Alcock

1821 Henry Wemys Index to Griffith's Valuation of Ireland, 1848-1864 *Wemys, Henry, Esq County: Danesfort, Rathclogh, Kilkenny.*

SOURCES: *The military in Kilkenny 1800-1870 by Liam Bóiger B.A. Chapter V Kilkenny's forgotten armies: the yeomanry 1830-1834 and the militia 1800-1870*

Otway Cuffe, 1st Earl of Desart (1737 – 1804)

On 6th January 1781, Otway Cuffe was *"advanced to the dignity"* of Viscount Desart, probably in recognition of his political influence as patron of half the borough of Kilkenny. Four years later, he married 30-year-old **Lady Anne Browne**. Lady Anne was a wealthy lady 25 years his junior. The Browne's, **Earls of Altamont**, descended from the great Pirate Queen, **Grace O'Malley**. (21) Lady Anne Browne's parents were, Peter Brown, 2nd Earl of Altamont, who in 1752 married Elizabeth Kelly, heiress to one of the largest Jamaican sugar plantations. In 1785 the marriage of Otway Cuffe to Lady Anne Browne must have brought a considerable fortune to the House of Desart.

Otway Cuffe, 2nd Earl of Desart (1788 - 1826)

Otway Cuffe, 2nd Earl of Desart, had a short but eventful life. He was born in Dublin on 20th February 1788, the only son and heir of the then Lord and Lady Desart. When he was five years old, his father was created Earl of Desart (1793) and Viscount Castle-Cuffe, the junior title of which was borne by the young Otway. He was educated at Eton from 1800 to 1804 whereupon, on the death of his father on 9th August 1804, he succeeded to Desart and the Earldom. Like his father before him, he studied at Christ Church, Oxford, matriculating on 29th April 1805. Another man who matriculated from Oxford that year became his good friend: (Sir) Robert Peel, a former Harrovian who would later become Prime Minister of Great Britain.

ELIZABETH CUFFE

The 2nd Earl had two sisters - **Elizabeth** and Dorothea. The first married **Henry Wemyss of Danesfort, County Kilkenny,** and had a son, Otway Wemyss, who served with the Buffs (The Royal East Kent Regiment).

Description of Lady Elizabeth Cuffe Wemys

Her great-nephew, Hamilton Cuffe, 5th Earl of Desart, recalled her as:

"a sort of cross between a housekeeper and a Grand Duchess (who) might have come straight out of the pictures in a Dickens's book. She wore a stupendous white cap, had a very handsome, rather roman profile, and carried a large bunch of keys hung on one side from her belt, with a large reticule on the other side. Also, she had generally in her hands a basket of eggs, or a jug of milk or cream".

SOURCE: Kind permission of Turtle Bunbury www.turtlebunbury.com/history/history_family/hist_family_cuffe.htm

MAJOR HENRY WEMYS

Son of James Wemys Mother Martha Blunden

Henry b. Feb 1785, d. 31 March 1860, Danesfort, Kilkenny. He was Major of the Militia, magistrate and deputy lieutenant for Kilkenny and served as high sheriff in 1819.

Henry married Lady Elizabeth Cuffe

Elizabeth was b.1789 d. 03 Mar 1864 Danesfort. Married Dec 1822 Lady Elizabeth Mary Cuffe of Desart, Kilkenny. Father: Otway Cuffe b. 25 Nov 1737, d.09 Aug 1804 Dublin, First Earl of Desart Kilkenny, Cuffe Castle. Mother: Lady Ann Browne her father was Peter Browne, 2nd Earl of Altamont.

*Marriage of Henry Wemys & Lady Elizabeth Cuffe

On Thursday, at Ballycallan Church, by the Rev. Hans CAULFIELD, Henry WEMYS, of Danesfort, in the County of Kilkenny, Esq, to Lady Elizabeth CUFFE, sister of the late Right Hon. the Earl of Desart. The populace would not suffer horses to be put to the carriage of the happy pair, but drew it themselves from Ballycallan to Desart House, and from thence the whole of the way to Danesfort House, the ancient family mansion of the bridegroom and in the evening bonfires were lit on all the eminences of the surrounding country as marks of respect to an excellent landlord and to the virtues of the most kind-hearted and benevolent of women.

**Obituary of Henry Wemys of Kilkenny

On Thursday at his residence, Danesfert , Henry Wemys esq, JP,Danesfert ,late lieutenant Colonal ,commanding the Kilkenny Fusiliers Regiment of Militia . His family, the branch of a Noble Scottish house, became connected with the county of Kilkenny in the beginning of the seventh century ,when James afterwards Duke of Ormond ,having formed the resolution of seeking by marriage his kinswomen ,Lady Elisabeth Preston to restore himself with his descendents the greater portion of the Ormond property which had been alienated through her mother from the head of the house , in that enterprise received the assistance of Sir Patrick Wemys a near relative of the young lady's father , Sir Richard Preston, one of the Scotch favourite of James 1 ,and through whose interest Preston had obtained in marriage the only daughter of the Thomas 10th Earl of Ormond along with the property which ought to have descended in the male line. In acknowledgement of the service which Sir Patrick had done the Duke in this important matter, the latter granted to him and his decedents forever, in fee farm, one of the most ancient of the Ormond Manors and castles in the county of Kilkenny, modernly transformed into Dansfert, which has since been the residence of the Wemys family, a name always from the period prominent amongst our local Aristocracy. Colonel Wemys married in 1823, Lady Elizabeth Cuff, eldest daughter of Otway, Earl of Desart (grandfather of the present Lord) who survives him; and he leaves an only son, Captain Otway Wemys 2nd battalion 3rd Buffe,at present quariered with his regiment in Malta who succeed to the family property.

SOURCE: *Connaught Journal Galway, Ireland, Thursday, January 2, 1823/Volume 69 Price 5 Pence **04 April 1860 - Wexford Independent - Wexford, Wexford, Republic of** Ireland https://en.wikipedia.org/wiki/James_Butler,_1st_Duke_of_Ormond

They had three daughters who died young. James Henry Wemys died at birth 1824 Danesfort.

John Otway Wemyss (Major)

Born June 1826 Jeri point Kilkenny Ireland. d. June 1891 at 30 Ovington Square, in the county of Middlesex Holy Trinity, London, Kensington, England. Without issue. Military: Occupation: Soldier in the 71st Highlanders, Captain, promoted to Major 3rd Foot. He gained the rank of Major in the Buffs (The Royal East Kent Regiment). Justice of the peace for Kilkenny.

Census- Listed in 1876 Landowners census of Danesfort, Kilkenny, Ireland. Census: 1891, Holy Trinity, London, Kensington, England.

Married Julia Sophia Browne

Julia Sophia Browne b.1838 d.13 September 1926 London. She married John Wemys in Kensington, London on 31 January 1872, daughter of John Denis Browne and Esther Wells who lived at Mount Browne, County Mayo, Ireland. Julia was a cousin of his mother, Lady Elizabeth Cuffe.

John Otway Wemyss Will: All his estate was left to his wife. The land was sold on the request of Thomas Palmer Chapman (petitioner) by public auction by Mr. Justice Ross in Dublin in 1896.

John Otway was the father of a number of illegitimate children, however, he failed to father a legitimate heir.

Local Historian Danesfort: According to Mr Frank McEvoy the local historian in Danesfort Henry and Elizabeth had three sons, two of them died and when the third John Otway fell sick the housekeeper took him to the local priest a Fr. Nesboro and he cured him.

*SOURCE: *England & Wales, FreeBMD Death Index: 1837-1983. District: Kensington County: Greater London, London, Middlesex*

Landowners in 1876 County Kilkenny, Ireland: The land survey was actually completed in 1876 and first published in a London book that same year. It only represents those who owned one acre or more. Some owned property in Co. Kilkenny but lived elsewhere.

JOHN OTWAY WEMYSS* Census London: Maj. Otway Wemys, address Danesfort, Kilkenny, owned 1,870 acres. Julia Sophia Browne Wemys: In 1896 they sold off land and family mansions, Annamult, Rathclough, Croan and Ballyda, due to their lavish life style. (Annamult house and land was sold to Jerimiah Nolan).

John Wemys* of Danesfort 1811 7th March: John Wemys of Danesfort, Co Kilkenny & Harriet Colclough of the City of Kilkenny, sister of John Hannagan, of Crossford Hill, Kilkenny City, for an annuity of £100.00 p a. witness W. Walley

Unknown family: *Kings Inn UCD 1607-1867 -James Wemys Clerk, James Wemys Attorney exchequer 1734____*He was a Capt. James Wemys In Lord Homes Regiment of Foot TSPI, May 12 1752.

Diocese of Ossory Kilkenny Marriages

Husband ROBERT WEAIN **b.abt 1732** Ossory, Leinster Ireland. Marriage: **1758** Ossory, Ireland. **Elizabeth Williams b.abt 1737** Ossory, Leinster Ireland.

JAMES WEMYS 1.10.1774 Danesfort, seat of James Wemys esq Death from lime fumes. [FLJ copied] -Finns Leinster journal.

JOHN WEMYS b. 03March **1755** St Marys Roman Catholic church Kilkenny. Father: John Wemys b. abt 1730 Mother: b. abt 1730 Catherine Meagher. Sponsor Denis Dwyer Sponsor Honor Coghlin

John Wemys deserter from French Army: 1755 March 14, Examination of John Wemys aged about 25 years born at Kilkenny, deserter from Lally's Regiment of the French army, having previously been a gentleman's servant and before that a soldier in Colonel Pool's Regiment in Ireland.

Ireland, Catholic Qualification & Convert Rolls 1701-1845:

JOHN WYNES Year 1783 Court county: Catholic often swear an oath of allegiance to the crown to keep their property or have a business.

Land -1811,7th March John Wemys of Danesfort, Co Kilkenny & Harriet Colclough of the City of Kilkenny, sister of John Heanagan, of Crossford Hill, Kilkenny City, for an annuity of £100.00 p a. witness W. Walley RoD 634/347.

Marriages from Irish Genealogy records Vol. 8 No.2 for Dioceses of Ossory 1739-1804.
1st May 1773 James Wemys/Margaret Blundell

SOURCE: * Examination of John Wemys aged about 25 born at Kilkenny, deserter from... Date: 1755 Mar 14. Description: Folios 46-47. Reference: **SP** 36/129/2/46. *Held by: The National Archives, Kew.* Https://discovery.nationalarchives.gov.uk/details/r/C17015462

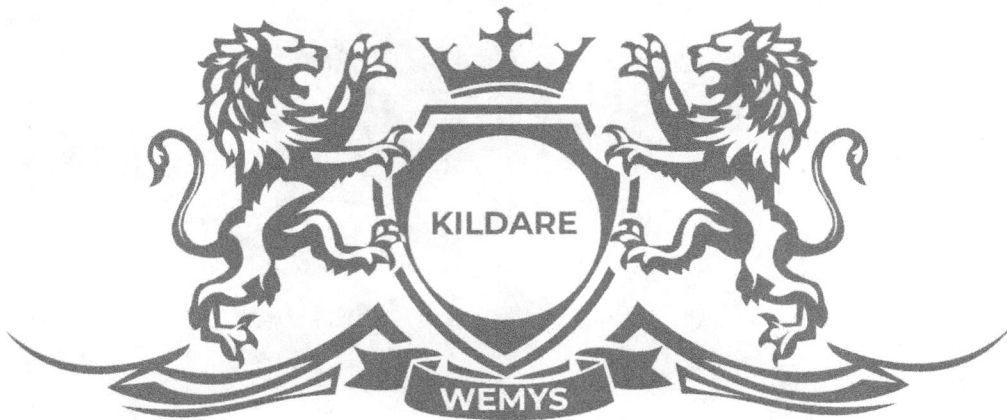

KILDARE

WEMYS

Maynooth Castle. - Alexander Taylor's map of County Kildare in 1783. *Picture National Library Ireland.*

JOYCE BLUNDELL WEMYS

Francis Wemyss Sir Patricks grandson married Joyce Blundell

Baronet Sir George Blundell was **Elizabeth Blundell's Wemys** father and **Joyce Blundell Wemys (married Francis Wemys)** grandfather. Joyce's father William was Elizabeth's Blundell's brother making Elizabeth Joyce's Aunt.

Coolestown-Now Edenderry. borders on Kildare, Meath and Westmeath and the Wemys settled in these counties.

Edenderry-In the 16th century, it had the name of Coolestown, after the family of Cooley or Cowley, who had a castle there. Henry Colley a soldier in the royal service was given the manor and castle of Edenderry in 1562 along with Drumcooley and other lands. Edenderry was then known as Colleystown. George his eldest son inherited in 1581 and when he died, his in 1614 and was succeeded by his son William. William had two children, Sarah who married Sir George Blundell and George, who married in 1648 but had no family. When William died Edenderry, estate passed to his sister Sarah, Lady Blundell. Sarah Colley married George Blundell and land became owned by the Blundell's.

Edenderry was sacked 1599 and defended against the Earl of Tyrone's rebellion. Castle sacked in 1691 by the army of James II. The Blundell family probably occupied the castle on the hill until then but it was never rebuilt. Edenderry -during the 18th century it remained with the Blundell family who resided at the elegant, East Hampstead Park in Berkshire, England. On his death in 1756, Lord Blundell left Edenderry in the hands of his three daughters. The ownership of Edenderry next passed into the hands of the Marquis of Downshire's family in 1786.

Viscount Blundell-Sir Francis Blundell, 1st Baronet (1579–1625) Sir George Blundell, 2nd Baronet (died 1675) Sir Francis Blundell, 3rd Baronet (1643–1707) Sir Montague Blundell.4th Baronet died 1756, no surviving male issue and the titles became extinct on his death in 1756.

SIR GEORGE BLUNDELL 2nd Baronet

Son of Sir Francis Blundell & Joyce Sergeant.

George married Sarah Colley, daughter of Sir William Colley d.1666 and Elizabeth Gifford, d.bef. 1642. He was a Commissioner of Customs and Excise. M.P. for Dingle [Ireland] between 1639 and 1648. M.P for Philipstown [Ireland] between 1661 and 1666.Sheriff of King's County in 1657.

Prerogative WILL Index -Sir George Blundell -WILL granted to Joyce Blundell and Sara Roster sister's granddaughter December 1711.

Sir George Blundell & Sara Colley-Children

William Blundell b. 1643 D 1732

Sir Francis Blundell, 3rd Bt. b.30 January 1643, d.1707.

Winword. Exact dates unknown.

Daughter -**Elizabeth Blundell** was married to Sir Henry Wemys (son of Sir Patrick Wemys) of Danesfort) Kilkenny.

William Blundell- Married Anne Taylor d.1732

William & Anne's Blundell's Children

George Blundell

William Blundell, who died unmarried.

Joyce Blundell married **Francis Wemys of Roestown** (grandson of Sir Pattack Wemys) in the County of Kildare. See chapter

Mary Blundell and Sarah Blundell

Married Christian Forster, Esq; a Colonel in the Eleistor of Brandenburgh's Service, whose Widow died 22 April 1744, and was buried at Monasteroris in the King's County, (the Burial-Place of many of the Family) having had several Children.

Murder of Thomas Preston -In 1674 William, Francis, and Winword killed Thomas Preston, son of a Catholic peer, Lord Tara Last Viscount. They were acquitted of murder and pardoned by Charles II.

Viscount Tara (or Taragh) The title was created by King Charles II in 1650 for the soldier Thomas Preston (1585–1655). He was the second son of Christopher Preston, 4th Viscount Gormanston. The 1st Viscount's son Anthony succeeded him as 2nd Viscount Tara. The title became extinct in 1674 on the death of Thomas, 3rd Viscount, at the hands of Sir Francis Blundell and his two brothers.

KING'S COUNTY. The Rev. W. G. Kittson, Rector of Ballyburley, has kindly sent me the following interesting inscription of the Wackly [Wakely], Handcock, and Blundell families, and for which I beg to thank him. In the next Report I propose to give an account of the Communion plate in Ballyburley Church.

BALLYBURLEY PARISH CHURCH, EDENDERRY.MONASTERORIS PARISH CHURCH, EDENDERRY.

"Near -his place lyes burred the Body of SARAH LADY BLUNDELL Relict of SIR GEORGE BLUNDELL baronet & sole daughter and Heiress of Sr WILLIAM COLLEY of Edenderrry, (Who dyed ye 25 of February 1701) and was a person of most exemplay Piety and Charity to whose memory this Marble is dedicated by her son SIR FRANCIS BLUNDELL Baronet who with her consent marry'd two Excel- lent wives, viz in December 1671 URSULA daughter of Sr PAUL DAVYS Secretary of State Privy Councillor and Clark of' the Council who dyed in May 1673 delivered of a dead child and ly's buried near her Father in St. AUDEONS Church, and in Dec. 1675, he marry'd

*ANNE the daughter of SIR HENRY

INGOLDSBY Barr & Privy Councillor who dyed ye 14th of July 1705 & lyes burid

by her Father in St. BRIDGETS Church in DUBLIN. He had by her seven sons and

two daughters, GEORGE, HENRY, FRANCIS, WILLIAM, WINWOOD, CHARLES, and

MONTAGUE, ANNE and SARAH."

The above is inscribed upon a plain white marble slab, inserted in the wall of the church, and underneath it is inserted another marble slab bearing the following inscription: -

"THE ABOVE GENEALOGICAL TABLET WAS SOME TIME BACK FOUND IN THE

RUINS OF THE OLD CHURCH OF MONASTERORIS AND REMOVED TO THIS SITE BY

MARY MARCHIONESS OF DOWNSHIRE AND BARONESS SANDYS,

THE LINEAL HEIRESS AND DESCENDANT OFMONTAGUE LORD VISCOUNT BLUNDELL 1814."

NOTES: Burials-The last Blundell burials to take place in Edenderry which were recorded in the Monasteroris Church Register, were Sarah Blundell, died in 1701 and Francis, died in 1707. *MONASTERORIS, a parish, in the barony of COOLESTOWN, KING'S county,*

*SOURCE: *Andrew J. Morris https://archive.org/stream/journalforyear01asso/journalforyear01asso_djvu.txt. Inscriptions 1617 – 1814 From: "Memorials of the Dead in Ireland" - Vol. 1, #1; Dublin 1890. Transcribed by Roy McMenamin*

In 1669, the future King James II (reign 1685 to 1688) converted to Catholicism and took a stand against a number of anti-Catholic moves. This did not impede his succession to the throne on his brother, Charles II, death in 1685. In 1687 he issued a Declaration of Indulgence aiming at complete religious toleration. James's second wife Mary of Modena, gave birth to a son, James Francis Edward June 1688.

The Church of England nobles and Parliamentarian did not want a Catholic on the throne and asked James eldest sister Mary an Anglo-Catholic and her husband William of Orange, to fight for the throne. Unfortunately for James his army and navy deserted him and when William landed in 5 November 1688 in Devon he fled to France. Parliament took this as an abdication and crowned William (King **William** III) and Mary as joint monarchs. James then raised an army of Scot's and Catholic Irish supporters with the support of the French and returned to Ireland in March 1689.

He was defeated by William at the Battle of the *Boyne in July 1690*. James died in exile in Saint-Germain in France on 16 September 1701. With the defeat of Catholic the Ascendancy (established Church) sought to ensure dominance with the passing of a number of laws to restrict the religious, political and economic activities of Catholics and Protestants.

These laws ensured that Catholic could not passed their land on to a single heir and all land had to be divided over the generations. Because of this some Catholic gentry converted to the Church of England to keep their lands but some got one member of the family to convert to but they remained Catholic. Following the defeat of the Jacobite's in Scotland at Culloden in 1746, the threat to Anglican Church diminished and many penal laws were relaxed or slightly enforced.

NOTE: *It was rumored at the time that James Butler the duke of Ormond d.1688 whose father and Uncle were Catholic indulged in late-night card games in his castle with members of the remaining Catholic gentry, that were readily interpreted as being the prelude to a Catholic uprising. James had been a close friend to Sir Patrick Wemys Danesfort.*

WEMYS IN THE BARONY OF KILDARE

There are two distinct branches of Wemys, both families are found under Wemys and Weymes

The first branch are descendants of:

Kildare: Francis Wemys grandson of **Sir Patrick Wemys** (see section on Kilkenny). Francis lived in Kill, Kildare moving there after inheriting land from his Uncle James Wemys. Francis was an Army officer who later became MP for Harristown. He had **six sons** and eight daughters, from which this branch grew.

Wemys of Frankford (see the section on the Offaly Branch) can trace themselves back to Kildare.

Wemyss from Colchester (see the section on the Colchester Wemyss) in England originate from Kildare branch (they changed their name to Colchester-Wemyss after the marriage of Francis Wemyss to Elizabeth Colchester in 1808). I was unable to find their ancestor a Francis Wemys who married a Miss Agar connection for that time period.

Catholic Branch: The other branch of Weymes in Kildare is Catholic. Records relating to this branch start in 1820 - there are no records prior to this and no indication of their origins. There was also catholic Wemyss in Offaly Frankford from 1800.

FRANCIS WEMYS *b. 1673*

Grandson of Sir Pat -Parents Maurice & Elizabeth

Francis Wemys* b. 1673 in Danesfort Kilkenny. d. 1738 Blind Quay, Cadogan Alley. Dublin.

Francis Estate** He resided and owned an estate at Kill Kildare which he inherited the year of his birth. Francis was Co Heir with his uncle Henry to his uncle James Wemys d.1670 estate who married Judith Usher from whom he acquired the estate but had no male issue. According to records Francis father Maurice died the year of his birth 1670 and his Uncle James died when he was just one year old. Francis also inherited land in Coolestown Offaly from Viscount George Blundell his wife's Joyce's grandfather.

KILL Kildare   *Gaelic name is "An Chill" meaning "The Church"*

Kill is a village and parish in Kildare, on the main road from Dublin to the south and south west of Ireland. The village was a staging post on the old toll road to Kilcullen, it was the first turnpike to be built (1729). It was here that horses were changed on the three-hour mail coach journey from Dublin to Kilcullen. Kill is said to have been the burial-place of the Christian kings of Leinster.

When Francis was living at Kill the parish church was the Catholic church of St. Brigid and St. Mary built about 1650, it was rebuilt in 1821 but this time as an Anglican Church, St. John's Church. A new Catholic church was built in 1820 called St Bridget's. There are many Catholics buried at St John cemetery from the earlier times.

At the time that Francis Wemys lived in Kill, Ireland was ruled by King George III and a declaration in 1720 stated Catholics could no longer sit in Parliament. In 1731 in Kill Parish the number of Protestants was 80 and Catholics were 800.

Francis died in 1739 and the year after the famine of 1740-41 broke out. It was caused by extremely cold and then dry weather in successive years, which resulted in poor grain crops, milk shortages, and frost damage on potatoes, killing approximately 400,000 people.

NOTE: *There was a manor owned in Kill by to St Thomas' Abbey Dublin, until the Dissolution of the Churches then it passed to Richard Aylmer. Stella Wyndham Alymer b. 16 Feb 1889 Kill Kildare married Lt.-Colonel John Maurice Colchester Wemyss in 03 Mar 1909 at Kilcock Kildare. He was a descended of Francis Wemyss Kill.*

Leases: *Wemys Frank-Dublin: Lease by Sir Henry Wemys & Francis Wemys to George Kennedy of House in Blind Quay and Cadogan Alley Dublin May 5th 1697. Francis gave deeds in 1711 to William Alcock City of Dublin St Nicholas St, Dublin – (next to Nicholas Gate).*

NOTE: *Harristown was a townland in the parish of Ballyboggan and Francis was MP there. Ballyboggan graveyard is where William Weymes b. 1801 my ancestors is buried.*

Army: Francis Wemys Major was a professional soldier. Firstly, **he was in the 20th regiment of foot which was r**aised 20 November 1688 as Sir Richard Peyton's Regiment of Foot. Secondly, he was a Captain in Duke of Norfolk's Regiment of Foot on 20 June **1689 which** fought from 1689 to 1691 in the Williamite War in Ireland, including the Battle of the Boyne, the Capture of Waterford and the Siege of Limerick in 1690. He was a Captain in Sir Henry Belasyse's Regiment of Foot, possibly joining them after the October 1691 Treaty of Limerick, when the regiment returned to England before being transferred to Flanders. When the Nine Years' War ended with the 1697 Treaty of Ryswick, the regiment was saved from disbandment by becoming part of the Irish establishment, then spent the War of the Spanish Succession in Jamaica.

Francis was an MP for Harristown County Kildare-from 1695 to 1699 *******. Harristown was a townland in the parish of Ballyboggan and is where William Weymes b.1801 Westmeath is buried.

SOURCE: HISTORY OF IRISH PARLIAMENT' 1692 – 1800. https://en.wikipedia.org/wiki/Henry_Belasyse_(died_1717)

Marquis of Ormond, Kilkenny

It is unclear if Francis was in the army in Jamaica at this time but he now asks Ormond to be transferred to a regiment in Ireland or England suggesting he is abroad. Francis and Joyce had 12 children in 13 years.

Francis Wemys to Ormond**** 24 January 1706: Asking to be preferred to be raised in Regiments in England or in the Irish Guards. He mentions how ill Irish rents are paid, and his 12 children, and hopes his Grace will not impute he's not waiting upon him in London as a neglect of duty. (extract)

Francis Wemys to Ormond 17 February 1711: Asking the same favour as his uncle Wemys. He is his uncle's eldest brother's son and heir to Sir Patrick Wemys, who was a constant attendant in the war of 1641 on his Grace's grandfather. Francis had 15 children. (extract)

NOTE: The name Francis may have come into the Wemys family because Joyce's Blundell's great grandfather was Baronet Sir Francis Blundell b.abt 1579.

Wemys Frank -Belfast PRO t662/5. Lease by Sir Henry Wemys & Francis Wemys to George Kennedy of House in Blind Quay and Cadogen Alley Dublin May 5th 1697. Shared estate given from James who married Usher.

SOURCE: *Index to Chancery Pleadings 1682-1687 Ireland Diocesan and Prerogative Wills & Administrations Indexes 1595-1858, ** National Archives Dublin, Inheritance D/366/18. ***Genealogical Memoirs of The Members of Parliament for The County and City of Kilkenny- Harristown, Kildare in the Irish House of Commons until 1800. ****The manuscripts of the Marquis of Ormond, Kilkenny Two pieces taken from Ormond Manuscripts. Day Book of Clerk Crown & Hanaper 1684-8, Birth, Marriage, Death & Parish Records Crossle Genealogical Abstracts Transcription Offaly Kings County (Fras Weymes, Event date 11 Nov 1693, Offaly (King's) Ireland, Married No, Dead No

FRANCIS WEMYS first marriage in abt 1690 was to Joyce Blundell Abt. 1674 b. d 15 July 1717. His second marriage abt.1734. to Mary Mc McCullough b. 1710. d.1747, Blind Quay, Cadogan Alley Dublin. Mary McCullagh, and Henrietta Wemys (1747) Joyce daughter resided at the same address Blind Quay Dublin. *Francis had 6 boys and 8 daughters* (said to have had 15 children)

JOYCE BLUNDELL (See Blundell's chapter) Joyce was b.abt 1684 in Philipstown Offaly Ireland. Her father was William Blundell, her mother was Anne Taylor. Joyce was the granddaughter of *Baronet Sir George Blundell*, Cobally Kill Kildare. In Georges prerogative WILL land was granted to Joyce Blundell wife of Francis Wemys of Kill Kildare and Sara Foster sister admin granted____ Granddaughter. Probate - Land granted 7 December 1711. **The 17th Century Blundell family Blundell Estate-** Sir Henry Colley a soldier in the royal service was given the manor and castle of Colleystown now Edenderry in 1562 along with Drumcooley and other lands. In 1581 he left Edenderry to his eldest son George who died in 1614 and was succeeded by his son William. William had two children, Sarah who married **Sir George Blundell** and George, who married in 1648 but had no issue. On George Colley death the Edenderry estate passed to his sister Sarah, Lady Blundell.

Francis Wemyss & Joyce Blundell -Children 6 sons and 8 daughters

Maurice Wemys b.1693. d. abt.1777, Brierfield (Toole) Townland Abbeyknockmoy, Galway.

Francis William Wemys b.1708 d.1782 Mountrath St, Coolderry Offaly

Rev William Wemys b. abt.1709, Edenderry, Co Offaly. bef. 1748 Bumblim Roscommon.

Dr James Wemys b. abt. 1710, Kill, Kildare, Ireland. bef. 1792

Dr Patrick Wemys b. abt. 1717, Kilcock Kildare. d.1792, at 4 George's Street, near Poolbeg-street.

Ann Wemys b. abt. 1696. d. 1740 Danesfort.

Elizabeth Wemys b. Abt. 1699.D. 03 Mar 1792

Martha Wemys b. abt. 1697.d. 1787 Dublin

Sara Wemys d. abt. 1698. Married Christian Forster

Henrietta Wemys b. Abt. 1700 D. aft. 1747 Blind Quay Dublin

Mary Wemys b.1703 d. after 1747. Married Christian Forster (otherwise McCullagh) Blind Quay Dublin.

Catherine Wemys. b abt 1710

Antionette Wemys b. abt. 1716.d.1804. Mentioned in Martha's Wemys WILL Dublin spinster 1787.

SOURCE: Parish/Church/Congregation -St Werburg, Betham Genealogical Abstracts Transcription-National Archives of Ireland written Jocose Wemys Als B, married. Record set Ireland Diocesan and Prerogative Wills & Administrations Indexes 1595-1858, Crossle genealogical abstracts, and miscellaneous military records, -04 Apr 1684, Dublin Archives Wills: D/366/18.

MAURICE WEMYS Heir

Son of Francis Wemyss & Joyce Blundell-no issue

Maurice was b.1691 Kill Kildare and married Elizabeth abt 1720 no issue. Maurice lived in Coolderry Offaly as did Francis Wemys b.1708 who I assume was bequeathed Maurice property. Maurice was already at University Trinity at the tender age of 14 years old.

Army -In the Year 1714, Maurice was rank Cornet in the Regiment of Richard Morris's Dragoons. *Maurice Wemys of the city Dublin esquire captain in major general Bolsconvens regiment of foot in Ireland- taken from memorial of deeds 1758.* * Lt Maurice Wemys In Col Boscawen's Regt of Foot 1754 Feb 11.

History of the 29th (Worcestershire) Regiment by H. Everard- Chapter 4 1751 Quarters of the Army in Ireland. XXIX FOOT. Colonel Peregrine T. Hopson. 1 L. Maurice Wemys.} Castlecomer Kilkenny.

Land in Coolderry Maurice was Heir to his mother's estate in Coolderry Offaly passed the land onto his brother Francis William Weymes of Coolderry (Ann Duane) 58th regiment of foot who died in 1782.

Leases***

White to Butler-Henry White Edward Butler

Made between Richard Eames of Bark Kings co son and heir of the late Thomas Eames of the city of Dublin merchant of the first part Maurice Wemys of the city Dublin esquire captain in major general Bolsconvens regiment of foot in Ireland of the second part Henry white of Dublin esquire of the said Thomas Eames of the third part Sarah Palmer and Francis Palmer of the for-4th part spinster of the forth part Edward Butler of Dublin of the fifth part and Francis Butler of Dublin of the sixth part.

Wemys of the lands of; Killchancorkerry otherwise killclon 142 acres, In the barony of Coolestown kings co, 60 acres Clonbrook, 26acres Fanmore under lease to William Nelson Clerke_____agreed to the share of Joyce Wemys otherwise Blundell mother of Maurice Wemys and her heir James Bantly gent at Kilmantog 33acres and moity sir William king and Richard Waller moity Sir George Blundell in Clonbrock containing 74 acres moity Captain John Eames in Brackragh and Kilcloncorkerry containing 52acres all in barony of Coolestown and Kings co. Thomas Eames to lease for 999years.

SIGNED -Maurice Wemys, Richard Eames, Henry Whyte

NOTE TC I have several leases of property in Dublin for Maurice.

SOURCE: * Military, armed forces & conflict-Establishment Irish-Record set British Army, List of Half-Pay Officers 1714. ** The records were transcribed by the Deputy Keeper of Northern Ireland from the records held in PRO London. *** Memorial of deeds of lease and release 27 May 1758 deed number 120504 book 192 page 511. / Alumni Dublineneses- By George Dames Burtchaell Maurice Wemys. pen (Dr Scott., Dublin) feb 14 ,1705-6 aged 14years, s.of Francis, generosus;b. Kilkenny BA vern 1710.

REVERAND WILLIAM WEMYS

Son of Francis Wemyss & Joyce Blundell

William Wemys b. abt. 1688 Edenderry, Offaly. d before 1748 census. *William went to Trinity College in 1709. William was in the British Army, List of half-pay Officers 1714, Cornet, Regiment Richard Morris's Dragoons (same regiment as his brother Maurice). Vicar for Parish Bumlin, County Roscommon in Census of Elphin 1749.

Court of Exchequer Ireland Bills- of payment for Maurice Wemys and William Wemys to pay Penelope Read which was due to her father Samuel Medlecotte of late of Dunmurry Kildare who died 1738 and bequeath all his goods to his daughter Penelope. That Maurice Wemys and William Wemys since deceased of Kill Kildare executed their bond of £100 dated 16 June 1726.

Rev William married Elizabeth Montague-child**** William Wemys junior died without issue.

NOTE William***** is mentioned Court of Exchequer Ireland Bills, 27 May 1756 and written William Wenys

HENRY WEMYS b.1706

Son of Francis Wemyss & Joyce Blundell

Henry Wemys (Lt) b.1706 Kill Kildare, d.23 Mar 1765 Temple bar Dublin.

*Faulkner's Dublin Journal: Died- (1765) On Temple-bar, Lieut. Henry WEMYS, descended of a noble Family, and a near Relation of the Right Hon. the Countess of Brandon.

Henry married

Jane Rogers** b. abt 1726. Married 20 Feb 1747 St Andrews Dublin. Henry is written as Weymes of Danesfort Kilkenny no issue.

NOTE: There was a J Rogers in the Census of Elphin 1749, which is where Reverend William Wemyss was at that time but Joyce had married Henry in 1748. In Ireland, Society of Friends (Quaker) there is a Jane Rogers in Ireland for 16 August 1738.

Countess of Brandon-Ellis Bermingham- was born in 1708 as Ellis (Elizabeth) Agar, daughter of James Agar and Mary Wemyss. She married, first (1726), Theobald Bourke, 7th Viscount Mayo.

*SOURCE: *Alumni Dublineneses - 1924 edition Transcription-Trinity University. Record set Alumni Dublineneses - 1924 Edition. **Establishment Irish-Record set British Army, List of Half-Pay Officers 1714-Alumni Dublineneses - 1924 edition Transcription. ***Betham Genealogical Abstracts. ****PRONI Will Belfast. *****Collection Thrift's genealogical abstracts- Bundle 4 nos. 793-1051-File 944.Source Court of Exchequer Ireland Bills Archive National Archives of Ireland. PRONI Will -Written-William Wenys. *Faulkner's Dublin Journal-Dublin, Ireland, Tues., 19 Mar 1765-Sat. 23 Mar 1765. **Betham Genealogical Abstracts Transcription -Index to The Act or Grant Books, And to Original Wills, Of the Diocese of Dublin 1272-1858 -Prerogative Court of Armagh*

JAMES WEMYS DOCTOR

Son of Francis & Joyce Blundell

BALLYBOY OFFALY* -Prior to the Plantations of Ireland, Ballyboy was ruled by O'Molloy in a territory known as Firceall which was allied to the Kingdom of Meath. When the Gaelic chieftains were removed from power following the English Plantations, Firceall was broken up with Ballyboy forming its own barony within the then newly formed King's County (now County Offaly).

Ballyboy Calvary in 1700 Ballyboy had a garrison of Calvary station at the Castle. This was the penal times which lasted from Cromwell to 1640 to Queen Anne in 1714. There was a reprieve when the Catholic King James 2 was on the throne from 1685 to 90. This rule came from England and there was persecution of Catholics especially Bishops and Priest. However, many protestants did not hold to this and sheltered run-away priest from the Ballyboy Calvary at great risk to themselves. During this time there was no church and Mass was held in various secret locations. **School -**In 1820 the Landlord of Ballyboy *Lord Lansdowne* built a school for mixed Catholic and protestant. In 1815 a church was built. *SOURCE: * Wikipedia*

The **Constitution of 1782** freed the Parliament of Ireland.

Penal Laws were a series of laws imposed to force Irish Catholics and Protestant to accept the established Church of Ireland. Catholics and Presbyterians—who together made up a large majority of the Irish population—were completely excluded from public life at this time under these Penal Laws, in force in Ireland from 1691 until the early 1780s.

The most constraining restrictions arose in Poynings' Law of 1495 ("An Act that no Parliament be holden in this Land until the Acts be certified into England"). These restrictions were lifted in 1782, which freed the Irish parliament. The Irish Appeals Act 1783 commonly known as the Renunciation Act, by it the British Parliament renounced all right to legislate for Ireland, and declared that no appeal from the decision of any court in Ireland could be heard in any court in Great Britain.

This period was **Grattan's Parliament** after Henry Grattan. This new constitution gave the Parliament greater control over the Royal Irish Army. Unfortunately, it was short-lived because of the 1798 uprising by the United Irishmen. By the Acts of Union, the Parliament of Ireland was abolished, and the Kingdom of Ireland absorbed into the new United Kingdom of Great Britain and Ireland, with effect from 1 January 1801. Henry Grattan was a leader of the Patriot Party. He was an Anglo-Irish statesman, lawyer, who campaigned for Irish independence from the British parliament and he also favoured Catholic Emancipation. In *1792–93*, he succeeded in carrying a Roman Catholic Relief Act which allowed Catholics to buy land in most places. Some laws against Catholic clergy and worship were lifted. It also enabled Catholics to sit once again in the British Parliament. Meanwhile, Presbyterian ministers were permitted to carry out marriage ceremonies.

In 1783 Dr Patrick was thrown out of his brothers James house in in Mountrath St Birr Offaly. He was brutally beaten and thrown in a fire and all his medical equipment destroyed. I believe this was because of the following: his brother view (he was in the west indies at this time) from an article in the Newspaper some months before.

Dr Patrick Wemys-Court case -Febuary.4, 1784

_____Mr Wemys refers to Colonel Bernard, of the Volunteer Mountain Rangers, whose Corps, he belongs to, or any other gentlemen, he has the pleasure of being acquainted with, for his character. _____Supporting the interest of his brother, the late Francis Wemys, esq; the children's property, and the property of his brother, **Mr James Wemys**, serving his majesty in the East or West Indies, son in law and heir in law to the late Walter Pritchard, of Frankford, Esq **as some time ago advertised in the public papers, supporting the line of the Protestant interest**, has occasioned said Mr Wemys to be so barbarously treated, but having the honour of half pay from his Majesty's , prevent distress. PAT. WEMYS

This article may shine some light on what Dr James may have written in the Newsletter.

However, this James could also be James Wemys b. 1743 d. 08 Aug 1820 of Danesfort Kilkenny who signed it.

FRANCIS FLOOD. HON. P. BUTLER, BENJAMIN KEARNEY, APPENDIX. **JAMES WEMYSS**/ r~ April, **1782**

We do declare for ourselves, **that we do deny** the authority of the British Parliament to make Laws to bind this Kingdom and that we will resist the execution of any laws so made, that we are ready to support our parliament in declaring it exclusive right with our life and our lives and fortunes. Resolved unanimously—That we are ready, with our lives and fortunes, to cooperate with every **Volunteer Corps**, to obtain the Constitutional rights and liberties of our country.   SOURCE: Appendix Historic Memoirs of Ireland, Volume page 353

Historic Memoirs of Ireland Extracts from By Jonah Barrington book p 90

My veering opinion as to a choice of profession was nearly decided by that military ardor which seized all Ireland, when the whole country had entered into a resolution to free itself for ever from English domination. The entire kingdom took up arms—regiments were formed in every quarter—the highest, the lowest, and the middle orders, all entered the ranks of freedom, and every corporation, whether civil or military, pledged life and fortune to attain and establish **Irish independence**, but with the same constitution, and under the same king as England, inseparably and forever united. England tried to evade, as she could not resist this; but in **1782** Ireland was pronounced a free and independent nation._____The Irish parliament had refused to grant supplies to the crown or pass a mutiny bill for more than six months. The people had entered into resolutions to prevent the importation of any British merchandise or manufactures. The entire kingdom had disavowed all English authority or jurisdiction, external or internal; the judges and magistrates had declined to act under British statutes: —the flame had spread rapidly, and had become irresistible. _____ every man swearing, as he kissed the blade of his sword, that he would adhere to these resolutions to the last drop of his blood, which he would by no means spare, till we had finally achieved the independence of our country. We were very sincere, and really, I think, determined to perish, (if necessary) in the cause—at least, I am sure, I was. _____ Having carried our point with the English, and proposed to prove our independence by going to war with Portugal about our linens, we completely set up for ourselves, except that Ireland was bound, as I before said, constitutionally and irrevocably, never to have any king but the King of Great Britain—whether de jure or de facto, however, was not specified.

About this book: Excerpt from Historic Memoirs of Ireland, Vol. 1 of 2: These historic memoirs comprise of secret records of the National Convention, the 1798 Rebellion and the Act of Union. They are included to back-up statements, so that no unfounded charges are present in the memoirs.

Sir Jonah Barrington (1760–1834) was a member of the late Irish Parliament for the cities of **Tuam** and Clogher. He was a lawyer of landed background and then later a MP for **Tuam 1792**–8 and Bannagher 1799–1800. Also, in 1798 he was appointed an admiralty court judge and knighted in 1807. However, he was removed from office for embezzlement in 1830, by which time he had long retreated to France to escape his creditors.

SOURCE: Historic Memoirs of Ireland, Vol. 1 of 2: Comprising Secret Records of the National Convention, the Rebellion and the Union; With Delineations of the Principal Characters Connected with These Transactions. By Jonah Barrington.

DOCTOR JAMES WEMYS

Son of Francis Wemys & Joyce Blundell

James b. abt. 1705, d. bef. 1792 Kill, Kildare, Ireland. Baptised St Werburg Church Dublin. Resided at **Silver Court** Dublin City Ireland. On the prerogative Will Index of Francis William Wemyss this James was written Dr James so I am assuming this is him. He was a Navel Surgeon in the Royal Marines from abt.1724. **James Wemyss*** Occupation *Chirurgeon* belonging to Her Majesty's Ship Weymouth. **Will** *Date Proven 01 December 1724. (nationalarchives.gov.uk)*

HMS Weymouth was a 60-gun fourth rate ship of the line of the Royal Navy, a navigational error on 16 February 1745 brought her too close to the shore of Antigua (Caribbean), where she was wrecked upon a submerged reef.

Entry from Sea surgeons' *examinations 1709-**1745**- James Wemyss. Date of court 8 July, 1733. Examiners Maurice (Master), Woodward, Barnwell, Serjt. Dickins, Ferne.*

Commissioned sea officers of the Royal Navy Written Wemys (S), James (1), L 26 Sept.**1745**. Appears to be home based in Dublin from abt **1764 to 1775**. In 1783 he is based in Canada. James Wemyss 6 May **1769** Surgeon **40th regiment of foot** based in Ireland (from 1764 -1775).

Taken from the military register; or new and complete lists of all his Majesty's land forces and marines for the year 1770.

*The 40th Foot was formed on 25 August 1717 in Nova Scotia as Phillips' Regiment. In the first 44 years of its existence the Regiment garrisoned the **Canadian frontier** and took part in numerous actions against the French and their Indian allies, becoming adept early practitioners of Light Infantry tactics. The 40th Regiment left Nova Scotia for Ireland at the end of **1764** and was based in Dublin. They stayed in **Ireland for 10 years** but with the American War of Independence with Britain, the 40th arrived in Boston in 1775. In 1778 the 40th left America for the West Indies but returned to New York in September, 1781. In 1782 the 40th was given the distinction of a county title, and was to be known as "The 40th Regiment 2nd Somersetshire". The 40th returned to England in 1783 after the peace treaty of Versailles.*

When James brother Francis was in prison, he mentioned his brother serving in the Indies. Francis was still in prison in 1784 so it looks unlikely that James was back from Canada, even though the regiment was in England.

Full Context of U.K. and U.S. Directories, 1680-1830. **Wemyss, James Esq. Lancaster, 1738**
Subscribed to A description of the sea coast of England and Wales, from the Black-Comb in Cumberland to the point of Linus in Anglesea ... with proper directions to avoid all dangers, and sail into any harbour ... as also many prospects of the same ... according to an actual survey, 1738, FEARON, Samuel, EYES, John. Liverpool, Subject: geography.

*NOTE Not to be mixed up with Dr James Wemys there was another James Wemyss from Edinburg b.1748 that joined the 40th Regiment of foot in **1771** and he arrived Boston in 1775 as a captain in the 40th Regiment of Foot. By all accounts he was a barbarian under the leadership of Lt. Col. John Simcoe. (40th became Queens Rangers 1783).40th regiment of foot Ireland 1763 to 1773 based in Ireland. More details here: https://archive.org/details/historicalrecor00smytgoog/page/n94/mode/2up?q=wemyss*

*SOURCES; PCC *Abstracts of Wills: Wills Proved at Prerogative Court of Canterbury. 1st December 1724, Source: UK Data Archive, LL ref: Wills_1720_1729_2531154_708259, Unique Project ID-2531154. **TNA Item and Image ID.** 708259. https://www.londonlives.org/browse.jsp?id=persNamewills_1720_1729_2531154_708259&div=wills_1720_1729_2531154_708259#highlight.***https://archive.org/s tream/historicalrecor00smytgoog/historicalrecor00smytgoog_djvu.txt. **https://archive.org/stream/historicalrecor00smytgoog/historicalrecor00smytgoog_djvu.txt.P49 & P81*

Dr James Wemys married *in abt 1727, Dublin.* Elizabeth Pritchard* b. abt 1710, d.1792 father Walter Pritchard b.abt 1690, d 1782 of Frankford, Esq Elizabeth is listed as a widow at her death in 1792.

James Wemys & Elizabeth Pritchard *Children*

JOYCE WEMYS** (*written Joice Wyems etc*) bap. 21 July **1728**. St Mary Dublin (COI). Father James Wymes Mother Elizabeth Wyems. Died 1732 Coles Alley Dublin City Ireland

HENRY WEMYS ***- Baptism of Henry Wemys of *Silver Court Dublin* on *7 November 1736 at* St Werburgh - Dublin (COI). Died 1761, buried St Andrews Church Dublin.

POSSIBLY James Wemys Children

JAMES WEMYS Married Margaret **Blundell.** 1st May 1773, child **James** baptised 20 Nov 1798 St Catherine Dublin (COI), (*James mother was Joyce* **Blundell,** *hence why I have attached them here*).

PATRICK WEMYS b.abt 1745. Married Mary Miller, June 25 1773 St Nicholas Without, Dublin, Ireland. *Residence 4 Great Georges Street. Dr Patrick lived here during his trial.*

GEORGE MORICE WEYMS *of LAZERS HILL (later called* **Townsend St***)* on 8 April **1768**. Baptism of St Marks Dublin (COI). *NOTE TC: *Dr Patrick Wemys lived in* **38 Townsend** *St Dublin in* **1789,** *as he often took care of his brothers' property while he was abroad. This was 20 years after the birth of George Wemyss 1768. George was most probably Captain James Weymes grandson his wife Elizabeth was too old to bear a son, she died in 1792.*

Henry Wemys maybe descendent of *Dr James* as he had property in Mountrath St which his brother Dr Patrick took care of it in 1780. James's other *brother Francis Williams Wemyss d.1779, owned houses on Mountrath, and his grandson Francis Wemys d.1856, in Cornwell, had four properties' in High street Frankford no ,40,42,45,48.*

HENRY WEMYS b.1776 d.1864 Parsonstown, Birr Offaly. Henry, lived **44 Mountrath St, Birr**. *Henry Wimms Death age 88, 28-May-1864 Workhouse P. Town Married Pauper, Birr Co. Offaly, cause of death: Debility.* According to Griffith Valuation Henry (Wim's) leased this property from 1845 and possibly earlier until his demise in 1864. Nevertheless, in Griffith Valuation the lessor was Catherine Coughlan in 1854. It consisted of a house and yard.

Dr Patrick Wemys-Court case -*February 4, 1784 (see Patricks chapter). Newspaper article. _____his brother, Mr James Wemys, serving his majesty in the East or West Indies, son in law and heir in law to the late* **Walter Pritchard,** *of Frankford, Esq as some time ago* **advertised in the public papers, supporting the line of the Protestant interest___**

British Army-East & West Indies- *From the 17th through the 19th century, the European colonial territories of the West Indies were the French, British the Danish and the Spanish West Indies. The West Indies- is known as the Caribbean. It includes the islands in the Caribbean Sea, off the east coast of America. East Indies- are the lands of South and Southeast Asia, consisting of India.*

*NOTE: James is written as a Doctor in his brothers Francis William Weymes (Wemys) Will in 1782. SOURCES: *PRONI prerogative will index. **St Mary Dublin (COI) Parish records. ***Area - DUBLIN (COI), Parish/Church/Congregation – St Werburg. Ireland Diocesan and Prerogative Wills & Administrations Indexes 1595-1858. Transcript List of State Papers, Ireland. ttps://archives.gnb.ca/Exhibits/FortHavoc/html/BritishOfficers.aspx?culture=en-CA#linkTop*

ANCESTORS THROUGH HISTORY

Dr Patrick Wemys was a member of the Irish Volunteer corps in 1782. He was in the Irish Volunteer Corps-Queen's County Mountain Rangers 15 August 1779 Colonel Bernard; Major George Clare; **Captain John Drought***, Scarlet, faced black. (uniform).

The Irish Volunteers were a local militia raised by local initiative in Ireland in 1778. Their original purpose was to guard against invasion and to preserve law and order when British soldiers were withdrawn from Ireland to fight abroad during the American Revolutionary War and the government failed to organise its own militia. The Volunteers however were also marked by liberal political views. For instance, although only Anglican Protestants were allowed to bear arms under the Penal Laws, the Volunteers admitted Presbyterians and a limited number of Catholics, reflecting the recent Catholic Relief Act of 1778.

The **Renunciation Act**, was passed by Westminster in 17 April 1783. It acknowledges the exclusive right of the Parliament of Ireland to legislate for Ireland. However, The Act of Union 1800 abolished the Irish parliament, and thus ended legislative independence.

Catholic Gentry *After the effective demise of the Jacobite cause in the 1750s, many Catholic gentry withdrew support from the Stuarts. Instead, they created organisations like the Catholic Convention, which worked within the existing state for redress of Catholic grievances. When Charles died in 1788, Irish nationalists looked for alternative liberators, among them the French First Republic, Napoleon Bonaparte and Daniel O'Connell.*

American War of Independence 1775- 1783- Thomas Jefferson drafted the Declaration of Independence, which argued that the goals of the United States of America were 'life, liberty and the pursuit of happiness'. In September **1783**, the Treaty of Paris formally ended the war. Some say that the American revolutionary war helped change the British government approach to Ireland on such developments as Catholic relief, the removal of restrictions on Irish trade, and Britain's recognition of Irish legislative independence.

IRISH REBELLION 1798

Napoleon's Irish Legion 1796- 1798 The French revolutionary government had launched two unsuccessful Irish invasions—in 1796 and 1798—believing that Britain's naval superiority would be much reduced by the loss of Ireland. In 1803 Napoleon approved the formation of an Irish Legion, to spearhead another invasion. This new unit comprised many United Irishmen who were exiled in Paris following the recent rebellions and former officers from the ancien régime Irish Brigade. ___Following the defeat of the Franco-Spanish fleet at Cape Trafalgar in 1805, the anticipated invasion of the British Isles was cancelled.

NOTE*: It was Captain John Drought bother the Rev Drought who refused to return Patrick watch worth a lot of money so that he ended up in the debtor's prison see chapter. Captain Drought was known for his hard line against Catholics.

SOURCE: https://en.wikipedia.org/wiki/Irish_Volunteers_(18th_century). https://en.wikipedia.org/wiki/Jacobitism . https://www.historyireland.com/18th-19th-century-history/napoleons-irish-legion/.Apothecary picture: Nation Gallery Ireland

PATRICK WEMYS DOCTOR b.abt 1717

Son of Francis Wemys & Joyce Blundell

Patrick was b.abt 1717 Kill Kildare Eire. According to Army records he was listed as an Apothecary in the Army in Senegal West Africa from 1750 to 1798. Dr Patricks was married to abt 1747 **to** Mary Weymes b. abt 1730. d. 1771 at Frankford Kings county Offaly.

Freemans Journal 15 February 1771 Parish Burials*. -Died -Mrs Wemys Frankford Kings county, wife of Apothecary Frankford. Kings County Offaly (King's).

OFFALY WEMYS-*I cannot prove that Dr Patrick had a son Patrick below but all my research has pointed to this been the case. However, this Patrick to the best of my knowledge is the Westmeath ancestor.*

Dr Patrick & Mary Weymes Children**

Jane Wemys b.1750 d.1787, baptised Nov 1750 St Werburg Church of Ireland Dublin City. Burial of Jane Weymes (as written) of Goat Alley Dublin, 5 August 1789 at St Peters Church Dublin. *In 1536-1810 Index Prerogative Wills of Ireland there is a Jane Wemm 1780 Dublin spinster.*

Patrick Wemys *(written Patt Wymbs)* b.1748 d. unknown. Married **Mary Concannon** 1771 Tuam Galway. *Written Patt Wymbs on marriage certificate.* Their son Patrick (written *Wheims on marriage cert)* b abt 1772. The Wemys were mainly military or Vicars but I could not find anything on this Patrick there. During Dr Patrick trial, he only mentioned his brother Dr James who was abroad perhaps Dr Pat son Patrick was also abroad or died young. The Weymes were known as gentlemen farmers and Dr Patrick did have a small farm so perhaps this Patrick became a farmer.

Patrick married 1771 **Tuam Galway** the widow Mary Concannon (born Concannon) b.abt 1749. Mary Concannon* is on the Catholic conversion roll on the 7th March **1771** Ireland. I believe this is the Catholic line in Offaly and where William Weymes b 1801 Westmeath came from that my tree is attached to also. **Mary Concannon** *(possibly her parents) Baptism 20 Mar 1749, Parish St. Catherine's, Dublin. Her fathers were Hugh Concannon, mother's Eleonor Concannon.* Ireland.

Patrick Wemyss and Mary Concannon Children:

Patrick Weymes (written Patt Wheims**)** b. abt 1772 d.unk. He married September 27th **1794** Anne Ward Athboy Meath. Witnesses -John Currin Daniel Lynch, Honor Brady. Patrick and Ann were Catholic. Their son William Weymes b.1801 was the ancestor of the **Weymes of Westmeath.** *See chapter*

NOTE: *During the 1700's, Catholics were restricted from owning property, holding public office, and voting. Due to these restrictions some chose to renounce their religion and convert to the Church of Ireland. In addition to church rites participation, they were also required to file a certificate in a court of law. There are still Concannon's living in Tuam today. Wards still live in Athboy.*

SOURCE: *Francis Williams Wemys prerogative Will index 1782- NLI Dublin *BMD by HF Morris. Dublin Archives- Ireland Diocesan and Prerogative Marriage Licence Bonds Indexes 1623-1866, Category Birth, Marriage, Death & Parish Records. Repository National Library of Ireland. National Library of Ireland link http://registers.nli.ie//registers/vtls000633519#page/1/mode/. ***Familysearch.com, Affiliate Image Identifier: IRE/CATHQUALCONV/004150581_00145*

Patrick Wemys residence: It seems as Dr Patrick was the youngest by many years, he did not inherit any property unlike his three brothers. Patrick seems to have had these residences all belonging to his brother James: Coles Ally Dublin City, Mountrath Street Birr Offaly 1782(brother James house), 4 Great Georges Street also bother James house during his court case and 38 Townsend St Dublin-1789. (His brothers Francis William Wemys house in Mountrath Offaly in 1794 was let).

NOTE: I have not found any other Pat Wemyss for this period so this maybe Dr Pat although he was not living in Danesfort but perhaps they return to base when they do their Wills.
Ireland Diocesan and Prerogative Wills & Administrations Indexes 1595-1858- **Patrick Wemys 1792** Danesfort, Kilkenny.

Saunders newsletter 1789 To be let -new house -with a horse stable-- and in Stillorgan Deer park grounds are 2 acres proposals to be received by Henry Hartley esq, Cuffe St, Dublin or Patrick Weymes, **38 Townsends** St Dublin. **Thom's Almanac** and official directory for the year 1862-Library Ireland -**38 Townsends St** - Mac **Nevin** Patrick, pawnbroker and auctioneer. Barlow Arthur Sol, to the governors of the schools founded by the late Eramus Smith esq, 80L.Barlow Arthur Junior, solicitor.

NOTE Dr James son Patrick Wemyss who married Mary Miller in 1771 lived at 4 Great Georges Street. According to Court case 4 Great Georges Street was Dr Patricks residence in 1783.

The term 'apothecary' traditionally described a person who dispensed medicines and who would now be called a chemist. They were mmore than a druggist: In colonial times, the apothecary was more than simply a druggist. He often: provided medical treatment, prescribed medicine, trained apprentices, performed surgery, served as man-midwives. A colonial apothecary practiced as a doctor. Records kept by 18th-century Williamsburg's apothecaries show that they made house calls to treat patients, made and prescribed medicines, and trained apprentices. Some apothecaries were also trained as surgeons and man-midwives. It is generally conceded that is from the apothecary's that the general practitioner arose, and by the 1700 some were called "surgeon apothecary". Apothecaries used mortar and pestle sets to grind herbs into fine powders and to make their pills and ointments. Many recipes included herbs, minerals, and pieces of animals (meats, fats, skins) that were ingested, made into a paste for external use, or used as aromatherapy. Some of these are similar to natural remedies used today, including catnip, chamomile, fennel, mint, garlic, and witch hazel. Their listed stock was, "medicines, perfumes, spices, herbs, comfits, antidotes, aphrodisiacs, antiseptics, tonics, purgatives, laxatives, emetics, astringents and general cure-alls". Apothecaries needed great skill to recognize plants, and learn their properties and qualities, as well as how to extract their essences. They weighed and mixed compounds and prepared medicines with sophisticated techniques of fermentation, filtration and distillation. Apprentices served seven years and passed an oral exam. Up to the 1700 there was very little respect for Apothecary's possibly due to the fact that some were "Quacks" and did a lot of damage leading to fatalities. Nevertheless, in 1704 the House of Lords ruled that apothecaries could both order and administer medications. This was a landmark ruling because it gave legitimacy to the apothecary as a physician and thus an apothecary could say he belonged to a profession's body, rather than still be considered a tradesman.

Apothecary Patrick Wemys Senegal

*Goree had been taken from the French in **1758**, but restored to them at the Peace of Paris, in **1763**, in return for the **Senegal**, which was retained by us for several years, during which interval many medical officers of the regular army were quartered there. The nature of their duties may be surmised from the foregoing lamentable picture, almost the earliest record of the African service handed down to us. On the cession of the Forts to the Crown by the African company, a regiment to garrison them had been raised, and styled "A Corps of Foot serving in Africa."*
*_____The regiment consisted of a lieutenant-colonel commandant, three captains, three lieutenants, three ensigns, a and a regimental agent, but no regimental medical officer, the hospital and corps being in charge of Garrison Surgeons," some of whose names appear in the older Army Lists. The succession of Colonels in this corps was as follows Charles O'Hara 25th July, 1766. John Clarke 28th September, 1776. Joseph Wall 16th February, 1780. It was disbanded in **1783**, with two independent companies of Foot raised for service in Western Africa in 1781 and 1782, viz., Mackenzie's and Captain the Honourable Charles Cranston's. Both of these companies had a captain, two lieutenants, and an ensign.*

The Officers of the Hospital, *" as they were at this time called, then serving at the **Senegal,** were Surgeon John Boon. William Bishop. **Apothecary Patrick Wemys.** Brocklesby insisted upon the good elects of discipline and minute attention to the laws of health as essential to the welfare of an army. He drew up for General Draper, previous to his expedition against Manilla and the Philippine Islands (at that time a two months' passage from Madras), the following excellent regulations for the preservation of the health of the soldiers embarked on board the transports. _____*

SOURCE: *The Story of Our Services Under the Crown: A Historical Sketch of the Army Medical Staff Hardcover – 19 May 2016 by Albert Augustus Gore* https://www.forgottenbooks.com/.../TheStoryofOurServicesUndertheCrown_10118191=PAGE 98-

The Medical Register for the Year **1783**

1783 SSS WEMYSS PATRICK Hospital Senegal.

18th Century Medics (-b- means before) b1745 a (-a- means after).

Master Apothecary to our Army hospital,15 January 1762, 659.

1762- Patrick Wemyss. "Master Apoth. to Our Army Hospital," 15 Jan. 1762.

1766-Apoth. h.p. Hosp. at Senegal, c. 1766.

Genealogical Society London-Roll of Army medical Service 1727-1898 -Pat Wemyss (Page 37 -(659)

1779- In the Medical Register-1779 Mr. Patrick Wemyss, *late* apothecary at Senegal.

Officers of The Land Forces and Marines on The English Half-Pay 1760

1787-A List of the Officers of the Army and Marines. Irish half pay *P209*

Senegal apothecary Patrick Wemyss

1787 -A List of the Officers of the Army and Marines. *P314*

Staff Officers and Officers of the Hospitals placed on sundry Periods on half pay -1787

Senegal apothecary Patrick Wemyss

1791-A List of the Officers of the Army and Marines. *P582*

Senegal apothecary **Patrick Wemyss.**

Apothecary HP Hospital at Senegal C 1760-**Pat Wemys**s Apothecary Senegal **1794**

NOTE TC: In the Prerogative WILL index from PRONI of his brother Francis W Weymes he is written **Patrick Wemys MD**

Patrick earlier years he was resident at Kilcock Kildare Ireland.

SOURCE: Army List 1787 - Military, armed forces & conflict, Collections from Great Britain

FOUR COURTS MARSHALSEA DUBLIN

FOUR COURTS MARSHALSEA DUBLIN

Debtors Prison: The Marshalsea was a debtor's prison, allowing debtors along with their families to take refuge from their creditors. The majority paid rent for their lodgings with the destitute being fed with bread. The building was laid out around two courtyards that housed the prisoner's accommodation, guard rooms, a chapel and an infirmary. The keeper of the prison was the Marshal of the Four Courts, a role filled after 1546 by the Constable of Dublin Castle. The Marshal had his own accommodation in the upper yard. It closed in 1874

Dr Patrick in prison from November 1783: There was an illegal possession of Doctor Patricks house (belonging to his brother Dr James) in Birr Frankford where he was brutally beaten, thrown into a fire and all his medicines and equipment broken which left him destitute. *See newspaper articles.*

Judge John Gamble 1783, **said _____Wemys** *still had the humanity sufficient to forgive the villainous offender, imagining a prosecution might have brought him (the offender) to the gallows."*

The Gold Watch: Dr Patrick had a gold watch to pay his debt, but he gave it for safe keeping to the Rev, James Drought, who refused to submit it to him. He ended up at the Marshalsea without money so that another inmate kindly shared his bed with him and gave him food. Dr Patrick assisted those who required medical treatment and refused payment. His brother James Wemys an officer in the British Army was at this time away in West India's. *He was acquitted Tuesday 24 August 1784.*

SEVERAL MURDER ATTEMPTS ON DOCTOR PATRICK WEMYS LIFE

In 1782 Dr Patrick brother Dr James Wemys put an article in the paper supporting the stance of the British Government in Ireland while he was in the army in West Indies. Perhaps this may be the reason that Dr Pat was under attack. There were no police at this time only Volunteers Corps which Dr Pat was a member under John Drought.

By all accounts of what I have read he was a kind man and looked after the poor in Birr and even did not report the burning attack for fear the man might be executed. The attacks were done by gentlemen meaning they had money and influence. They swore to kill him and threatened to main his cattle wanting him to leave Ireland, but he fled to Dublin. From Debtors prison in *29th January 1785 he writes to The Lord Chancellor* via the newspaper saying his letters were not been passed on to him and pleading for assistance.

SOURCE: The Four Courts Marshalsea - taken by Elinor Wiltshire at Dublin's Marshalsea Barracks 1969 *wiki*

DR PATRICK THROWN INTO A FIRE.

Sworn before me, the 30th September 1783, John Gamble

*N.B. The said **Mr Wemys** was thrown in the fire about the **20th of last October** was twelve months, by **Hugh Molloy**, an inhabitant of the town of Frankford , and burnt in a shocking manner, the men and women of the house knocked down by attempting to save his life, he still had the humanity sufficient to forgive the villainous offender, imagining a prosecution might have brought him to the gallows.-Said Wemys never received any fee or reward for the injury, or the loss of his practice, & c.*

*On the **26th of last July**, the said **Doctor Wemys** was dragged out of his house, his Medicines and Goods thrown on the street and illegal possession taken from his house by one **John Ellwood** and his family, the Medicines and Goods lost and destroyed said Wemys leaving them in the street. The aforesaid **Doctor Wemys, about** a month or six weeks ago, was attacked with a violent gripping and cutting in his bowels, attended with bloody stools, on examining the same, found the powdered glass had been administered to him, as he is fully able to prove.*

Dr Patrick was resident at 15 Mountrath St Birr on the 15th September 1782 along with George Batson this was perhaps his brother Francis William house while they were waiting for probate of his Will in 1782. Francis had several houses on this street 40 to 45.

On the 20th of October 1782 *Hugh Molloy* threw Dr Pat into a fire causing severe burns. He must have taken up other residence in Birr because new residence was at 15 Mountrath St by 9th *July 1783* a Roger Larkin and James Jackson. On the 26th of July of 1783 Dr Pat was thrown out of house by *John Ellwood.*

By the time of his trial in debtors court in February 1784 he was living in his brother Dr James house in 4 George St Dublin. Prior to this in 28th August 1776 no 5 Mountrath St had: Issacs Shephard, George Jackson, *Robert Drought, Thomas Drought, Patrick Molloy.* Pat Molloy was also there in no 20 in 28th August 1790. From 15th February 1785 there was Steward Drought.

It seems even with severe burns Dr Patrick continued as an Apothecary in another house until *John Ellwood* took his house and destroyed his livelihood. He now had no means and fall into debt. He did however have a gold watch he gave to Rev Drought for safe keeping but Drought refused to give it back to him so he could pay his debts.

NOTE: *Elwood is a name from Gloucestershire England.* Griffiths Valuation of Ireland - Ballyboy, County Offaly *of 1856 there is an Anne* Elwood, Ford (Part of) Main Street Ballyboy Offaly.
Source Doc: no 519 Frankford Ballyboy 7th February 1775

DR PATRICK WEMYS SEEKS JUSTICE

DUBLIN EVENING POST **9th March 1784**-Kings county to wit

This day **Dr Patrick Wemys** *Of Frankford came before me , and made Oath on the Holy Evangelists ,that he is hunted up and down by a set of fellows, with an intent to murder him, or deprive him of his senses: they threaten to murder him and hough his cattle ,desiring him to quite the country,(constantly night and day under cover)which deprives him of his rest and being in danger of his life , is obliged to lay down his practice , greatly to his injury and loss .-This method has been followed a considerable time,* **Hurt said Wemys** *practice and a great number of the poor has perished for want of his assistance.-These are therefore in his Majesty's name, by me John Gamble, one of his majesty's Justice of the peace for the said Co. Charging every one of his Majesty's peaceable and loving subject, strictly to find out such offenders, and give proper information to me thereof: If they are dread or danger of such a set of combined villains, any just information will be received, and the informer not mentioned; by giving intelligence for the proper person to prosecute, a reward will be given to the humanity of the informer.*

DUBLIN EVENING POST – Dublin- 9th March 1784 - ~~February.4th, 1784~~

Mr **Wemys** *refers to Colonel Bernard, of the Volunteer Mountain Rangers, whose Corps he belongs to, or any other gentlemen he has the pleasure of being acquainted with, for his character.-Supporting the interest of his brother, the late Francis Wemys, esq; the children's property, and the property of his brother, Mr James Wemys, serving his majesty in the East or West Indies, son in law and heir in law to the late Walter Pritchard, of Frankford, Esq as some time ago advertised in the public papers, supporting the line of the* <u>Protestant interest,</u> *has occasioned said Mr Wemys to be so barbarously treated, but having the honour of half pay from his Majesty's, prevent distress.* **PAT. WEMYS**

No 4. George's Street, Said Dr Wemys is well assured that the great injuries he received, was propagated and encouraged by men, who call themselves gentlemen, divested of, every honour and principle.

Colonel Thomas Bernard (c.1769-1834; M.P.) Of Castle Bernard Birr King's Offaly. Colonel Bernard commanded a local volunteer corps called the 'Mountain Rangers' in the 1798 Irish Rebellion. He was appointed High Sheriff of King's County for 1798–1799. He was then elected at the 1802 general election as a Member of Parliament (MP) for King's County (now County Offaly), holding the seat until 1833. He died intestate in Dublin in 1834.

Dr Patrick Acquitted August 1784

Dr Patrick Wemys Acquitted 1784_____Lang, for perjury, to remain in jail till next alhzes; James Cunningham, Philip Keon, Francis Murry, Dom. Feenaghty, Barth. Wemys, and Pat. Horrm, were severally tried for different offences, and acquitted_____

DOCTOR PATRICKS SUPPORT FROM OTHER PRISIONERS

Four Courts Marshalsea, **January 24th, 1785**

We, the under named prisoners, do hereby certify, that Dr. Patrick Wemys, on the 25th of November last, year was, on his commitment to this prison, put into a common hall, in the greatest distress, being destitute of every means to obtain support; and was it not for the great humanity of William Freeman,-in the same hall, who gave him part of his bed, and credit for his maintenance, he might have perished. That the aforesaid Dr Wemys has carefully attended the poor sick prisoners since his confinement without recompense.

Patrick Martin, William Ellis, John Bradbourn, James Fitzgerald, William Freeman, Denis Lawlor, Patrick Mulvaney, Mathew Mc Mahon, John Preston, Thomas Phillips, James O'Brian, Charles Mc Doniel. * The printer certifies that a number of names are left out to save expense.

DR PATRICK WEMYS PLEADS FOR MERCY

DUBLIN EVENING POST **January 29th, 1785**

To the right honourable THE LORD CHANCELLOR

My Lord

It is with infinite pain that I have to address your Lordship in this public manner, to obtain redress for the various wrongs and injuries I have suffered. After refereeing your worship to the copy of my examinations, and the partiality of the Grand Jury of Phillipstown, in throwing them out, my application by letters not having been attended to, makes me imagine your lordship never received them, which occasion this public and never -failing method being Taken, the liberty of the press never denied to freeman.

Being illegally dragged out of my house, my medicines and goods thrown into the street, and taken away by sundry individuals, and possession taken of my holdings without any authority by law; obliged to lay down my practice worth 200L.per ann. every attempt made to destroy me, I am now confined for 32L-178. which I offered a considerable time ago to settle with the late Robert Drought of Ballygowan the Kings County, which was refused, he having joined me in a note to Joseph Maniford, at the same time leaving a note of mine in the said Drought's hands for the said value payable at the same date, with a double cased gold watch, which cost 27 guineas, as a security for the aforesaid joint note ,

I beg leave to represent to your Lord, that the note and my watch are with-held from me by Rev, James Drought, and Robert Drought, attorney, sons to the late Robert Drought, of Ballyoran, and executors to him, --------Drought, attorney to the said plaintiff.

Such attempts made to destroy a subject induces me to lay my case before your Lordship, being confined here in the common hall, and in a manner destitute of the common necessaries for support. I hope your Lordship will be pleased, out of great humanity to order protection to the injured. -My Lord, I have the honour to be, very respectfully your Lordship's most obedient, and most humble servant. **PAT WEMYS**

NOTE this is Patrick brother Francis house.

Newspaper: Saunders's News-Letter- Published: Tuesday 24 August 1784: House Birr, Kings county_____ adjoining, containing three acres and an_____ A dwelling house and garden, in the town of Frankford, formerly inhabited by **Captain Wemys**. *It is commenting the beauty the gardens, or the situation of the house_____*

THE THREE DROUGHTS BROTHERS Cappagolan, Litter, Whigsborough.

Rev James Drought refused to return Dr Patricks gold watch and is one of the reasons he ended in Debtor prison.

The one in Whigsborough. (John) was known to be a very hard Protestant. There was a story that the Cappagolan and Whigsborough were having supper with the Sheriff of Ridgemont and Drought of Whigsborough informed him that there was a Priest in hiding and that he could bring him to them. The Ballyboy Cavalry went to arrest him the next day but the hut was empty. The servant overhead the conversation and alerted the priest and warned them. However, when Drought of Cappagolan, got home he brought the priest to his homeland hide him and then dressed the priest in his own clothes so he passes as him and then drove him to safety in Banagher. The Droughts were Landowners, Droughts of Droughtville and Whigsborough, King's County. Rev James Drought -b.1738, Ballyboy, Offaly, Ireland. He was a teacher and Professor of Divinity at Trinity College, Dublin. He died at Bath Jan 1820, aged 82 years, and was buried beneath the floor of the Abbey Church on January 20, 1820. John Drought Whigsborough - High Sheriff of King's County 1780/82. Robert Drought abt 1770 Park (Ridgemont) King's County – d.12 Apr 1827. 1823: There was a Fran Drought esq, Croughan House. John Drought esq Whigsbourogh. In Griffith Valuation 1854 Fran Drought was a landlord of Ballyboy Village with 34 houses. The last surviving member of this Drought family died in Canada and his ashes were sent to be buried in Birr.

*NOTE: Frankford Offaly Ireland 1799**_____ of assignment 20 November 1799 (daughter of Francis and Ann). Between Ann Wemyss Widow of Frankford Kings County of the first part* **John Dought** *Gentleman of the 2nd part and Francis Wemys esq Lieutenant (24 egiment of Foot) and Ann Wemys spinster of the 3rd part. Reciting the assignment of an annuity of £50 per annum to Ann Wemys out of the Frankford estate. Note £50 was about £3600 in 1800.*

OFFALY

WEMYS

THE SQUARE, PARSONSTOWN, 1805, W.L.

FRANKFORD WEMYSS

Descended from Francis Wemys Kildare d. 1684

Frankford Wemys are descended from Francis Wemys Grandson of Sir Patrick Wemys (see Kildare and Kilkenny). This family had significant property in Birr, Frankford and Dublin (Blind Quay, Cadogan Alley, Dublin), which was originally owned by Maurice Wemys and was passed down through many generations. This was most probably land inherited from the Blundell's through marriage. They were originally Protestant and had a tradition of serving in the Army and Navy. A notable member of this branch was **Francis Wemys**, who in 1811 became Paymaster for the Southern District of Ireland. He finally went to England and lived in Falmouth, Cornwall, where he descended are today.

Chronicle of the Wemys of Frankford Estate

Dublin Ireland 1769/77*_____ Lieutenant **58 Regiment** of foot Francis Wemys leased land for thirty years at Merrion St, City of Dublin to Murtagh Lacy Bricklayer of Dublin in 1769, mortgage. Offaly: Francis Wemyss **24th regiment of foot** leased land in Mountrath St, Frankford in the barony of Ballyboy in 1777 to Issacs Honey for three life times. Frankford Offaly Ireland 1799**_____ of assignment 20 November 1799 (daughter of Francis and Ann). Between Ann Wemyss Widow of Frankford Kings County of the first part John Dought Gentleman of the 2nd part and Francis Wemys esq Lieutenant (24 Regiment of Foot) and Ann Wemys spinster of the 3rd part. Reciting the assignment of an annuity of £50 per annum to Ann Wemys out of the Frankford estate. Note £50 was about £3600 in 1800. Dublin Ireland 1800***_____between Francis Wemys lieutenant in his majesty's regiment of foot Dublin City esq and Ann Wemys of Dublin City Spinster the Sister of Francis the first part and John Mac Donald senior of Frankford shopkeeper the lease of Land in Frankford.

Griffith's Valuation 1847-1864- Ballyboy, Parsonstown (Birr)Offaly (King's)

Francis Wim's, Role Lessor,1854-08-17. Occupier's Francis Feighery, 40 and 42 Main St Frankford, House Yard Garden.

Francis Wim's Lessor date,1854-08-17, Occupier Edward Walls, 45 Main St Frankford, House Yard Garden.

Francis Wim's, Lessor, date:1854-08-17, Occupier Patrick Reedy, 48 Main St Frankford House Yard Garden.

Francis James Wemyss**** Year 1854, Dwelling House Parish Cork.

Francis James Wemys of Lancaster leased it for life to Andrew Honey. - Mountrath Offaly 1859.

NOTE The House in Mountrath St was leased from 1777 to 1759 to an Isaac and then Andrew Honey

Frances Wemyss, Head*****, W, 73, District Paymaster, - Ireland, (Half Pay) Army. Cornwall England 1864.Sophie H Wemyss, daughter, U,34, Lady, Ireland. Catherine A Wemyss, daughter, U,26, Lady, Ireland. 1864 Harbour Terrace.

*SOURCE: * Deeds from Dublin Archives **Memorial of Deed-of assignment 20 November 1799 (Daughter of Francis and Ann), Source: Eneclann Report ***Memorial of Deed- Release April 22 1800(I 581 98 389738) Source: Eneclann Report ****Landed Estates Court Rentals 1850-1885-Census, land & surveys *****Cornwall Online Census Project-1851 Landowners, circa 1870s - King's County- NO Wemys listed. Cumberland Square c.1880-1900 Birr Offaly. Picture National Library Ireland-wiki*

FRANCIS WILLIAM WEMYS

Son of Francis Wemys & Joyce Blundell.

Portsmouth England Line

Francis William Wemys*s. b.1708 Kill Kildare. Francis Weyms *(as written)* of Coolderry Offaly died aged 71 years buried July 6th 1779, at St Thomas Dublin. Probate 1782. Residence Mountrath street (off main street) King's County. Francis Williams eldest brother Maurice Wemys inherited his estate (came down from his great-grandfather Sir George Blundell of Edenderry) and having no Heir Willed his estate to Francis William in 1777. In the prerogative Will he is registered as Toole, (written *orwise* Latin) otherwise Coolderry Kings county (Ofally).

Army 24th regiment of foot. *LT Francis Wemys June 5th 1762, 58th Regiment of Foot Ireland. (His brother James served with him). He became a Major Francis Wemyss in 25 May 1772, in 20th Regiment of foot America in 1777.

Francis William married- 07 Feb 1767 Ann Frances Duane at St Michan Dublin (COI). He was 59 years old. **Ann Duane** Ann was b. abt. 1745. Ireland, d.14 March **1789,** St Audoen's. (written Wymes in Parish records.) (COI) Married: Francis Wemys and Ann Duane on 11 February 1767 St Michan (COI)Dublin. *Resident in Dublin.*

*In Calendar of Converts: Ann Francis Duane** was a Catholic married 07 Feb 1767 and she swore an oath to the sovereignty in order to guard their property as Catholic could not own property. However, it seems she remained an Anglican as she was buried in St Michan (COI)Dublin.*

Prerogative WILLS***: Written as Ann Frances *W (orn) Duany,* date 10 Sep 1781. Spouse's Francis Wemys, of Toole otherwise Coolderry. Married of County Offaly (King's)Ireland.

NOTE The W stands for Weymes, her name was Duane not Duany.

Francis William Weymes & Ann Duane Children

Francis Wemys b. abt 1768 Mountrath St Ballyboy Kings county, d.1856 Falmouth Cornwell, England.

Anne Weymes b. abt 1769 Coolderry Offaly. d. aft 1800. Memorial of Deed 1800.

*SOURCE: for Ann Duane *Collection -Betham's genealogical abstracts **Calendar of Convert Rolls Vol. 1. Record set Ireland, Catholic Qualification & Convert Rolls 1701-1845 ***Notebook Betham's Genealogical Abstracts. Prerogative Wills: (Phillips Mss.) W. 1779-1787*

REGIMENT OF FOOT

Francis Wemyss *Army He appears to have changed regiments a few times but seems mainly based in Canada.

1762- June 5th, 24th regiment of foot. *LT Francis Wemys, 58th regiment of foot (His brother James served with him). Became Major Francis Wemyss in 25 May 1772. 1777- 20th Regiment of foot in Canada

20th Regiment of Foot (1751–1782), *1688 raised as Sir Richard Peyton's Regiment of Foot in Devonshire 1751 became the 20th Regiment of Foot, 1782 became the 20th (the East Devonshire) Regiment of Foot, 1881 became The Lancashire Fusiliers*

During the American Revolutionary War, the regiment was sent to Quebec in April 1776 serving under General John Burgoyne for the remainder of the Canadian campaign, they later surrendered at Saratoga 1777 (Ontario). The 24th returned to Britain in 1781 but was reposted to Canada between 1789 to 1800 to help guard the frontier from Revolutionary America.

24th Regiment of Foot was formed in 1751. It took part in the Siege of Fort St Philip in Menorca in April 1756 during the Seven Years' War. They fought in France and were defeat at the Battle of Saint Cast in September 1758. In June 1776 they were sent to Quebec to fight the American rebels who had invaded the province during their War of Independence. The regiment was part of the 5,000 British and Hessian force, under the command of General John Burgoyne, that surrendered to the American rebels in the Saratoga campaign in summer 1777 and remained imprisoned until 1783. In 1782 it became the 24th (The 2nd Warwickshire) Regiment of Foot.

58th Regiment of Foot (1756) They were first formed in 1755 during the Seven Years' War (1754-1763). The French and Indian War was fought between the colonies of Great Britain and New France, supported by American Indian allies on both sides.

1755 raised as the 60th Regiment of Foot

1757 became the 58th Regiment of Foot

1782 became the 58th (Rutlandshire) Regiment of Foots

*SOURCE: *Army list Kew London archives and Genealogical Society London. Army List 1765 (P.112), Army Lists 1785 (P. 78), Army List 1777 (P.74). Taken from Army List 1765 page 112, LT Francis Wemys J Une 5th 1762 58th Regiment of foot Ireland. (Also, Lt James Wemys June 4th 1762 58th Regiment of foot brother) Wikipedia*

FRANCIS WEMYSS *b. abt 1768 d.1856*

Son of Francis & Ann Wemys

Francis Wemys b.abt 1768 Mountrath St Ballyboy Kings County, d.1856 Falmouth Cornwell, England. He was lieutenant in his majesty's regiment of foot Dublin. Francis married abt 1810 Elizabeth Wemys***** b. about 1790.d. unknown.

Will Archives Gloucester- Gazette Issue 16201, published on the 15 November 1808. page 1558- Memorandum

The Appointment of Francis Wemyss, Esq; to be Paymaster of a Recruiting District in Ireland, as stated in the Gazette of 2d February last, has not taken place. At a later date: Francis Wemys was Paymaster master general, Southport. NOTE: Colchester Wemyss were from Gloucestershire.

British Newspaper Archive, Family Notices / Obituary, 18 Feb 1857, Cork, Ireland: **Wemyss** *Titles and Terms Esq Paymaster.*

Francis Wemys & Elizabeth -Children

Francis James Wemys * b. 1812 Mountrath St, Coolderry Offaly. d. March 1880 Poole, Dorset, England. Married Ann (Bennett) Anderson.

James William Wemys*** b. abt. 1820, Mountrath Frankford Ballyboy Ireland. d. September 1862, unknown, at 64 Harbour Terrace, Falmouth, Cornwall. James was mentioned in Will as abroad.

Sophia Ann Wemys**** b. 1817 Mountrath Frankford Ballyboy Ireland. Married 1899 Long fleet Poole Dorset. In 1891 lived alone 2 Ardley Rd Long fleet Poole. 2, North Parade,1, Sophia Wemyss, Head, U,55, Independent (Fundholder), Ireland.

Catherine Augusta Wemys**** b.1825 Mountrath Frankford Ballyboy Ireland.

Memorial of Deed of assignment 20 November 1799 .522 395 342732: Between Ann Wemyss Widow of Frankford Kings Co of the first part John Dought Gentleman of the 2nd part and Francis Wemys esq Lieutenant in the 24 Regiment of Foot and Ann Wemys spinster of the 3rd part Reciting the assignment of an annuity of £50 per annum to Ann Wemys out of the Frankford estate.

NOTE Master Mariner-Most mates or Master will have served their time as ordinary seaman or apprentices before gaining their certificate. Before1845 Masters and other officers were not separately registered

SOURCE: *Betham Genealogical Abstracts Transcription. * England and Wales Death Registration Index 1837-2007. **Cheshire Marriage licence bonds and allegations 1606-1905. *** England & Wales Deaths 1837-2007-Devon records. ****Cornwall Online Census Project-1861. Enumeration District 9-Civil Parish of Budock, Eccl. District of Penwerris-Folio 90 Page 1

FRANCIS JAMES WEMYS *b.1812 d.1880*

Son of Francis Wemys & Elizabeth Weymes

Francis James Wemyss *married Anne Anderson a widow, b.abt. 1814, Ireland, married 30 Aug 1851, St Pauls church Liverpool, Lancaster, England. She died 1897 age 83 Birkenhead, Cheshire. Her father was Joseph Bennet.

Francis Wemys & Ann Child: Marie Ann b.1854, Birkenhead Cheshire England, d unknown, Chesterfield Derbyshire.

Francis James Wemyss** and Ann returned to Mountrath Frankford Ballyboy Ireland but Francis died in Poole, Dorset, England in 1880.

In the 1871 census Tranmere Cheshire, Ann Wemyss age 53, Francis James Wemyss age 54 Ireland Head Tranmere Cheshire, daughter, Maria **Ann Wemyss** age 17 Birkenhead, Cheshire, England. Residence: Holt Hill, Tranmere, Birkenhead, Cheshire.

Maria Anne Wemyss*** Lodger Head, -26 1855, Ireland. Residence :144 Northbrook Street, Toxteth Park. She died in Chesterfield Derbyshire.

Francis James Wemyss**** was mentioned in Landed Estates Court Rentals 1854 in Cork Ireland.

This seems to be the Francis William Weymes line

SOURCE: *England Marriages, 1538-1973. **Census Frankford 1861/1871, ***1881 England, Wales & Scotland Census. ****Volume 027 Document 006, Landed Estates Court Rentals 1850-1885

CATHOLICS WEMYS OFFALY *Parsonstown, (Birr) Offaly Ireland*

WILLIAM WEYMES(Wimms) According to the Census 1821 he was *b.1783* (Pensioner age 38 years). Residence 29 Charles St, Birr, Offaly. William married Mary Wimms b.1785. Their children were: *(* Census 1822.)* Mary Ann Wimms b. 1813 age 8 years. Eliza Wimms b.1820 age 1 year. *Note William is possibly Patrick, Martin and Thomas father.*

PATRICK WEYMES *b.1815* in Birr Frankford, Offaly.

Patrick was accused with his brother for swearing an unlawful oath in 1841 and sent to Australia but he must have had very influential family as they were both brought back within 6 months and it was paid for by the British government which was unheard of. In 1842 he was again in court and imprisoned, this time falsely accused of been part of the Whitboys and threatening a farmer. Again, a friend a Judge proved that the accuser was James Levins police informant who admitted he lied and Patrick was released. Finally, in 1849, at the hight of the famine Patrick was accused of robbery *(bearing in mind robbery could be a loaf of bread).*

He was transported to Hobart Town Tasmania. Some four years later his wife Sara had an illegitimate male child and she died before 1855. Patrick must have been freed as in Sep 6 1855 he married a second time in Hobart Town Tasmania Margaret Martin a widow but no issue from this marriage that I could find. By all accounts he must have done well because in 1862 he was at an engineering conference doing speeches *(see below)*. It was difficult pinpointing Patrick in Hobart town as there were other Wemyss sometimes spelt Weymes there from 1800s. In 1907 there is mention of a *Weymes* that had private property where there was a gold mine claim.

As my father Joe said we were related to this Patrick and as we are descendance of Francis Wemyss and Joyce Blundell. I have no doubt there are from the same tree. Also, they are in the same town of Birr as the line of Sir Patrick Wemys. I was intrigued why Patrick and his brother were accused so often falsely perhaps someone had a vendetta against them, possibly because their relatives were Anglican and British army. I feel it was through these that they were reprieved from prison. Also, 35 years before Patrick was born *Dr Patrick Wemys* by all accounts a kind man in 1783 in Birr was very savagely threated even thrown into a fire and his livelihood destroyed and house taken from him. (See chapter)

NOTE: My father Joe said we had a relative that had been to Tasmania but I thought he was mistaken until I found Patrick this year 2020.

Patrick Marriage: He married on the 1 Aug 1837, Kilcormac RC Church Offaly, Sarah Nevin b. abt 1820 d.bef 1855. His second marriage was to Margaret Martin b.1806 in Tasmania Australia in 1955.

Patrick Weymes & Sarah * children *Ireland Roman Catholic Parish Baptisms*

William Weins (as written) Baptism date 23 Aug 1840, Kilcormac Offaly *(must have died young as they had another William later)*.

Patrick Weins Baptism, 27 Sep 1843 Kilcormac Offaly

Ann Weymes baptised ,02 Sep 1845, Kilcormac Offaly Twin of Mary

Mary Weymes-Baptised 02 Sep 1845, Kilcormac Offaly

William Weymes. baptised August 1853 Kilcormac Offaly. *Baptism cert written bastard.*

Court case 1842**** *At the spring Assizes 1842 the following cases occurs in the Kings county. James Levins police informant 1842 accused* **Wemys Michael Nevin and Martin** *but when he was imprisoned confessed, he had lied. About three months earlier three men named Martin, and Pat Wemys, and Michael Nevin, were, upon his testimony, and contrary to the charge of the Judge, found guilty of a whiteboy offence, for putting Levin's on his knees, and threatening to shoot him if he did not resign as caretaker of a farm for Mr. Biddulph. They were sentenced to transportation... and had actually been sent to Dublin when their pardon had been obtained by the magistrate of Frankfort, who knew them to be innocent. They now reside in Frankfort.*

NOTE: In 1797, an Act was introduced which made the swearing of unlawful oaths illegal. The swearing of oaths was the basis by which the working class organised successfully, and ensured both secrecy and solidarity. Not only did the ancient guilds, and later the unions organise around oath-taking, so did all manner of working-class organisations, from political clubs to insurrectionist movements. By banning oaths, the Government hoped to end the methods by which clandestine working-class organisations had been operating for hundreds of years. The importance the Government placed on undermining working class organisation by attacking the oaths system can be seen from the severity of the sentence for conviction could led to up to 7 years transportation.

*SOURCE: *1821 Census Record -29 Charles St, Birr, Offaly – Householder. Other householders John Whelan labourer age 58 Householder -Mary Whelan age 56 wife Martin Kennedy age 46, Anne Kennedy age 30 Wife, Patrick Kennedy age 2 son.*

Irish Prison Registers 1790-1924 *Transcription****** Patrick Weymes, age **26**, Birth year 1815. Residence county Kings (Offaly). Date 12-Apr-**1841**, Role Prisoner, Offence Administering an unlawful oath, sentence commuted to 6 months. Prison Kilmainham, Dublin. Patrick Weymes- Australia-Transportation 10 years-*height 5ft 5.*

Irish Prison Registers 1790-1924: Patrick Weymes age **30**. Birth year 1819, Residence county Kings (Offaly). Date 05-Sep-**1849,** Role Prisoner, Offence Robbery, Prison Newgate, Dublin. Transportation 10 years.

NOTE- *1849 was the last year of the Irish famine. Discrepancy with the ages as Patrick is written 1815 this one 1819.*

Hobart Town Tasmania Australia **, Marriages, 1810-1980*****

Margaret Martin & Patrick Wemyss, Marriage Sep 6 **1855,** Hobart Town Tasmania, Australia. Patrick Wemyss widower age 40 years, Margaret Martin 49 years widow. Married in St Joseph Church. Witness Sarah Mc Lean, Nathanial Martin.

SOURCE: indexing Project (Batch) Number M31046-8 Australia-ODM GS Film number 1368292-familyseasrch.com

Launceston Examiner (TAS) In Australian Newspapers Mar 4 1862

Dun Mountain Railway **Mr Weymes** *proposed "the engineers of the Dun Mountain Railways and said that undoubtably a large amount of scientific knowledge was due. _____ Mr. Fitzgibbon, who was received with very loud and repeated cheers, said he really felt very proud of the way in which they had received his name.* **Mr. Weymes**, *in praising him for his engineering skill, had most properly paid a tribute to the toaster mind of Mr. Doyne to him, to his large experience and knowledge, the construction of the line was due, _____*

Daily Telegraph (Launceston, TAS) Feb 14 1907. Weymes had private property where there was a gold mine claim.

NOTE: From 1800 Hobart Town Tasmania was a British penal colony. My father Joe mentioned a Weymes that transported to Tasmania but I only just found him 2020. I believe this is Patrick of Offaly. At first, I thought it could not be him because William was born in 1853 but it is written bastard on baptism cert. *On his marriage cert to Margaret he is written as labourer.* There are other Wemyss in Hobart Town from the 1830 but they are not related_ *Daniel Pring Wemyss*

*SOURCE: *Ireland Marriages 1845-1958 Transcription -Parsonstown, Birr Offaly Ireland -Repository National Library of Ireland. **Register title DUBLIN-KILMAINHAM PRISON GENERAL REGISTER 1840-1850. ***Register title DUBLIN-NEWGATE (RICHMOND) PRISON GENERAL REGISTER. **** Report on the Irish Coercion Bill by T.M. Ray secretary to the Loyal National Repeal Association of Ireland. 17 March 1846. *****Launceston Examiner (TAS) In Australian Newspapers*

Thomas Wenns* was born abt 1820 and married on 27 Sep 1842, Ballyboy Offaly, Margaret Feighery.

Thomas & Margaret's Wenns child- Margaret Wems Baptism 09 Feb 1847, Parish **Ballyboy** and Killoughy, Diocese Meath, Offaly (King's). Ireland, Petty Sessions Court Registers- Birr. John Weymes 11June 1886, Role: Complainant, Birr Court, Parsonstown, County, Offaly.

MISCELLANEOUS-Parsonstown, Birr Offaly Ireland

Henry Wimms b. 1776 d. 28 May 1864, age 88. Workhouse P. Town Married Pauper, Birr Offaly. Cause of Death: Debility.

Possibly Henrys Children if he married at 16 years old in 1792 in: Jane Wems: b.1792, d.1867, Parsonstown, Ireland. Age:75. *(possibly daughter of above)*. Mary Anne Wim's b.1803, d. 16 Aug 1870, Age 67, Birr Offaly. Status: Spinster.

Patrick Wyonas b.abt 1795 Marriage 28 Oct 1814, Parish, Rahan and Lynally, Diocese Meath, Spouse's Eliza Dumpres, Offaly (King's)Ireland.

James Wyennis b.abt 1820, married Biddy Maher abt 1835, child Mary Wyennis, Baptism date, 29 Feb 1836. Parish Moneygall, Offaly (King's).

Michael Wynes b. abt 1840 married Anna Kelly, child James Wynes, Baptism date Sep 1867, Parish Rahan and Lynally, Diocese Meath, Offaly (King's), Ireland.

Charles Wenes d.10 Nov 1846, Killinagant Parish Ballyboy and Killoughy, Diocese Meath Offaly, Ireland.

Peter Wynes, d. 14 Oct 1850, Parish Ballyboy RC.

James Wynes RC, Baptism Sep 1867, Parish Rahan and Lynally. Diocese Meath, Offaly (King's). Father's Michael Wynes Mother's Anna Kelly National Library of Ireland.

LONGFORD WEYMES, I have included these families below because of the similarity of names. However, there is also a Bridgit Scanlon b.abt 1780 and Danial Weymes from Bunduff Sligo who had 7 children who may be related to the Scanlon below.

Martin Weymes b.abt 1880, married Mary Scanlon their children Thomas 12 June 1804, Peter 3 Nov 1806, Margaret 10 Jan 1807, Ann 1 March 812.

William Weymes. b.abt 1820 married Elizabeth Mullen, child Peter b. July 1823.

Weymes widow- Tax Assessment .1826 Temple Michael, Town Parks, Longford, Ireland

NOTE: In 1820 Census in Charles Street there were 39 housed and 200 Inhabitants and the Robinson distillery was beside the town.
SOURCE: Ireland Roman Catholic Parish Marriages, baptism and deaths Dublin Archives

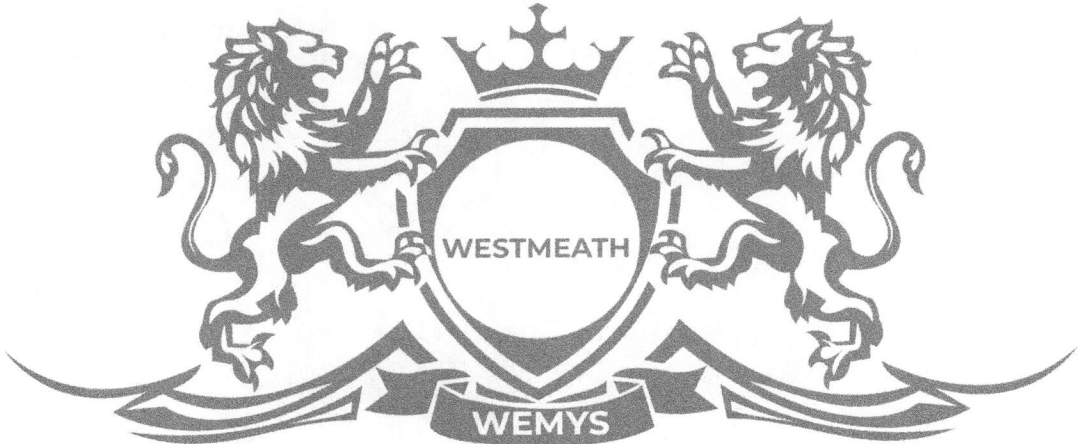

WESTMEATH

WEMYS

SIR DAVID WEMYSS Of Wemyss		Cecilia Ruhven
SIR JAMES WEMYS Bogie		Margaret Melville
PATRICK WEMYSS Reverand		Elizabeth Preston
SIR PATRICK WEMYS Kilkenny		Mary Wheeler
MAURICE WEMYS Kildare		Elizabeth
FRANCIS WEMYS Kildare		Joyce Blundell
DR PATRICK WEMYS Kildare		Mary
PATRICK WEMYS Offaly		Mary Concannon
PATRICK WEMYS Offaly		Anne Ward
WILLIAM WEYMES Westmeath		Mary Glynn
THOMAS WEYMES Westmeath		Bridget McDermott
PATRICK J WEYMES Westmeath		Ethel Shaw

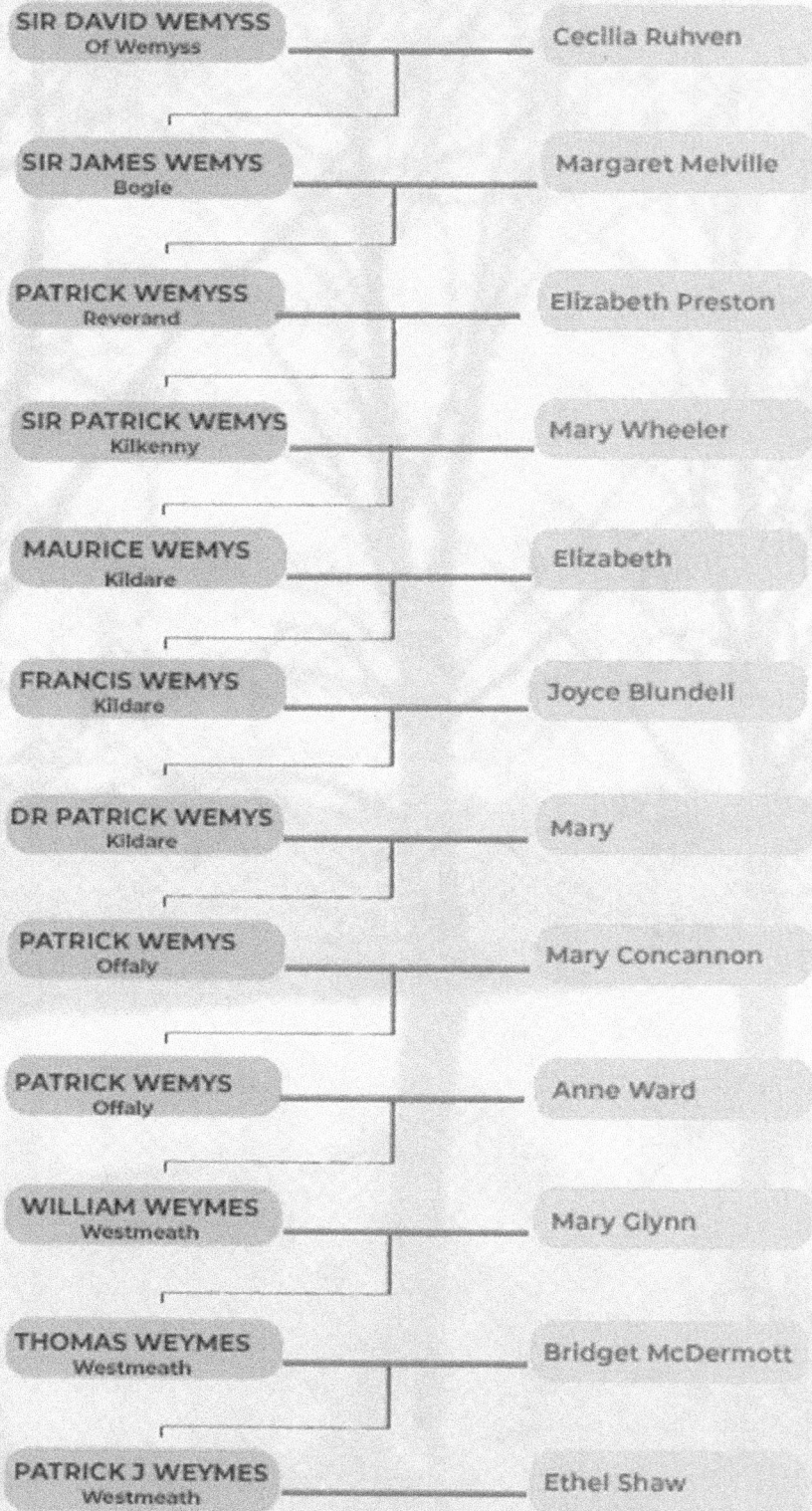

ANCESTORS OF PATRICK JOSEPH WEYMES

BARONET OF BOGIE TITLE

My Grandfather Patrick Joseph Weymes always knew he was descended from Sir Patrick Wemys grandson of Sir James Wemyss of Bogie Scotland. In 1900s he was approached by researchers who believed he had a claim to the *Title of Baronet of Bogie Scotland*. He was not successful possibly because he did not know who was the father of Sir Patrick Wemys b.1604. The title went to a Canadian Sir John Kessler Wemyss.

My Research. Unfortunately, research has been difficult because most of the Irish Births Marriages and deaths records were destroyed when the *Custom House* Dublin was burnt down in the Irish Civil war in 1922. However, I persevered over the next 30 years with the only piece of information that remained of my Grandfather PJ Weymes research written on a piece of paper.

Fragment of Will from PJ Weymes research. *Ref T. 559/41*

Weyms children

Dr Patrick

Dr James

Francis of Toole alias Coolderry Kings co will 1782 married Frances Derany

children -Francis, Anne

Mentioned in will of F.W. Lt. Colonel M Weyms: Jas and Capt Francis Weyms. Also, in will Rev William Weyms and his son William.

See Chapter on Prerogative Will Index Wemys Ireland

PJ Weymes Research/ WILL index of Francis William Wemys 1782.

Those on the index are the children of Francis Wemys b.1684 and Joyce Wemys (Blundell) Kill Kildare. I have traced and completed all the names in the index. Only Dr Patrick Wemys and his brother James Wemys were left that might connect to the Westmeath Weymes. Dr Patrick had a daughter Jane b.1750 Dublin, with his wife Mary who died in 1771. I surmise from all the evidence and research I have undertaken they had a son b.1748 Patrick who married Mary Concannon of Tuam Galway in 1771(Catholic). They in turn had a son Patrick that married Ann Ward of Athboy (Catholic) and their son was William Weymes b.1801 Westmeath. I believe our ancestors were as follows. Sir Patrick Wemys -son Maurice & Elizabeth -son Francis & Joyce, son Dr Patrick Wemys & Mary Concannon-son Patrick Weymes & Anne Ward -son William Weymes Westmeath. William sons had all the names of the Wemyss down the generation they missed however Henry and James.

See chapter on Francis Wemys & Joyce Blundell.

FAMILY HISTORY AND FOLKLORE

Family history from Joe Weymes stated that the Westmeath Weymes descended from Sir Patrick Wemys of Danesfort Kilkenny, the Weymes of Kildare, Ofally, the Wards of Meath and the Concannon's of Galway. In fact, he wrote the name Concannon down on a betting slip as I had never heard the name before. He also said that there were plaques to the Wemyss at the Cathedral of St Marys Tuam, Galway. There was a Thomas Wemys who died near Tuam at age 117 years in 1792 but I have not found whose tree he came from. Fortunately, several years ago I found both Wards and Concannon families married into the Wemys (husbands names Patrick) in the 1770s and 1790s both from the counties described.

Westmeath Weymes descendancy

They descended from Sir Patrick Wemys of Danesfort grandson, Francis Wemys and Joyce Blundell of Kill, Kildare. Francis sons settled in Birr, Offaly. Francis children were: Maurice and Henry who died without issue. Reverend William son William as best I can ascertain died without issue. At the time of Francis William Will, in 1782, it was just Dr James or Dr Patrick alive (*See chapter on Will*). The reason this book exists is because I had to complete several family trees in order to eliminate other family trees. Finally, I came to settle on Dr Patrick by trial, error and deduction as my ancestor. Because so many records have been destroyed, I have no documents to prove that Patrick Wemyss who married Mary Concannon of Galway in 1771 and the next Patrick who married Anne Ward in 27 Sep 1794 of Meath are the son and grandson of Dr Patrick Wemys our ancestor. But in a process over many years, I deduce that they are in fact Dr Patrick kin, and you will see why as you read this book. However, from William Weymes born 1804 all the Wemys/Weymes tree is documented and accurate to the best of my knowledge.

Tradition also stated that there were Weymes who were from Offaly who were deported to Tasmania and I only found this link in 2020. This all goes to show that Oral family history is very important even the smallest detail even if not totally correct can be a led, you just need to persevere and sometimes take a convoluted route to find them.

There was also a belief that we were related to Robert the Bruce, but I have found nothing to suggest this. However, the Wemyss supported Bruce and came to Ireland with him.

While, completing other tree even those in the Peerages books I found incomplete trees with the assumption that they belong to that line and others who have claimed Titles with no evidence of descendances.

*The Waterford herald -1792 * A few days ago, in the suburbs of the town of Tuam, Thomas Wim's in the 117 year of his age. He fought at the siege of Londonderry in the year 1691 and in different other skirmishes in the present and last century. Historical Books - Index of Authors and People Mentioned, 1811-2003- P38. Thomas Wimms, who died in 1791, near Tuam, in Ireland, had fought in the battle of Londonderry in 1701, and Phoebe Hessel, the Amazon, who received a bayonet wound at Fontenoy in 1745, lived to be 108, receiving a pension from the private purse of George IV. until his death.*

FAMILIES OF WESTMEATH

MILTOWN unknown family: *Patrick Weymes b.abt. 1838, Milltown Westmeath. Married Mary Hallion. Their daughter Bridget baptised 16 Mar 1858 C Witnesses Andrew Beglan Eliz Hallion. WINES: I have sometimes found the name Weymes spelt as Wines and for that reason I have included these. However, in the records from the church in Killucan (COI), I found many Wines which are not the Weymes. Edmundo Wines b.abt 1760 married Anna Wines. Their son was Thomas Wines Baptised 20 Feb 1781 Parish Milltown, Diocese Meath, County Westmeath, Ireland.*

WEYMES OF KINNEGAD WESTMEATH

The Weymes lived in Kinnegad from about 1800 until 1900 when they relocated to Mount St Mullingar. Maurice Weymes was living in Mullingar, from the 1860s. Slaters Directory of Mullingar for 1894 records a Maurice Weymes, wool merchant residing at Mount St.

Kinnegad is located on the border with Offaly, where the roads from Dublin to Galway and Sligo meet. The population in 1830 was 2812 of which 670 lived in the town. At that time there was also a police station and dispensary and 115 homes, with a market-house in the centre. In the 18 centuries, it greatly prospered due to being a staging post. This meant that weary travellers could stop and replace exhausted horses for fresh horses and receive food and accommodation. From 1729 Stagecoaches ran twice-weekly from Dublin to Kinnegad and Kilkenny at a cost of 5s.5d. The Kinnegad service extended to Mullingar in 1747; by the early 1750s this service was working four times weekly. It was a busy industrial area at the start of the 18th century, when hatters and nailers traded here, but its prosperity declined with the construction of the railroad track and canal.

NOTE: MOUNT ST MULLINGAR -Up until 1868, when public executions were stopped, crowds would gather weekly in Mount Street to get a good view of the hangings carried out in the jail.

MULLINGAR WESTMEATH HISTORY

Ruth Illingworth Archaeological Society Given by kind permission

By the eighteenth century, Mullingar was a major centre for the sale of wool and the local livestock fairs attracted buyers and sellers from all over Ireland and beyond. The majority of the population were Roman Catholic and by the 1760s, despite the Penal Laws, they had built a fine slate roofed parish chapel. There was also a substantial Church of Ireland community, and by the early 1800s, there were some Presbyterians and Methodists too. The nineteenth century brought a transport revolution to the town with the arrival of the Royal Canal in 1806 and the railway in 1848. Mullingar was also an important coach stop.

The rise of a Roman Catholic middle class and an active Clergy led to the building of a Cathedral in 1836 and the founding of schools by the Presentation and Loretto Sisters and the Christian Brothers. There was also a Church of Ireland National School.

Nineteenth century Mullingar was an important military centre and many British army regiments were stationed in the town. Many of the soldiers married local women and settled in town. The army also supplied a source of employment for locals and men from Mullingar served all over the British Empire. In 1858, Lord Grenville purchased the town and his family remained Landlords until the 1920s.

As well as a Cathedral, a military barracks, a railway station and the canal, Mullingar in the 1800s also had an infirmary, a workhouse, a jail, a courthouse, a market house, a post office and a police barracks. There was also a racecourse. The town was lit by gas from 1859 and a telegraph office opened in 1853. Mullingar Town Commissioners were founded in 1856. A District Dispensary opened in the 1850s, as did St. Loman's Mental Hospital. Sports played in the town included Rugby, Cricket and Gaelic games. Confraternities, Temperance Clubs, Freemasonry and the Foresters provided a social life and welfare.

Poverty was also a feature of 19th century Mullingar. There was much poor housing and periodic outbreaks of Cholera and other disease. A lack of sufficient employment and the ravages of the Great Famine led to an upsurge of emigration to Britain, America, Australia, Canada and Argentina. Changing agricultural practices, recession and unjust land laws led to many evictions and much violence in parts of the rural hinterland during the 1860s and 1870s. The twentieth century began with the arrival of the first motorcars and electric light in Mullingar. James Joyce visited the town in 1900 and recorded his impressions of Mullingar in his novels, 'Stephen Hero', and 'Ulysses'.

During the First World War, scores of Mullingar men served in the armed forces and many were killed or injured. The town was also a major military training depot. During the 'troubled times' of 1916-1921, many people from Mullingar, a largely Nationalist town, took part in the struggle for Irish Self Government. Sean McEoin was shot and wounded while trying to escape arrest in Mullingar in 1921. Early in 1922, the British Army left Mullingar and the Irish Army took over the barracks. Mullingar would remain an important garrison for the rest of the century. The first Gardaí arrived at the end of 1922. Mullingar escaped the worst of the Civil War, although there were a number of deaths and other serious incidents.

United Irishmen Catholic Emancipation

Prior to William's Weymes birth, there was the American war of Independence (1775–1783) and French Revolutions (1789 -1799). In 1793 France declared war on England.

The French revolution in particular produced a wave of interest in reform, especially amongst Presbyterians in the north of Ireland who wanted a more democratic state. From 1774 Roman Catholic were starting to be allowed to acquire their own property and land. In 1791 a bill was passed that enabled Roman Catholics to practice their religion without fear of civil penalties. The Relief Act of 1793, granted Irish Roman Catholics the admission to most civil offices. However, this seemed to be too little too late.

Irish Uprising-Catholic Emancipation-1798 Wolf Tone

In 1791 the Society of United Irishmen was founded in Belfast and Dublin by Wolfe Tone who was Church of England (*his mother had been Roman Catholic*). He wrote a pamphlet in 1791 titled "An Argument on Behalf of the Catholics in Ireland "He wanted a non-sectarian Irish Republic, and his compelling pamphlet called for the emancipation of Ireland's Catholic. The real importance of his society was the alliance for the first time with Catholics with protestants in order to gain political rights for all.

In May 1798 an Irish uprising occurred with the demand for Catholic Emancipation and removal of the penal laws and others. Wolf Tone believed aided by Napoleon that this would help them bring down the monarchy and he did send some ships that landed in Mayo with little success. Wolf Tone was arrested and died on 19 November 1798 at the age of 35 in Provost's Prison, Dublin. He is buried in Kildare where he grew up.

The uprising was suppressed by the British army with a death toll of between 10,000 and 30,000. The rebellion failed mainly due to lack of leadership and the uncoordinated uprising nationwide. The British army also had many high officials in the Society of United Irishmen who were also Government spies.

The Irish lawyer Daniel O'Connell

In 1820s Daniel O'Connell became the new liberator for Ireland. He was born at Carhan Kerry to a wealthy Roman Catholic family that had twice been dispossessed of lands. He went to a Jesuit college at Douai France and had to flee for his life during the French revolution been mistaken as an aristocrat. In 1823 Daniel persuaded the Roman Catholic peasantry and middle class to strive for full emancipation and formed the Catholic Association with hundreds of thousands of members.

The British government was faced with the threat of a nationwide rebellion in Ireland. In the Clare by-election of 1828, O'Connell decided to exploit a loophole in the Act of Union. It stated that Catholics could not sit in Westminster as a Member of Parliament (MP), but there was nothing about them standing for an election.

He won the Clare election and it was the first time since the reformation that an openly Roman Catholic MP, was elected, but he refused to take his seat until the anti-Roman Catholic oath required of members of Parliament was abolished. With great opposition especially from the anti-Roman Catholic King George III the Government conceded and with the Emancipation Act of 1829 in Parliament. It would take another 100 years before Ireland gained her freedom in 1922.

William Pitt was Prime Minister of England. William (who was elected at the young age of 24) believed that Ireland could not be allowed the luxury of an independent parliament, because they might decide on an independent nation and make Ireland a base for England's enemies. Pitt therefore decided on an Act of Union which would totally tie Ireland to Great Britain. It was given by both the Irish and British parliaments despite much resistance. It was signed by George III in 1801. Pitt intended to follow the Act of Union with other, more far reaching reforms, including Catholic Emancipation, but was thwarted by George III, who refused to break his Coronation Oath to uphold the Anglican Church. *Pitt resigned because he wanted reform and Catholic emancipation.*

BALLYBAGGON CEMETARY

Medieval Augustinian Priory of Ballyboggan Co. Meath near Kinnegad, Co. Westmeath

Ballyboggan graveyard is not a parish graveyard and is about four miles from Kinnegad on the Edenderry road. It is situated in the grounds of the former Ballyboggan Abbey a well-known Augustinian Priory and important pilgrimage shrine. The abbey was burned in about 1570 by the forces of King Henry and was passed – along with 5,000 acres – to: Sir William Bermingham (later know as Lord Carberry). Burials have taken place there since early 1500 and the oldest gravestone was 1754. Both Catholics and Protestants are buried there as the basis of being interred there is on the fact that one's ancestors were probably buried there.

Michael Weymes research on Ballyboggan: Michael talked to the parish priest of the nearest parish (Ballinabrackey) he felt that the fact that William Weymes (1804) family stone was of such quality that they were of considerable standing. He checked the local parish records, but without success. There is no RIP anywhere on the stone which could be an indication that they were Protestant at one time although he was Catholic on his death certificate. The location of the graveyard so close to the Offaly and Kildare border is most interesting as Francis Wemys (b abt 1718) lived there. For William Weymes to be buried there is a clear indication that the family must have lived close to where the cemetery at one time. NOTE Sir William Bermingham was related to the Wemys- Patrick Wemys (1707-1762). Married Catherine Bermingham Athenry in Kilkenny 1750. She married Cullen one month after his death a folklore says she murdered him. Died without issue. SOURCE: Picture www.panoramio.com/photo/56470005, Author Robin Pollard

133

MAURICE AND THOMAS WEYMES

IN MEMORY OF THEIR BELOVED
PARENTS

MARY WEYMES DIED 21 JUNE 1876
AGE 59 YEARS

WILLIAM WEYMES DIED 23
OCTOBER 1879 AGE 78 YEARS

ANN GLYNN SISTER OF THE ABOVE
DIED 14 APRIL 1878

THOMAS WEYMES

& MARY CHRISTINA

HIS DAUGHTER

DIED 10 JANUARY 1887 AGE 10
YEARS

First Records of Weymes in Westmeath: The wool business passed from Marcella down to Patrick Joseph Weymes who eventually became bankrupt and lost the business.

Official records of this branch start with the Land Title book of 1823 of the Widow Waims (Marcella)land holder who owned 5 gross perches with house and garden in *the district Killucan Kinnegad, Westmeath*. She was written as "In fee Lands held 'in fee' were freehold tenures, derived from a grant from the Crown. *Free-hold, signifying that they were hereditable or perpetual owners.*

Marcella Weymes b. 1792 d.15 the October 1879. On her death certificate she died of old age, age 87, a 'widow of a dealer in skins'. Ann Weymes, probably the daughter of William was present at her death. Marcella was married to Williams older brother most probably named Patrick who had the Wool business that passed from Marcella death to Williams sons. First Patrick who married Ann Connolly in 1880 who became bankrupt, then taken by his brother Maurice, when he died in 1894, it passes to his brother Thomas the father of PJ Weymes and finally to PJ Weymes and then to PJ himself.

Griffith's Valuation (1848-1864) written-Weymes, Marcella, Parish of Killucan, Kinnegad, Westmeath -owner small property, house, office, small garden, total annual valuation 9.10.0. She continued to own this property according to Griffith Valuations until her death in 16 Oct 1879. In1860 William Weymes b.1804 is listed in the property that adjoins Marcella until his death in 1879.

Griffith evaluation in 1856, there is a **Henry Weymes** but he is no longer there in 1860. He leased land from Darby Cole a house, office and garden in Kinnegad. He is possibly Williams brother.

NOTE TC: William Weymes and Marcella Weymes died 8 days apart. William moved next door to her with his wife Mary Glynn in 1860. Marcella was 9 years older than William.

*Tithe Applotment - were compiled between **1823** and 1837 in order to determine the amount which occupiers of agricultural holdings over one acre should pay in **tithes** to the Church of Ireland (the main Protestant church and the church established by the State until it dis-establishment in 1871).*

Griffith's Valuation is the Primary Valuation of Ireland, a property tax survey carried out in the mid-nineteenth century. The survey involved the detailed valuation of every taxable piece of agricultural or built property on the island of Ireland and was published county-by-county between the years 1847 and 1864.

Quakers Woollen factory in Edenderry Kildare: By 1716 there was thriving woollen cloth manufacturing, established by Quakers, which employed around 1,000 people. Some of the Wemyss were Quakers but continued having their marriages and baptism in the Church of England. Interesting that the Westmeath Weymes were in the woollen industry and this is where my grandfather PJ Weymes made his fortune.

SOURCE: WEYMES MARCELLA – Westmeath Barony Farbill Union Mullingar Parish Killucan Townland Kinnegad. *Publication Details P36 Printing Date 1854 Act 15&16 Sheet Number 27,28,34 Map Reference 63 12.* Waims Tax Assessment 1830 Killucan, Kinnegad Town, Westmeath, *Ireland 004625678, 1576 (Marcella). Index to Griffith's Valuation of Ireland, 1848-186. Tithe Applotment in the NAI, Tithe Applotment 1823 and 1833.*

EARL ST, MULLINGAR, CO. WESTMEATH. 8093.W.L.

WEYMES OF WESTMEATH THE BEGINNING

William Weymes *Presumed Son of Patrick Wemys & Ann Ward*

WILLIAM WEYMES. b. 1801 Kildare d. 23 Oct 1879 Kinnegad, Ballyboggan graveyard Meath. Married in 1840 in Kildare Mary Glynn b. 1819d. d. 23 Oct 1879 Kinnegad and they had seven boys and three girls. On his death cert his occupation was a Hatter. I have given William brothers and sister, although I do not have any records to indicate this except, they all lived in Killucan and all had their children baptised in the Kinnegad church. All records after this are accurate as I have documentations.

Hat Factory-William by profession was a Hat maker. The National Library stated that there was a thriving hat making industry in Athlone in the 17th century, and up to 1860 the area where the trade was carried out was named Hatters Lane.

Athlone Hats were highly regarded all over Ireland. It is possible that William worked in Athlone from Killucan and he could have got to work -in two ways horse or the Royal canal (built 1789). However, there are some reports that there was a hat factory in Kinnegad but I could not find anything on that.

Travel in Westmeath- The Royal Canal was originally built for freight and passenger transportation from the River Liffey in Dublin to the River Shannon in Longford. The canal winds its way through the North Dublin suburbs, the green pastures of Kildare, Meath and Westmeath, through the town of Mullingar and on through Longford.

These canal boats passed through Kinnegad in 1789 but are now abandoned. The surrounding villages have prospered throughout their history due to their excellent land and transport links to Dublin. The railway age signalled the demise of the canal.

The Midland Great Western Railway. On December 2, 1796 the first passengers were ferried between Dublin and Kilcock at a cost of 1/1 (one shilling and a penny) which was considerably cheaper than the stagecoach. The Midland Great Western Railway reached the town in 1848, when their railway line was extended from Hill of Down to Mullingar, the station, officially called Killucan Station closed in 1963.There was also a railway station on the line between Dublin and Galway/Sligo.

NOTE: Kinnegad is a town in Westmeath, on the border with Meath. Athlone is a town on the River Shannon by the terms of the Local Government Act of 1898, six townlands on the west bank of the Shannon were deemed to be part of the town and, therefore, part of Westmeath. NOTE: In Frankford Michael and Patrick Weymes brothers married two sisters by the name Nevin*

SOURCE: *Surname Registry Heritage centre Westmeath, Roman Catholic Church Baptism Record, Kinnegad **Surname Registry Heritage centre. Earl Street, Mullingar, in the late 19th century Picture National Library of Ireland-wiki

Patrick Joseph Weymes b.1841 HEIR. Kinnegad Westmeath. 1905 Kinnegad. He married 1871 Mullingar Westmeath Anne Connell's. 25 June 1854, d.10 Feb 1914, School Teacher in Mullingar and lived at The Cottage Sowerby Bridge Park St Kinnegad Westmeath.

Maurice Weymes b.1842, Kinnegad d.14 Dec 1894. buried Coralstown graveyard Westmeath. He married Feb 1866 Mullingar, Rose Mullingar b.1850, d. Feb 1908, live at 2 Mount St Mullingar Westmeath.

Thomas Weymes b.1846 Kinnegad, d.20 Mar 1919, buried Coralstown Westmeath, Ireland. He married 31 Jan 1876 Kilcock Kildare. Bridget McDermott b.1854 Kilcock Kildare, d 21 Jan 1916, buried Coralstown Westmeath

William Weymes b.1849 Kinnegad Westmeath, d.abt. 1849 Westmeath.

Laurence Weymes b.1853 Kinnegad Westmeath. Died unknown.

Phillip Weymes b.1854 Kinnegad Westmeath, Died unknown. He acquired a dog licence in Killucan court Westmeath. Ireland Dog Licence Registers, 31/03/1874.

William Weymes b.1858 Kinnegad Westmeath. Still alive 1885.

Ann Weymes b.1843 Kinnegad Westmeath. d.aft 1883. She married 27 Jan 1866, Kildare, Patrick Glynn b. 1840 Kildare.

Mary Weymes Born 1851 Kinnegad Westmeath. Living 1885, she married 1882 Mark Cribben b. 09 May 1866 at Carbury Kildare. Born 09 May 1866 Carbury 0575 Kildare.

*__Taken from death cert*__ **William Weymes** Residence Kinnegad, William Weymes widower died age 78 years in the year 1879, Profession Hatter, died of old age. Present at death Tina Bolance. Register Killucan Mullingar. Buried Ballyboggan Graveyard Clonard, Ballyboggan. At William death Elizabeth was present and Andrew was present at Marys Glynne death.*

*__Mary (Glynn) Weymes*__ Died 21 June 1876 age 57 years Kinnegad, Buried in Ballyboggan graveyard.*

*__Mary Glynn__- Found in: Rosey Kinney (Keeney) m. Peter Moran 7 Jan 1834, sponsors were Anne Nevin and Mary Glynne, in Collinstown parish, Co. Westmeath. Two children found in the parish records are: Mary Moran, b. 1 Aug 1836, Sponsors: Mary Glynne, Judy (Julia) Moran, b. 23 Oct. 1837, Sponsors: John Fitzsimmons and *Anne Nevin She was 17 years old.*

SOURCE: Surname Registry Heritage centre Westmeath. Roman Catholic Church Baptism Record, KINNEGAD

PATRICK JOSEPH WEYMES

Son and Heir of William Weymes & Mary Glynn

Patrick Weymes was b.1841 Kinnegad Westmeath's. 1905 Kinnegad. He married in 1871 Mullingar Westmeath Anne Connell b. 25 June 1854. d.10 Feb 1914. Anne was a teacher at the local Mullingar school and their residence was *The Cottage Sowerby Bridge, Park St, Kinnegad Westmeath.*

Wool Factory- Patrick Weymes inherited the wool business from Marcella Weymes who died 1879 and sold it a year later due to bankruptcy.

Flint & Co's Mercantile Gazette page 942-Ireland bills of sale

Patrick Weymes Kinnegad Skin & Hide dealer sold to George A Wells 19 Temple st Birmingham &ano Sept 22 1880 filed 29 Sept £26 :10 shillings. Principal creditors petitioning to force a bankruptcy (but often close relatives of the bankrupt helping to protect his assets): and solicitors.

Patrick Joseph Weymes & Anne Connell Children

Mary Bridgit Weymes b.1872 Kinnegad Westmeath. d. unknown

Catherine Frances Weymes b.18 Sep 1875. unknown

Rose Anna Weymes b.17 Feb 1877. unknown

Elizabeth Anne Weymes* b.16 Aug 1879. d. -Mount Alton Templeogue Dublin. Husband Maguire. Info on marriage taken from Ellis file 1930: from Reverend Maurice Weymes trip to America.

Anne Weymes b.1881. Died unknown

Margaret Weymes b.1883 Died unknown

Theresa Weymes* b.31 July 1885 Kinnegad Westmeath. d.1960 Philadelphia, Pennsylvania. She went to New York October 31, 1915, 30 years.

She married 1920 Upper Darby USA, John Patrick Byrne b.abt. 1880 Philadelphia Pennsylvania. Children: Maurice, John, Jack, Ann, Mary. Right up to the present day here family thought she was 15 years younger.

Anne Patricia Byrne b. 17 Mar 1924 Camden, New York. She married John (Jack) Turcotte b.1921 Philadelphia in 1960. Children Joseph Jay Turcotte and Theresa. Ann died 16 Mar 2001 Somers Point, New York.

*NOTE: His brother Maurice took over the Wool business, but I am not sure what George A Wells had to do with it. SOURCE: *Ellis Isle US Records. Roman Catholic Church Baptism Record, Kinnegad. Information on Theresa Wemyss of Westmeath family from America from Jay Turcott.*

Patrick Joseph Weymes & Anne Connell Children (continued)

William Weymes b.11 May 1873 d. unknown. William died in **India** along with his wife and had no children.

Thomas Joseph Weymes b. 09 Sep 1878 d.38 Bishop gate St Mullingar. He m**arried** June 1895 Kinnegad Westmeath, **Mary Reilly b**. abt. 1875 Unknown.

Christopher Weymes b.1886 d. age 2 years.

Rev Maurice Weymes b.7 Apr 1888 Kinnegad Westmeath. d. October 1969 Glasson, Athlone. He was the Reverend PP for: Glasson, Athlone and he taught Music and was very accomplished. Maurice went back and forth from America whilst visiting his relatives.

Ellis Isle Records -June 1921, Described as Brown hair Blue eyes, visit 60 days, New York Passenger Lists, 1820-1957 Visiting his sister **Mrs J Judge** address Down Mullingar. Went to see his brother John C Weymes several times in. Jamaica. Ellis Isle records Date: 14 Jun 1925 visiting friend **George Wemyss-** *George Weymes was the son of Patrick Weymes and Mary Byrne.* Ellis Isle records **Bost**on: 8 Jun 1930, age: 42 years, visiting brother **J C Weymes.**

John C Weymes b.abt 1886. d.17 Farquhar St Rolindale Boston.

Information taken from Maurice Weymes Ellis island document June 30 1930. He was visiting his brother **JC Weymes** who lived at 7 Labillille place. Jamaica. Second address taken June 1921 Ellis Visit of REV Maurice Weymes.

Patrick Joseph Weymes b. 04 Apr 1882 *The Cottage Sowerby Bridge Park St* Kinnegad Westmeath. d. abt. 1955 Rockland New York. Patrick married abt.1914 in Philadelphia, **Mary Mercedes Byrne** b. 31 Jul 1885, d.abt. 1960, Rockland New York. Her father was John Byrne b abt 1830 Kinnegad, mother, Margaret Sullivan b.abt 1860. Their children were Mary, Kathleen, Patricia, William Maurice George, John (Jock).

Mary Weymes b. 28 Feb 1917, married in Boston America 1935, Frederick Ritter b.1900, Germany d. 24 Feb 1996, Aiken South Carolina America. They had one son William Ritter b.1937, Aiken South Carolina US, he married in Margaret Dodd.

NOTE: History From: Margaret D. Ritter Wife of William. America. Fredrick Ritter parents were German who immigrants to the America just before he was born. Fredrick was a Colonel in the Air Force. Charming but with a rather cool and controlled nature and he preferred to be alone, write novels and paint. However, Mary emotional, romantic and free-spirited nature. They divorced when their son William was 12 years old. Mary was a catholic but when she remarried her second husband was Jewish and she reluctantly converted according to the family. Apparently all the Wemyss were characters in one way or another. Good looking, intelligent. **Immigration to America** *Some of Patrick and Anne's children immigrated to America. Theresa went to New York and married Byrne and had several children. Patrick Joseph junior who was also a teacher married and settled in* **Boston.**

MAURICE WEYMES

Son of William Weymes & Mary Glynn

Maurice Weymes b. 1842 Kinnegad Westmeath.d.14 Dec 1894 buried Cornalstown graveyard Westmeath. He married Feb 1866 Mullingar, Rose Mullingar b 1850 d. Feb 1908 2 Mount St, Mullingar Westmeath (where PJ Weymes was born 1879 and lived. Directory-Slaters Directory of Mullingar for 1894 records a Maurice Weymes, Wool Merchant residing at 2 Mount St.

ROSE WEYMES In Census 1901 there was Patrick Weymes and Bridget Carney listed in the Rose Weymes household. **Rose Weymes***. She died on 25th Feb 1908 at Mount St, Mullingar, age 83 years, widow of a Wool merchant, her daughter Mary Shiel 'caused the body to be buried. Mary Shiel was at one time in the Bolivar parish as some of her children were born there. Roses mother's name was Annie Leech. When Roses son William J Weymes died on 29 September 1897 Rose was the primary beneficiary. Rose was also the primary beneficiary for Thomas Mulligan who died 21 Feb 1897 Meath. On her death certificate her Primary beneficiary was Mary Shiel her daughter.

Maurice Weymes & Rose Mulligan *Children*

William Weymes b. 24 Jul 1871,317 Mullingar rd. 28 Sep 1897, Coralstown cemetery.

Bridget Weymes b. 01 Jan 1870,361 Mullingar.

Marie Ann Weymes b. 28 Dec 1867 399 Mullingar's. Ballivor Meath. Marie married 04 Feb 1891 St Saviour Dublin William P Shiel, Ballivor Meath. (taken from marriage cert father John Sheil Shopkeeper).

Marie Ann Weymes & Dr William P Shiel Children

John Shiel B. 04 Mar 1892, Ballivor Meath.

William Francis Shiel B. 25 Aug 1893, Ballivor Meath.

Laurence Shiel B. 18 Jan 1895, Ballivor Meath.

Gravestone -Erected by Rose Weymes Son William also buried there. On William Weymes his father's tomb:

MAURICE AND THOMAS WEYMES IN MEMORY OF THEIR BELOVED PARENTS MARY WEYMES DIED 21 JUNE 1876 AGE 59 YEARS WILLIAM WEYMES DIED 23 OCTOBER 1879 AGE 73 YEARS ANN GLYNN SISTER OF THE ABOVE DIED 14 APRIL 1878 THOMAS WEYMES & MARY CHRISTINA HIS DAUGHTER DIED 10 JANUARY 1887 AGE 10 YEARS

NOTE: *Maurice, I assume bought the Wool & Hide Business from his brother Patrick who after inheriting from Marcella Weymes in 1879 went bankrupt and sold it in 1880. It was then passed onto his brother when he died Thomas Weymes whose son my grandfather PJ Weymes the inherited.*

SOURCE: *Death Certificate-Official death certificate*

ANN WEYMES & PATRICK GLYNN

Daughter of William Weymes & Mary Glynn

Ann Weymes b.1843 Kinnegad Westmeath. d. about 1883. Ann married **Patrick Glynn** b.1840 Kildare, his father was Matthew Glynn. Patrick Glynn was also related to Mary Glynn Ann's mother. Ann and Patrick married on the 27 Jan 1866, Killucan. Patrick was a Blacksmith as was his son Thomas they had a forge in Bogtown Mullingar. The forge was sold in 1964 when John from the 2nd marriage died, he never Married. Some of their children settled in America.

Ann Weymes & Patrick Glynn Children

Patrick Glynn b. 4 April 1876-Killucan Westmeath

Thomas Glynn b.10 December 1874 Killucan Westmeath. d.28 September 1957 Bogtown Mullingar.

William Glynn b. 7 December 1871, godfather was Thomas Weymes

Matthew Glynn b. 2 February 1870

Bridget Glynn Born b. 6 July 1873

Kate Glynn b. 10 September 1868, godparent Weymes. **Mary Anne Glynn** b. 30 May 1867, Killucan. Mary married Mark Adamthwaite in 1887, New York America. Her godmother was Mary Weymes.

Mary Anne Glynn & Mark Adamthwaite children

Kate Adamthwaite married William Piers New York.

Patrick Glynne second marriage -Married a second time to Elizabeth Graham 25 November 1879. Step family.

Christopher b. 23/12/1882 John b.1887 Margaret b.1890 James b.1892 William b.1896 Elizabeth b.1899.

Picture: Mary Anne Glynn

MARY WEYMES

Daughter of William Weymes & Mary Glynn

Mary Weymes b.1851 Kinnegad Westmeath. Living 1885. On her passport she is written as 5 ft 4 fair hair, grey eyes. *Mary married* 1882 Mark Cribben b.09 May 1866, Carbury Kildare, his father was Patrick Cribben b. abt. 1848, Mother **Catherine Nevin* she was b**aptism roman Catholic 14-May-1846 Kinnegad and her father, Patrick Nevin, and mother was Alice McKeon.

Mary Weymes & Mark Cribben *Children*

Michael Cribben b. 1899 Dominick Mullingar Westmeath. d Mullingar aft 1970. Spent 5 years in New York. In New York.

Rosanna Cribben b.1888 Dominick St Mullingar. d. 27 East St New York city America. Rose is in the -New York Passenger Lists, 22 Sept 1915, age 29 years and worked as a waitress. Rose married aft. 1915, William E **Steaton** b. abt 1880. Rose stayed with brother in Law H Smeaton New York who lived Manhattan Ward 19, New York.

Mary Cribben (Nan) b. 1886 Mullingar. Still living after 1970. Married O'Brian, New York. In Ellis island records Mary went to America on -Cribben, Mary, Irish, British, Mullingar, Ireland. May 14, 1907, 19 years, Ship Cedric Queenstown, Cork, Munster, Ireland. Mary Cribben went in 1915 to New York. Occupation Servant. Stayed with her sister Rosanna Cribben and Mrs Sullivan 27 East St New York city.

NOTE: *There were 2 sisters Sara and Jane Nevin who married brothers Patrick and Martin Weymes in Kilcormac Offaly in 1840. The brothers were deported for an unlawful oath to Australia and brought back paid by the British government after 6 months. My father Joe Weymes mentioned we were related to them.* **Also,** *Unknown family: Catherine Cribben b. 1899 d. 1970 New York City. Husband Morris Carney b.abt. 1967 New York. America.*

SOURCE: *Church Baptism Record-Roman Catholic church Kinnegad. Ellis Isle records New York Ship records*

THOMAS WEYMES b. 1844 Kinnegad Westmeath. d.20 Mar 1919 buried Cornalstown Westmeath, Ireland. Thomas married Bridget **McDermott** 31 Jan 1876 Newtown and Kilcock Kildare. Sponsors at their wedding were Kate McDermott, Maurice Weymes. *In 1916 he was living at 47 Mount St Mullingar and the Lesser was Rose Weymes, John Halon. Thomas Weymes appears to have inherited the Wool Business from Maurice Weymes his brother who died in *1894*. In Thomas Will primary beneficiary was Patrick Dunne, County Meath. Directory-Slaters Directory of Mullingar for 1894 records a Maurice Weymes, Wool merchant residing at Mount St. Mullingar. Maurice widow held the lease until 1932 when it reverted back to Lord Grandville.

BRIDGET MC DERMOTT b.1854 in Kilcock Kildare, *d. 22 Jan 1916 buried in Coralstown Westmeath, Ireland. She was a very strong-willed woman and kept the business together when Thomas died. Bridget was very frugal and used to keep sovereigns in the coal bucket beside the fire. She sent her eldest son Patrick Weymes to Bath in England to learn the Wool business. Father -Michael Mc Dermott b.1820 Kilbrook Enfield Kildare.d.1904 buried at Newtown Cemetery. Mother Catherine Hogan Kildare, Westmeath. In Bridget's Will in 1916 her primary beneficiary Edmund Murphy, Meath Country Ireland

Thomas Weymes & Bridget Mc Dermott Children

Patrick Joseph Weymes b.18 Mar 1879 Kinnegad Westmeath, d. 01 Oct 1966. He resided at 2 Mount St Mullingar. Patrick married 20 Apr 1904, Ethel Josephine Shaw Turin Chapel Mullingar Westmeath.

William Francis Weymes b.1884 Kinnegad Westmeath, Ireland. d.11 May 1912. William married 09 Jan 1912 Catherine Hugh. Died four months after his marriage.

Kate Wemyss b. 1881 Mount St, Mullingar Buried Coralstown graveyard. Kate married Westmeath Abt. 1906, Patrick Dunne. See back of book for tree.

Bridgit Weymes b. 1891. d. 23 Sep 1960, 9 Merrion Square Dublin. Bridget married 25 June 1919 Dublin Dr Henry Leo Barniville. Their children were Sean and Harry.

Mary Christina Weymes b. 24 Dec 1876. d.1886

Mary Ann Wemys b. 1887. d.12 Dec 1918, Ballyboggan graveyard Meath.

NOTE: *Interesting that both Thomas and Bridget left their estate to others then their children. New Zealand Newspaper-This piece was transcribed from New Zealand Tablet; Volume XX; Issue 27; 22 April 1892; Page 9, under the heading Irish News. At a sale at Kinnegad on 22 January the tenant's interest of 9 acres of land (part of Miss Megan's estate) without the house was purchased by Mr. Weymes for £300. This would have been £234,790 in today's retail price!! This is most probably PJ Weymes. SOURCE: *Valuation List 1916*. Ireland Calendars of Wills & Administrations 1858-1920- Original source Archive National Archives of Ireland. Irish Deaths 1864 - 1958 Dublin Archives, Ireland Census 1901, and 1911, 1919. National Library of Ireland.*

KATE WEYMES & PATRICK DUNNE

Kate Weymes b.1881 Mount St Mullingar, her p*arents were Thomas Weymes & Bridget McDermott*. Kate married abt 1906 **Patrick Dunne** b. abt. 1885 of Mullingar Westmeath. Patricks parents were Patrick Dunne and Jane Coleman.

Kate Weymes & Patrick Dunne children:

Tom, Fr Patrick, Andy, Fr John, William, Frank, Maurice, Michael and Harry, Kathy, Jane, Brigid.

Kate and Patrick Joseph Weymes her brother went on the same boat to New York in 1929, she stayed with her Uncle William Mc Dermott. The Dunnes were buried in Coralstown. At Clonard church there are windows to Kate and Patrick Dunne.

Picture is Kate and Patrick Dunne with their three daughters.

CLONYN CASTLE. CO. WESTMEATH 3198. W.L

PJ Weymes bought Clonyn castle on Thursday March 15 1923 (Was bankrupt July 1929). Irish Independent Newspaper: Clonyn Castle Delvin which was recently burnt. It was built by the late Lord Granville and completed in 1879 at a cost of £179,000. Some time ago PJ Weymes Co. Purchase the castle and demesne. SOURCE: Picture-https://commons.wikimedia.org/wiki/File:De_Lacey_Castle_01.jpg Picture: National Library of Ireland

PATRICK JOSEPH WEYMES

MULLINGAR WESTMEATH

A Department in WEYMES'S, Wool and Hide Merchant, MULLINGAR. (Copyright)

ANCESTOR IN TIME

HISTORY OF THE WEYMES

WOOL & HIDE BUSINESS

In medieval times, wool would have been harvested using a comb or just plucked out by hand. It was then placed in a barrel of stale urine and The Fuller spent all day trampling on the wool to produce softer cloth. There was an enormous demand for wool, mainly to produce cloth and everyone who had land, from peasants to major landowners, raised sheep. The monasteries, in particular the Cistercian houses played a very active part in the trade, which pleased the king who was able to levy a tax on every sack of wool that was exported.

Acts of Trade and Navigation from 1600

This Acts was mainly aimed at Irish woollen's and established a policy to crush the Irish woollen industry. Restriction on Irish trade prevented export of goods to England and the colonies of cattle, horses etc, leaving only the Linen trade. Both the English and Irish parliament passed these restrictions to the detriment of both Catholics and protestants alike. When the Irish landowners were prevented from exporting their cattle to England, they raised large flocks of sheep and began to manufacture wool. English clothiers did not wish continental rivals to have the benefit of Irish wool, so heavy taxes were applied and they were only allowed to export wool to certain ports in England. This was disastrous and caused 40 thousand Irish protestants reduced to poverty and 20 thousand left for New England. Smuggling became the norm in Ireland with an all levels of society participating, all due to unjust legislation.

The British Wool Act of 1699 restricted the trading of wool products by banning the export of wool from the colonies, limiting the importing of wool to that produced by Great Britain, and taxing wool sales. This was detrimental to Colonial America who reacted with anger, resentment, dissension and ultimately revolution. - *the American Revolutionary War (1775–1783) and the Declaration of Independence from Great Britain.*

In 1733 to encourage the market for woollen goods, they even passed an act making it obligatory for corpses to be buried in a woollen shroud. Restriction started to ease in the 1750, technological improvements increased demand for Irish yarn, thereby absorbing any surplus left over from home consumption. In 1770 the spinning of wool was mainly done by women and was almost universal throughout the country. The manufacturers would distribute the wool to local peasants, who spun it into yarn for the English market. Those industries where British producers had advantages, notably cotton and woollen manufacture, began to decline in Ireland from the mid-1820s.

Westmeath Wool In 1820s the principal trade was in wool, its central situation and facility of communication with the Shannon and with Dublin having rendered it the commercial centre of a wide extent of country.

HISTORY OF THE WOOL AND TANNERY BUSINESS

Marcella Weymes -The wool business was passed down from Marcella Weymes (b. 1796) who inherited it from her husband (possibly named Patrick) who died about 1823. When Marcella died in 1789 it passed to Patrick J Weymes.

Patrick Joseph Weymes b. 1841 d.1905, son of William & Mary Glynn lived at The Cottage Sowerby Bridge, Park St, Kinnegad Westmeath.

Maurice Weymes b 1847, d.1894 son of William & Mary Glynn, residence 2 Mount St Mullingar Westmeath.

Thomas Weymes b 1846 d.1919 son of William & Mary Glynn. Thomas inherited the wool business from his brother Maurice after his death in 1894.

Patrick Joseph Weymes b. 1879 d. 1966 son of Thomas & Bridget McDermott. He inherited from his father, Thomas when he died in 1919. Residence 2 Mount St, Mullingar Westmeath.

Bankrupt- Patrick Joseph Weymes became bankrupt in 1923 and lost the business

Flint & Co's Mercantile Gazette *(page 942) 1880. Ireland bills of sale -Patrick Weymes Kinnegad skin & Hide dealer sold to George A Wells 19 Temple St, Birmingham & Ano, September 22* **1880** *filed 29 Sept £26:10 shillings. Principal creditors petitioning to force a bankruptcy (but often close relatives of the bankrupt helping to protect his assets): and solicitors.*

New Zealand Tablet *1892- 22 April* **1892***; Page 9, under the heading Irish News. At a sale at Kinnegad on 22 January the tenant's interest of 9 acres of land (part of Miss Mayans estate) without the house was purchased by Mr. Weymes for £300.*

Slaters Directory of Mullingar for 1894 -Records a Maurice Weymes, wool merchant residing at Mount St. Mullingar.

(Maurice widow Rose held the lease until 1932 when it reverted back to Lord Grandville)

Kelly's Directory 1905 *-Thomas Weymes & Son Wool merchants and dealers at Mount St Kinnegad and Killucan.*

Kelly's Directory *of Leather Trades in Ireland 1915 -THOMAS WEYMES & SON Mount St Mullingar. Valuation List 1916- Thomas Weymes 47 Mount St -Lesser Rose Weymes John Halon*

THE COLOURFUL PATRICK(PJ) WEYMES TC. JP.

In the year **Patrick Joseph** was born in the 1880s, there was still poverty and many Irish immigrated to America, but there was also much change occurring with the Irish people. Ireland was part of the United Kingdom of Great Britain and Ireland between 1801 and 1922 and was ruled by the British Parliament in London through its administration of Dublin Castle in Ireland.

The **Irish Home Rule movement** was a movement that campaigned for self-government for Ireland within the United Kingdom of Great Britain and Ireland. It was the dominant political movement of Irish nationalism from 1870 to the end of World War I. **Patrick** Weymes was 12 when Charles Stewart Parnell died in 1891 as leader of the Irish Parliamentary Party 1882-91 and the Home Rule League. From 1886 to 1912 Home Rule Bill was defeated three times by the British parliament. Shortly after the outbreak of World War I it was enacted, but implementation was suspended until the conclusion of the war. **Patrick** joined the Irish party in later life and was nominated to stand for election as MP for Westmeath in the Irish first free vote in 1918 but was defeated by Laurence Ginnell Sein Fein candidate.

When Charles Stewart Parnell died, the hope of Home Rule seemed to vanish with him. However, from these ashes, Ireland grew intellectually and culturally with many new movements, ideas and practical organisations.

In 1916, Ireland's Republican Army, led by Padraig Pearse and James Connolly, fought in the Easter Uprising at the General Post Office in Dublin. They were unsuccessful and were executed along with 14 others.

Arthur Griffith, who in 1905 founded in Sinn Féin was one of the fathers of the Irish Free State. Michael Collins, another member of the Sinn Féin, is best known for his leadership in the War of Independence by the Irish Republican Army (IRA). He was assassinated in 1922. Eamon DeValera became the president of Sinn Féin (who had not participated in the insurrection) when they were elected in 1918. Irish MPs refused to sit in the British House of Commons, but instead created a separate Irish government – Dáil Éireann in Dublin. They proclaimed Ireland's independence and were banned by the British government. Subsequent negotiations between Sinn Féin and the British government resulted in the signing of the Anglo-Irish Treaty, which annexed six predominantly Protestant counties of Northern Ireland to oppose the unity under the free Irish state that still exists today. The second Dáil was held for the first time on 16 August 1921.

The 1919-1921 **Irish War of Independence** between the Irish Republican Army (IRA) and the British Army, together with the Royal Irish Constabulary (RIC) and the Ulster Special Constabulary (USC). The Black and Tans were members of the Royal Irish Constabulary (RIC) as reinforcements during the Irish Revolution. In May 1921, Ireland was divided according to British law by the Government of Ireland Act, which created Northern Ireland and signed the Anglo-Irish Treaty on 6 December 1921.

The Irish Civil War from 28 June 1922 to 24 May 1923 was a conflict following the Irish War of Independence between two opposing groups, the pro-treaty Provisional Government and the anti-treaty IRA, over the Anglo-Irish Treaty. In July 1921, a cease-fire took place and the Sinn Féin negotiated the Anglo-Irish Treaty.

IRA activity in Westmeath during the War of Independence, 1918-21* *From 1918-1921, Ireland made a transition from being ruled by Britain to self-rule but divided. In Westmeath in 1920 a car belonging* ***P.J. Weymes****, was fired at about a half a mile from Mullingar, the chauffeur was wounded by shards of glass. The police immediately set about investigating the incident and were fired upon but they managed to captured three of their four assailants.*

ELECTION FOR MP FOR WESTMEATH**

Given by kind permission of Westmeath Westmeath Examiner

In a newly unified Westmeath constituency – a union of North and South Westmeath, brought about by boundary adjustments on foot of franchise extension – the 1918 campaign pitted Ginnell against ***Patrick J Weymes, a Mullingar wool merchant and Irish Party candidate****, and the incumbent MP for South Westmeath, the independent nationalist Sir Walter Nugent.* ***Weymes*** *was Ginnell's main contender; Nugent, the ranking Irish Party MP in the county, was a Baronet and empire loyalist, whose hostility to cooperation with Sinn Féin during the Conscription Crisis had, according to historian John Burke, "alienated all but a tiny minority" in the constitutional nationalist ranks. As a result, Nugent's bid for re-election was not endorsed by the Irish Party in 1918, forcing him to run on an independent ticket. **

_____The Irish Party was confident of success, though when polling day arrived on 14 December 1918, their optimism was rocked by the sudden death of a sister of P J Weymes, removing their candidate from the campaign trail due to his attendance at her funeral.

_____ As the Irish Party's initial optimism turned to despair, there were some bitter complaints. For example, a Ginnellite sub-agent in Kilbeggan was compelled to publicly repudiate a Westmeath Examiner *allegation that some of Weymes' campaign drivers had been "waylaid at Derrygolan [south of Kilbeggan] by Sinn Feiners", while the Examiner also bemoaned "some cases of strong intimidation of voters by Sinn Fein advocates... armed with hurleys in their hands".*

However, the final result – Ginnell 12,435 (over 75 percent of the votes cast), ***Weymes 3,458*** *and Nugent 603 – spoke volumes, and not even the most acerbic of John P Hayden's missives could mask the death of the* ***Irish Party*** *on a local and national level.*

General Elections 1st Dáil *14 December 1918 Westmeath*
1 Seat, 3 Candidates. Electorate: 24,014 (Men: 16,355 Women: 7,659)
Laurence Ginnell Elected, *P H Weymes Defeated, Sir W Nugent Defeated*
Laurence Ginnell was the Sinn Féin candidate. Weymes and Nugent were the Irish Party candidates.

NOTE: PJ sister was Mary Ann Weymes 12 Dec 1918 Kinnegad, buried Ballyboggan graveyard Meath.

SOURCE: *http://mural.maynoothuniversity.ie/5300/1/Russell_W_Shortt_20140805105151.pdf. ** www.westmeathexaminer.ie/2018/12/14/the-1918-election-in-westmeath-100-years-on/. https://www.rte.ie/history/first-dail/2019/1112/1090360-who-was-who-in-the-first-dail-laurence-ginnell/

PATRICK JOSEPH(PJ) WEYMES TC. JP

See Michael Weymes book on PJ Weymes at back of this book.

PATRICK JOSEPH WEYMES was born in Kinnegad Westmeath in 1879, eldest son of Thomas Weymes and Bridget McDermott. He married Ethel Shaw in 20 Apr 1904 Turin Chapel Mullingar Westmeath. He was recognised as a handsome, charismatic person who was generous and well-liked by the people of Mullingar. He became well known as an entrepreneur, and politician. He was Chairman of the United Irish League 12 yrs. Chairman of Westmeath County Council and a Commissioner of the Peace. Patrick also was a contributing member of the Temperance Society, and a keen Amateur Dramatist and known for his singing.

Ireland's first Free State election-In Ireland's first Free State election he ran as a candidate and lost. He was one of the few millionaires of that era but he was declared bankrupt in July 27th,1923. Patrick tried to restart his business but the banks foreclosed on him and after several failed attempts he went to America from 1929 to 1932. When he returned, he worked in a Wool factory in Longford and died in the county hospital in Mullingar 01 Oct 1966.

PJ Weymes Inherited the Wool Factory from his father Thomas Weymes. His mother Bridget (McDermott) who was a very strong-willed woman built up the wool Business and sent, PJ to Bath England to do business studies. Patricks J office was in Kilcock where the Munster and Leinster Bank is today.

Bankruptcy -In 1923 PJ became Bankrupt due to several economic factors. One was the unexpectedly losing of the contract with the British Army for Wool for their uniforms at the end of WW1 which he had stockpiled the wool, expecting a large order. He pleaded with the Leinster Bank in Kilcock to give him a loan to restart his business but they refused and he became penniless. Apparently, PJ saved a lot of businesses by destroying documents before he was declared bankrupt, he was owed a lot of money from his tenants, but refused to take it from them. Nevertheless, he always managed to be well dressed due to the generosity of the people whose business he saved in Mullingar.

From 1923 to 1927 very little is known of him, but in June 1927 PJ was sentenced to 6 months imprisonment on the accusations regarding the withholding of owning Nigerian rubber shares. Two of his colleagues were charged with him, but the jury disagreed, and the case against them were dismissed. There is no documented evidence that he ever did the sentence nor did the family ever mention it. We suspect he did not do any time in prison as at one time he knew a lot of very influential people both in Ireland and England. His house was in Mount street was sold on the 18th August 1927 and stated occupier was Ethel Weymes. I suspect he left for England after the court case as he is on a census for Coventry, in 1929 with his family who were working in a factory.

England & Wales, Electoral Registers- *Cheylesmore, Coventry, Warwickshire England. 1929-Patrick Joseph Weymes, Ethel, Michael Fintan Weymes, St Margaret's Rd. Census 1930-Andrew Vincent Weymes, Ethel Weymes, Michael Fintan Weymes.* ***New York Passenger Lists*** *& Arrivals 1929 Ellis Island -PJ Weymes age 50 b.1879 Kinnegad Ireland. Arrival city New York.*

PATRICK WEYMES IN AMERICA

PJ left Coventry for New York on March 28, 1929, hoping to be joined later by his family. That was 6 months before the Great Depression began. He had numerous contacts during his business years there and went hoping to try to find a new life for himself and his family. That said, because of the crisis, he ended up as a porter at the main station in New York and doubtlessly glad to have work.

A wealthy Irish man recognized him as a Magistrate from Mullingar and asked him to work for him in a Speak Easy in Boston! (Up until then he did not drink). He eventually finished working in Florida before returning to Westmeath in 1932. He died at the age of 90 in Mullingar a happy and very old man- but also a pauper in the Hospital he helped to pay for. He is remembered by the people of Mullingar with affection and remains as part of the folklore there.

The Great Depression of 1929-1930 was a serious global economic depression which occurred when the US stock market collapsed on October 29, 1929 (known as Black Tuesday). The hardest hit was the Cities that dependent on heavy industry resulting in unemployment. Agriculture was affected by a decline in crop prices of about 60%. Starting in 1932, the economies of some countries began to improve until the start of the Second World War.

Kylemore Abbey -Folklore had it that PJ was the owner of Kylemore Abbey but he was not registered as the owner, although he did act as trustee while they waited for a buyer. However, he was registered owner of Clynon Castle from 1921 to 1928.

Patrick Weymes is on valuation list for leasing property from Rose Weymes from 1904-1932. T Weymes is also mentioned (possibly Thomas, the eldest). The property reverted back to Lord Grenville estate in 1932. Valuation List 1932, Westmeath Weymes 24 Mount St, Mullingar Tenant Kernisson, Lesser Rep PJ Weymes.

Spanish Flu Westmeath -In July 1917 the Spanish flu epidemic spread across the world, and over the next 20 months it claimed an estimated 100 million lives, most of whom were people under 40 years old. (100years ago we now have Coronavirus and are on our second wave 2020)

SOURCE: Patrick J Weymes 28 Mar 1929 born abt 1879 Male Co bh, Ireland Irish America went to America on the SS America.

SHAWS OF WESTMEATH

CHAIRMAN OF MULLINGAR TOWN COMMISSIONERS.

Shaw is originally Scottish and quite a common name in Ireland especially in north-east Ulster; in Leinster it is particularly associated with Mullingar. The main Shaw family in Ireland is that of Bushy Park, Terenure, Dublin. The first of these was William Shaw, an officer in the army of William III: he was grandfather of Sir Robert Shaw, first baronet and anti-Union M.P. George Bernard Shaw, was an Irish playwright, critic, and political activist. Other prominent Shaw's were Sir Frederick Shaw (1799-1876), M.P. for Dublin University and Recorder of Dublin for forty-eight years, and William Shaw (1823-1895) of Cork, leader of the Irish Party after Isaac Butt until superseded by Parnell.

Mr. P. W. Shaw, J P, T C.

At the opening of the recent Mullingar Petty Sessions Court Mr P W Shaw, Chairman Mullingar Town Commissioners, was sworn in as a Justice of the Peace or Mullingar. Mr Shaw, though it is only something over a year since he went into active public life (by his election on the Town Commissioners Board), gave during the year much proof of ability, interest in and aptitude for the work of the municipal body of Mullingar, that he obtained the high tribute of the members of a unanimous election to the chair last January. Mr Shaw will undoubtedly occupy the chair with much ability and benefit to the board and the affairs of the town, and will also fill the position of presiding magistrate of the Mullingar Court with much dignity and efficiency. We congratulate him on his appointments to positions to which we feel sure he will bring much credit, and in the discharge of the duties of which he should gain both approval and popularity. The brief period of his connection with active public work naturally does not give the writer many periods or events to deal with, but Mr Shaw has already done so very well that a long and useful career may be safely foreshadowed for him in the public work of his native town.

SHAW FAMILY Taghmon, Westmeath.

Garrett Shaw b abt 1760 d. unk. **Garrett** married Anne Donnellan b. abt 1760 in *1781* at Killynon Cooke, Taghmon, Westmeath.

Garrett Shaw & Anne Donnellan children:

Laurence Shaw baptised 27 Aug 1784, Taghmon Westmeath. Laurence married **Catherine Doyne** b.abt.1786.

Laurence Shaw & Catherine Doyne children:

Mary b.1818, Matthew b.1820, Bridget b.1824, James b.1826, Elizabeth b.1828, Laurence b.1833, Paul and Anne b.1835, all born in Killynon Cooke, Taghmon, Westmeath.

Matthew Shaw (son of Laurence, grandson of Garrett). Matthew b. 1820 d. 20 Jul 1944. He married on 11 Feb 1839, **Ester Quinn** b.1829 d. 04 Dec 1916.

Matthew Shaw & Ester Quinn children were:

Andrew b. 1842 d.1887,

Esther b.1841she married Mr. King and lived in Delvin, Westmeath.

Richard b.1844 d. 25 Jul 1899 Mullingar, Westmeath, Ireland.

Picture Matt Shaw

Andrew Shaw (son of Matthew, grandson of Laurence and great grandson of Garrett).

Andrew was a farmer b. 1842 d. 22 Nov 1887, Choughan Mullingar. Andrew married on 22 Nov 1882, **Anne Shaw b.**1858 d. 06 Jul 1931 Clonkill Westmeath.

*Anne's parents were **Patrick Shaw** b.1814 d.1872 and **Mary Connor** b.1831 d. 1916 at Clonkill, Taghmon, Westmeath. Patrick Shaw & Mary Connor children: **Annie,** Thomas b.1856 d.1931, Philip b.1860 d.1934, Catherine b.1863 d. 1944, Christopher b.1863 d.1944 and Mary b.1868 d. 1886. All from Clonkill, Taghmon.*

Andrew Shaw and Annie Shaw children:

Ethel Esther b. 12 Sep 1883, d. 1967, married PJ Weymes. **Matthew** b.1855 d. 1963, Taughmon Westmeath, Ireland. **Matthew** married in Jun 1925 Mullingar, **Mary Kiernan**, their children were Philip married and had a boy and girl, Matthew, Joseph, **Mary** married Mr. Smyth and had a son, Bernadette Jane, Eilish. **May** b.1887 d.1961 married **Richard Ham** and had a daughter Ann.

Notes for Mary Esther (Quinn) newspaper
Shaw Mary 3 April Probate of Will of Mary Shaw late of Clonkill Mullingar, widow who died 4th dec 1916 granted at Mullingar to Thomas Shaw farmer and Patrick J Weymes merchant effects £709.

ETHEL ESTER SHAW

Ethel Esther Shaw b. 12 Sep 1883, d. 1967 from Taughmon, Westmeath, Ireland. Her parents were Andrew Shaw and Annie Shaw. Ethel went to school at Rockford Bridge Mullingar. In 1901 census Ethel stayed with her aunt (Catherine) and uncle (Philip) in Mullingar. They owned a shop in Mullingar and are supposed to have known *James Joyce* well, who used to stay with them. Some say that one of the characters in James Joyce Ulysses was based on Ethel.

Westmeath newspaper 1904

Wedding Bells - Weymes married April 20th 1904 at Turin Chapel. Ethel Shaw eldest daughter of the late Andrew Shaw of Coughan Mullingar C Murtagh cousin of the bride Best man William Weymes. Bridesmaids Mary Shaw and Bridget Weymes, Groom Patrick Weymes eldest son of Thomas Weymes.

After PJ trial he went to Coventry and worked most probably in a car factory as PJ had had his own car company in Mullingar so he may have had contacts there. Ethels brother Matthew Shaw gave her the money for the boat to join PJ. In the census in 1929 the whole family are all living at 78 Bolinbroke Road Coventry. However, by June of that year PJ went to New York America for work at the start of stock market crash of which led to the great depression worldwide.

Ethel and her family worked in a factory in Coventry for a couple of years. By all counts they returned to Dublin to 2 Belton park Garden Park Donnycarney Dublin where she stayed until her death. PJ returned from America in 1932 but they did not reconcile so he went to work in a wool factory in Longford. It must have been very difficult to have come from a life of luxury and plenty to been penniless in England. Ethel was a very austere women may be due to life's trials and tribulations.

BRIDGET MARY WEYMES b. 3 March 1911 d. 23 Feb 1992, Kinnegad Westmeath. Bridget was a state registered nurse and health visitor. She was nursing as a member of the International Refugee Organization UNRRA and took part in the UN post WW2 relief operation in Bremen, Germany. In 1962 she lived in Winnipeg, Canada. Bridy was very tall with a sergeant major voice and never minced words, but was much liked in Kinnegad. Buried in Coralstown cemetery.

NOTE: *United Nations Relief and Rehabilitation Administration (UNRRA) was an international relief agency, largely dominated by the United States but representing 44 nations. Founded in 1943, it became part of the United Nations in 1945, and it largely shut down operations in 1947. Its ultimate objective was repatriation, within the camps relief expanded to include providing food, clothes, health care and accommodation, as well as child welfare, occupational therapy, education, vocational training and employment opportunities (Cohen, 2008).*

NAN (ANN MARY) WEYMES b.15 Apr 1912 Mullingar. d.1997 Bray Wicklow. Nan married Ron Forestall who worked as a Real Estate agent. They had no issue. She worked as an extra in Ardmore film studio Bray and was called " The Duchess " ever after.

MAY WEYMES b.abt 1914 Mullingar d.abt 1998 Kylemore Galway. May was an Army Nurse who met her English RAF officer radio engineer, husband Don Gibbins in Bahrain. May was a Public health nurse in the Kylemore Galway. In 1950, she nursed the Royal family of Bahrain, she also worked in the Far East and Thailand. Don Gibbins was what you would class as the typical strong man image and very muscular. He single-handed built a hotel in Kylemore beside the Kylemore abbey Galway. They died with no issue.

MONICA MADELINE WEYMES b.1925 Mullingar, Westmeath d. 2015, Mississauga, Ontario, unmarried. Monica went to Canada in 1957 and worked for 34 years as a nurse's aide at the Princess Elizabeth Hospital. She is remembered for her warmth, laughter, wonderful Irish stories, unwavering faith, and her loving kindness.

WILLIAM(BILL)WEYMES b.23 Dec 1909, 13 Mount St Mullingar, d. 1995 in Dublin. He was in the Army during WW2. Worked for the CIE (Bus Corporation). Bill married abt. 1941, Joan Connaughton b. abt. 1912, d. 04 Oct 2003 in Dublin. They had 3 daughters and one son.

THOMAS JOSEPH WEYMES b. 21 Jun 1905 Kinnegad, d. 09 Nov 1962. Living at Mount St, Mullingar. Thomas was married by Fr Maurice Weymes to Margaret Agnus Kenny. He was *Sergeant in the Garda Siochana in Kill Cootehill in Cavan; he was stationed there in 1926.

Thomas and Margaret children were: Helen, Annett, Ann, Bridge, Thomas Gerald Weymes.

Football career Thomas was a Gaelic footballer of high repute and he was one of the stars of the Monaghan team from 1927 to 1930. His team was Ulster champions in 1927 and 1929 and won the Dr McKenna Cup in 1928.

Picture Tom in middle

ANDREW VINCENT WEYMES b.16 Jul 1908 d.14 June 1960 Scotland. Andy was a daring character with a sense of fun. Andrew married in 1948 in Munster Germany. an Austrian, Margaret A Rakuscha (Graz) b. 1919 d. 2010, Dunfermline Cemetery Fife. They meet in Austria, when Andrew was there with the liberation army at the end of WW2. They had one son and one daughter.

Military Career -It appears Andrew joined his brothers Patrick and Michael in Spain with General O'Dufff and fought in the Bandera war for Franco. (Franco was to send a ship to Galway which never came). **Andrew is listed leaving Liverpool, 20 February 1937 on the ship Aguila, destination Lisbon, Portugal age 28 years, musician. British Army in the WW2. - Andrew Weymes*** joined the English army 1938. During WW2 Andy was sent on leave the week of the D-Day landing. When he returned his regiment had all perished.

SOURCE: *British Armed Forces and Overseas Banns and Marriages- Gro Index Army Marriages (1881 To 1955), Records year range,1948, ARM2, Page (10) 1001, Collections from Great Britain, UK None. **Passenger Lists Leaving UK 1890-1960- Destination Lisbon, Portugal. ***Royal Artillery Attestations 1883-1942 RECORDS- British Army regiments- Andrew Vincent Weymes. Attestation year 1938, Service number,1438670.

MICHAEL FINTAN WEYMES

b.17 Feb 1907, d.15 Jul 1937 Mullingar unmarried.

He was an Army sergeant who died in action in Spain under General Duffy's Regiment 15 July 1937 and some considered him to be a war hero.

SPANISH CIVIL WAR *17 July 1936- 1 April 1939*

Spanish Inferno-Dilemma *faced the men who lived like moles. Sunday Independent, July 3rd 1960.*

Michael Weymes Spain -Speculation in Ireland the headlines told of thousands at the RDS Spring Show. The great airship Hindenburg had crashed in flames at New Jersey with appalling loss of life. There was speculation on the marriage date of the Duke of Windsor to Mrs Simpson. A place with the queer name of Rineanna near Limerick was being drained by huge machines with the idea of making a giant air terminal. Among the Bandera were many natural soldiers, men who were gay and daring. One of them was Michael Weymes, son of Mr. P J Weymes, Mullingar, a former chairman of Westmeath Co. Council. Michael left to fight in Spain with his two brothers, Andrew (who died a week or so ago in Scotland), and Patrick, who is now in Canada. Michael Weymes, educated at St. Fenian's College, Mullingar, and at Castleknock College, served in the Irish Army, later joined the Civic Guards and then went to Spain with his former chief, Gen. O'Duffy. In Spain he became a leader man would follow willingly. But illness struck Michael Weymes and he was in Caceres Hospital when the Brigade returned to Ireland. Michael Weymes recovered in time to take part in the toughest battle of the Spanish war. He was leading his platoon at Villa Franco, Astilllo, when he was cut down by a stream of machine-gun bullets. 1937-07-15 – Michael Weymes (29) of Mullingar, County Westmeath and later 2 Belton Park Gardens, Donnycarney, Dublin – killed at Villafranca del Castillo on the Mardrid Front- buried in Cáceres, Spain.

JOSEPH WEYMES b.8 May 1913 Mullingar. d. Wicklow. He was an Army sergeant from 1940-50. During the war he brought supplies to the English Army in London. On one mission the "doodlebug" bombs exploded on the road he was travelling but he was not injured. Joe appeared to thrive in the army but the salary was not enough to support his family so he resigned.

He tried unsuccessfully to established several businesses. But success came in his 50s when he became bar, catering and transport manager for Ardmore studious Bray Wicklow. He was a good manager and knew how to as he said "play to their ego" and so for rich and famous making sure that the directors received their favourite cigars and drinks. In later years he worked as an extra for the Ardmore studio with his sister Nan. Joe married Gertrude Brady b.20 Jul 1911, 8 Harold's Cross Dublin in 1936. Bray, Wicklow. They had two sons one died at birth and 4 daughters.

PATRICK ALOYSIUS WEYMES b.14 Feb 1914, Mullingar Westmeath. Patrick died 1980 in Bray Wicklow while visiting his brother Joe from Canada. He went to Spain with General O'Dufff and fought in the Bandera war for Franco with his brother Michael. There were 40 men left Ireland on Nov. 20th 1936 to fight for the Bandera. He was in the Irish Army during WW2. He went to Canada in 1955 and stayed there. Patrick married *Anna M O'Reilly in 1953 in Surrey England. They had 2 boys. SOURCE: * *England & Wales Marriages 1837-2005*

ANTHONY WEYMES b. Nov 1918 Kinnegad, d.24 Mar 2002 buried at Tullamore Offaly. Tony married about 1944, Marie Page b. 1921 d. 06 Sep 1992, they had four boys and two girls. Tony was the youngest son of the Weymes clan. He was in the Irish army during the WW2.

Tony was a prison officer who became the founding Chairman of the Prison Officers Association (Union). He was first General Secretary of Prisons, prison Officers Mountjoy 25 years, probation Officer 25 years. His interests were writing poetry.

KNOWING PADDY WEYMES

By *MICHAEL WEYMES*

When Michael put an advert in the newspaper asking if anyone could give him any information on PJ Weymes he was overwhelmed with the response. He spent many hours going around the country interviewing people for what has now become a novelette on his life. He said he enjoyed it because PJ was such a colourful character. My deepest thanks to Michael and for all those that came forward with your stories of him. I never meet my grandfather but this has brought me close to him.

PATRICK JOSEPH WEYMES

P.J. WEYMES Born 18th March 1879 Died 1st October 1966

'Life is ours to be spent, not to be saved' (D.H. Lawrence)

This quotation by Lawrence could well have been written for P.J.

He lived life to the full measure in the spirit of the quotation.

I first heard of (Paddy) P.J. Weymes while researching my family history in the early 2000's. I came in contact with Theresa Cleaver (P. J's grand-daughter) who was on a like mission. While sharing information about our relevant research, Theresa told me of some details regarding Paddy. Because of the fact that so little was known about him, I decided to get in contact with as many people as possible that either knew Paddy or knew of him. I was overwhelmed by the amount and the content of the replies that I received in response to the letter of enquiry I placed in a number of newspapers. In the case of most of the replies (except those from abroad) I arranged to meet and talk to the person.

There was a recurring theme in all of those conversations and it was, Paddy was the kindest and best-read man I have ever known. So, I felt that Knowing Paddy Weymes would be an ideal title for the book.

My sincere thanks to the following people for the help and information that they gave to me;

Theresa Cleaver, Patrick Weymes, Kevin Weymes, Ann Ainsworth, Marian Diskin,

Michael Gaffney, Kieran Wynne, Brendan Lyons, Mr & Mrs. Dunne,

Michael Cully, Michael Coyne, Denis McDermott, Eddie Costello, Noël Flynn.

There were many more people who preferred not to have their names in print.

The Early Years

People will not look forward to posterity, who never look back to their ancestors

(Edmund Burke 1727-1797)

On a bright, pleasant, cool spring day, Patrick Joseph Weymes was born in Kinnegad, Co. Westmeath to his parents, Thomas Weymes and Bridget Mc Dermott. The date was 18th March 1879.

One month after Paddy's birth, on 20 April 1879 a meeting was held in Irishtown, near Ballindine, County Mayo. This meeting, which was attended by a crowd estimated at about fifteen thousand, arose out of a threat to evict a number of tenants from the estate of a local absentee landlord, because of arrears of rent. The meeting led not only to the cancellation of the proposed evictions but also to a general reduction of rents. Of far greater consequence, however, were the wider political effects of the meeting, whose reverberations were to be felt throughout the whole of Ireland over the next quarter of a century.

P J or Paddy as he was to be known as, could not have been aware of the extent that this meeting would impact on his life. For many years he would become committed to playing an active role to ensure that the dreams and aspirations of the people who attended that April meeting in Irishtown, were made a reality for all Irishmen.

This would not be the only reason he would be remembered. No, he would also be remembered as a provider of much needed employment in Kinnegad and Mullingar through his Wool and Hide business. He would also be remembered because of his involvement in one the longest running legal case in the history of the state; his bankruptcy; and also, his fondness of female company, which led him to leave his wife Ethel and his young family, and take a mistress. However, he would be best remembered as a kind, considerate, and caring person, who dedicated his life to improving the lot of his fellow beings; and in so doing many, many people remember him for his kindness, and his caring ways.

The first written reference to Weymes in Ireland (there is in excess of thirty variant spellings of the name) is that of a Ralph Wymes appearing at a Baronial court in Nobber, Co. Meath in 1304, concerning a land dispute. Ralph was called as a witness in this dispute. The original spelling of the name is Wemyss after the area in Fifeshire in Scotland. The Wemyss are the descendants of the Mc Duff clan.

Probably the best known Weymes in Irish history, is Sir Patrick Wemyss who came to Ireland from Scotland in 1631 as an officer in the army of the Duke of Ormond. He is mentioned in many official publications and also in the Ormond Manuscripts; it could be said he played a significant part in shaping the history of Ireland until he died in 1661. He lived in Danesfort in Kilkenny and served in the Irish Parliament, as did a number of his descendants.

Paddy believed that he was descended from Sir Patrick's line and had conducted research into this matter in an effort to lay claim to one of the titles of the family; however, no verifiable evidence is available now to support his claim as Paddy's personal papers have vanished.

Paddy's direct ancestors lived in the general area of Kinnegad for a number of generations. Many of them are in fact buried in the cemeteries of historic Ballyboggan Abbey, and Coralstown, which are part of Kinnegad Parish.

A Henry Weymes is recorded in the Griffiths Valuation Book of 1854 as residing in Kinnegad. His house, garden and office have a valuation of two pounds and six shillings, while the valuation of his land was four shillings. Also recorded was a Marcella Weymes whose house, office and garden have a valuation of ten shillings. These are probably ancestors of PJ.

Paddy's father Thomas had inherited the family wool and hide business from his late brother Maurice in 1895. Slaters Directory of Mullingar for 1894 records Maurice Weymes as a wool merchant residing at Mount street Mullingar. Kelly's Directory of Leather Trades in Ireland 1905 lists Thomas Weymes and son as wool merchants and dealers at Mount St, Mullingar and Kinnegad. A fire in the Kinnegad premises in May caused extensive damage.

The fire was first noticed by a member of the Dunne family, as he noticed smoke coming from the storeroom, which contained wool, skins, and tallow. Ringing the church bells raised the alarm, and hundreds rushed to the scene and assisted in putting out the fire. The fire damage was estimated at over £200. In the 1915 edition of Kelly's publication; T Weymes and son are listed as being in Mount St, Mullingar.

Paddy married Ethel Josephine Shaw in Turin R.C. Church on 20th April 1904. Ethel was the eldest daughter of the late Andrew Shaw of Cloughan, Mullingar.

On the following day the happy couple were present at the National Convention of the United Irish League of which PJ was a prominent member.

Thomas and Bridget were keen to keep abreast of all of the latest developments in the business, and to this end they sent Paddy to Bath in England to study and gain experience in the new processes and technologies of the wool and hide trade.

On his return he was placed in charge of the family business that was then located in Mount St in Mullingar. He revamped the business to meet the need of the day with new buildings and processes. He advertised extensively and in a manner that displayed his unique and forward-looking attitude to attract new customers. His newspaper advertisements were a feature in the local papers in that they were both topical and eye-catching.

Indeed, it could be said that he was displaying entrepreneurial skills that were well before there time. The Westmeath Examiner of 13th February 1905 carried the following report.

Mr. PJ Weymes T.C Mullingar has been giving the people of Killucan, Coralstown, and Kinnegad an exceptional treat during the past few weeks by recitals of gramophone records, for which he has a number of varied and interesting records, including several Irish songs. On to-morrow Sunday the venue is The Downs, where from 6.30 to 9pm the recital will be in progress. The small sum of sixpence will be charged for admission to a programme of over one hundred items. Schoolchildren one penny.

Paddy was an active member of the Amateur Dramatic class of St. Mary's Temperance Society and reports in the local press in November 1902 were loud in their praise for his performance as Robert Emmet in Pilgrims historic drama, Robert Emmet. One reporter stated; 'he gave a graceful exposition of the part, enunciated his dialogue distinctly, and in every way faithfully portrayed the patriot youth'

It was not only his acting that drew praise and appreciation from critics and audience alike; his fine singing voice warranted curtain call after curtain call; and was much in demand from organizations and promoters. His administrative skill was much in demand and an advertisement in the Westmeath Examiner listed him as joint secretary of Mullingar Feis in 1905. He was also President of the Kinnegad Branch of the Gaelic League who organised the Annual Aeridheacht in the town. This event was regarded an example of how such events should be conducted and it attracted competitors and spectators from far and near.

Politics and Business

No great deed is done by falterers who ask for certainty. (George Eliot 1819-1880)

In February 1908 Paddy was elected as chairman of Mullingar Urban Council. Newspaper reports in January 1909 of the Annual Meeting of North Westmeath Divisional Executive of the United Irish League carried a copy of a resolution proposed by Paddy. "This Executive has observed with dissatisfaction that some attempts in recent years to set up a rival authority in political affairs in North Westmeath, and that such efforts, whether of an open character or disguised under popular catch-cries are hereby condemned as detrimental to national unity and result in weakening the national forces". Paddy had moved this resolution, which was carried because of recent criticism of the Irish Party in regard to the Land Bill. He was aware that at a meeting of the Irish Party the member for North Westmeath had attempted to move a motion but failed to get a seconder for it.

In January 1910 there was an election for members to Mullingar Town Commissioners and Paddy was elected with the second highest number of votes –310. Patrick Shaw topped the poll with 400 votes.

At a public meeting in Ballinalee in Longford in May 1910 which was organized to welcome home released members of the League who were imprisoned for cattle-driving, Paddy said that if they had Home Rule there would be no need for agitation for the land for the people.

The Chief Inspector of Liverpool Police attended the September 1913 sitting of Mullingar Petty Sessions. Paddy presided at the sessions, and the Inspector expressed his pleasure at the efficient manner in which the court was conducted.

There is a story told about a local 'knight of the road' who frequently came before Paddy at the Mullingar Sessions at which he presided. It was well known that this 'knight' had little or no money and that whatever fine was levied upon him, Paddy always paid it. On one occasion that he came before the court, Paddy asked him, "What shall we fine you on this occasion" to which the 'knight' replied "whatever you like your honour, but go easy on yourself"

At the October 1915 Petty Sessions in Mullingar Paddy expressed his sympathy to the family of Captain Large and the other gallant soldiers who were killed in battle; and expressed a wish that many more in the country would answer the call to arms and help to put an end to the war in Europe which was launched at the instigation of the German Emperor.

In his hometown of Kinnegad he organized a collection for the Home Rule fund. This collection was taken up in Kinnegad, Coralstown, and Clonard.

The collection came to a total of £19 5s 6d. In today's terms this would amount to 9,525 Euro (based on average earnings). Mr. PJ Hayden the MP for South Roscommon duly recognized this gesture with a letter of acknowledgement and thanks. Hayden was also the proprietor of the Westmeath Examiner newspaper and a fellow member of Paddy's in the United Irish League.

He spoke often of his vision of Ireland, which was in keeping with the politics of his party and he never wavered from those beliefs. As a JP, he administered the law as it stood with both fairness and compassion, and as a consequence he was often literally in the line of fire.

During the War of Independence, the British authorities were seeking quite a number of prominent Irish leaders. To this end the British often mounted roadblocks in an effort to find and arrest these persons. Sean McKeon one of the most sought after was attending a meeting in Mullingar when news came through that a roadblock was in place on the Longford road. As McKeon would be returning home on this road Paddy arranged for him to dress up in women's clothes. When PJ was stopped at the roadblock that was manned by the Black and Tans, he passed McKeon off as his wife Ethel and proceeded to drive him to his home in Longford

In 1900 the Irish Parliamentary Party which had been split since the fall of Parnell, was concerned at the rise of the United Irish league and this led to the amalgamation of the two parties under the leadership of John Redmond. The United Irish League thus became the constituency organization of the Irish Party. The party was it could be said the main popular political force in the country until 1914. At local and national level Paddy was a prominent figure in the United Irish League and as such he had ambitions as to his political life. However, these ambitions were as good as shattered when the Irish Volunteers rejected Redmond's alliance with the British. This was borne out by the results of the general election for the first Dail, which took place on 14th December 1918. Paddy, standing as a Nationalist candidate in Westmeath was beaten by Laurence Grinnell. Grinnell standing as a Sinn Fein candidate polled 12,435 votes, to PJ's 3,458. It is interesting to note that Ginnell and Paddy were fellow member of the United Irish League, but Ginnell disagreed with some aspects of the party's direction and resigned. Paddy was declared as a Nationalist and Labour candidate for the Dail elections of 1923, but he did not stand.

The business of Weymes and Son had premises in Kinnegad and Mullingar. Paddy travelled throughout the entire country in pursuit of business and his Rolls Royce was a familiar sight on the Irish roads. He also had a shop in Mount Street in Mullingar. In excess of one hundred people were employed by him in his may enterprises.

The outbreak of war saw the rise of Paddy's star. Always to the forefront as a wool buyer his position was further enhanced when he was appointed as a buyer for the British army. As can be imagined the demand for wool for the war effort increased the price. In 1914 at the outbreak of the war, the price per lb of wool was on average 7.5 pence, whereas in 1916 the price had increased by 55%.

For the duration of the war all of the available storage space available at Hill of Down railway station was taken up by wool purchased by Paddy, on its way to Dublin for the British army.

During this period, it is known that he purchased a fleet of vehicles to collect wool from across Ireland, and that he contracted a company to maintain this fleet.

He also purchased a number of properties including, Clonyn Castle near Delvin in Co. Westmeath which was later burned, a licensed premise, general stores and a house in Derrinturn in Co. Kildare. He also had an interest in Kylemore Abbey in Connemara in county Galway, but the only record that pertains to this is an article in the Connacht Tribune of 16th October 1920, which refers to the fact that a Mr. Mackie of Joyce Mackie, in conjunction with Mr. PJ Weymes concluded the sale of the Abbey in London. He also invested in stocks and shares. Paddy's family residence in Mount Street in Mullingar was extended and renovated and a formal garden was laid out.

Over the years he became a collector of antique and modern furniture. He had a collection of fine oil painting and watercolours. In Derriturn he had a full-sized billiard table, a large collection of records and also a mechanical organ.

In March 1916, he started to cure and manufacture sheepskins. To this end he installed the most up-to-date machinery, methods, and processes. He acquired an office in Kilcock from which he carried on his auctioneering business.

His fondness of attractive female company increased as his opulence grew, and he was often seen parading these ladies in public without inhibition. They were usually attired in furs and diamonds, which were occasionally paid for by Paddy. It was well known that this behaviour was causing much concern and strain on his wife Ethel.

But he always showed his generously and his sense of caring for his fellow man. He paid for the renovation of the church in his native Kinnegad; and he had a new pulpit and altar installed in memory of his late mother and father in the church. Interestingly, the Pearse family completed this work. He also ensured that none of his employees were in any financial distress, and he was known to give aid and support to many local and national causes. Probably his greatest deed of kindness to his fellow man in this period was the fact that he keeps the poor of Mullingar fed and in comfort during the long hard winter of 1917. But for his generosity many a family would not have survived.

There was a robbery at the Weymes offices in August 1919, some bits and pieces were taken together with £40 in cash. It seemed that those responsible were of the belief that there was a large amount of cash there, the result of a recent auction; however, this had been lodged in the bank.

A further incident occurred in January 1920 when a car owned by Paddy was approaching Mullingar; shots were fired at the car that was been driven by a man named Harrison who was the only person in the vehicle. Six shots were fired at the car, the rear of the car was pierced and the windscreen was broken. The driver had a narrow escape although he required medical attention for injuries to his face from splinters of glass.

A further robbery was attempted robbery at the offices of Weymes & Son in January 1921 when the thieves got away with £100. Again, they probably expected to find the proceeds of a recent land sale to be in the office, but this had been lodged the previous day.

There are a number of unsubstantiated stories about Paddy and his wealth during this period that make interesting reading; and knowing of his life style and zest for life there is more than a smidgen of truth about them.

On one occasion when one of his female companions was unable to secure a hotel room he is reported as having purchased the hotel.

When he lived in Clonyn castle near the town of Delvin, which he purchased in May 1920, his dinners and entertainment were the talk of the county. They went on into the early morning and the cuisine was said to be the best in the land.

One of the many fine entertainers who sang there was a local man named Jim Bird who was regarded as the best tenor in Ireland bar John McCormack. To be on the guest list at Clonyn during Paddy's ownership was the ambition of many. The National Bank in Dominick Street in Mullingar had at one time a cheque for a quarter of a million drawn to PJ.Weymes on display in their offices in Dominick Street.

By May 1919 the ending of the war was starting to have an effect on Paddy's wool business, and he ran a series of advertisements in the national daily papers. He was unconcerned at the amount of wool he had in storage, as he was led to believe that the British army would honor the arrangement to purchase all of it.

As time wore on and there was no communication from the British, many of the wool buyers Paddy included arranged a meeting with the army as to the possibility of compensation; however, their request fell on deaf ears. Paddy decided to make an approach to his bankers with regard to a loan in order to allow him to reorganize his business, however he drew a blank.

Chapter 3

War and it's Casualties

The man who has done his best, as is conscious that he has done his best, is a success even though the world may write him down as a failure. (B.C. Forbes 1840-1945

When the war finally ends, great change takes place. Many are carried along by this change, but there are an equal number who are cut adrift, because of changing practices and policies, and priorities. Paddy Weymes was but one of many who were cut adrift. His main asset wool lost its value overnight. The reduction in the number of army personnel meant that the number of uniforms needed fell dramatically and as a consequence so did the demand for wool. His wool stores, which were full to the eves with wool bought at top price, were now like millstones around his neck and worthless. The British army just advised him they needed no more wool; there was no offer of compensation or even discussion. Bankruptcy followed and it was a long and ugly process.

Paddy made a valiant effort to 'keep the ship afloat' by trying to reorganize his business and his capital and also diversified into other venture, but he was losing the fight. Finance was scarce in the new state, other priorities and ventures were now competing for this finance, a new order was taking over and bank managers were not supporting perceived losers.

A report in the Irish Times of 5th April 1922 told the sad tale; Motor and Engineering, the company Paddy had contracted to maintain his fleet of cars and trucks were petitioning to have for a provisional liquidator to be appointed for the winding up of Paddy's business, Messer's Weymes & Sons Ltd, on foot of a debt of £690 due to them by Weymes.

It was stated that the capital of Weymes and Sons Ltd was held by PJ Weymes and amounted to £60,000; debentures amounting to £50,000 were held by the Munster and Leinster Bank.

The notice to creditors was posted in all of the national daily papers on the 11th May 1922; inviting them to advise their names and addresses together with details of the debts or claims to Stanley Stokes the official liquidator, and advising them that 29th June 1922 was the date for hearing and adjudicating upon the debts and claims.

So, the tide was going out for Paddy Weymes and his business.

The investigation into Paddy's estate and debts proved to be difficult and lengthy; the first sitting had to be adjourned again and again. Eventually Paddy made a proposal to pay 2s 6d in the £, payable in three instalments of four, eight, and twelve months from the date of court confirmation.

The first and second payments to be secured by provisionary notes of Paddy, and the last by joint promissory note of Paddy and Mr. Thomas McDonnell. There were objections by some of the debtors to Mr. McDonnell on the grounds of his solvency.

In order to overcome this impasse Mr. McDonnell agreed to lodge £2,000 with the assignee; and the cheque was paid over on 26th January 1923. (Later it was established that the £2,000 lodged by McDonnell was not his money, it was given to him by Paddy, and consisted of Paddy's own money and sums collected by him from various people in Westmeath).

However, Paddy paid none of the instalments. In June he made a new submission offering to pay 1s in the £, but having failed to secure the majority of creditors he was adjudged a bankrupt in July 1923.

In May 1923 Paddy went to America in an effort to secure finance to resolve his cash crises. However, despite his best efforts and personal connections, and the fact that he established some contacts in New York he had no success in securing finance, and he returned to Ireland in early June.

In July 1923 in the Bankruptcy court, he was questioned as to his connections with the Midland Counties Wool, Skin, and Hide Company. When asked if he bought the business from Mr. Gaunt of Bradford, he replied that it was Mr. Thomas F. McDonnell who bought it, but that he (Paddy) went security for McDonnell. When it was suggested that this was a plan to enable him to acquire the business when he was a bankrupt, Paddy replied that McDonnell was just trying to help him get back on his feet.

During the course of the questioning, it was discovered that in May1922, Paddy had returned his assets as £15,861, but in July 1923 he returned them as being £6,563. When asked how this could be Paddy replied that quite a number of the assets would have lost their value over that period owing to the changes in the economic climate.

The court made an order for the immediate realization of the assets.

On 18th September 1923 the national and provincial papers carried a notice of auction of antique and modern furniture the property of PJ Weymes of Derrinturn on the order of the Bankruptcy court. An extensive list of the items was included with the notice. In the same month there appeared a notice of setting of 33 acres of uncut meadows at Clonyn Castle on Tuesday 2nd October the property of PJ Weymes (a bankrupt).

At the resumption of the bankruptcy hearing in November 1923, further information placed before the court including the fact that Paddy had received £960 from the British Government for malicious injury. The examination of Paddy concerning his evidence continued for a number of days. At the conclusion of the hearing the judge directed that all of the evidence and the affidavits be sent to the Corporate Law Society. The Society referred the documents in the case to the Attorney General.

In March 1924 the licensed and general premises of "Weymes" at Kinnegad was advertised for sale at PJ Byrne sales office.

While all of this was going on Paddy was maintaining his sense of chivalry. One of the hardware shops in Mullingar with whom Paddy traded were feeling unsure if the goods Paddy purchased would be paid for, duly sent one of their female staff to his office with an invoice. She was shown into the office; on opening the envelope Paddy exclaimed, "Well we must not keep you dear boss waiting for his cash," he said, as he wrote out a cheque for the amount, while at the same time taking out a box of the most expensive chocolates and presenting them to the young lady.

In June 1927 the hearing of Paddy's case was listed for the Central Criminal Court as the investigation by the Attorney General' office in the course of their enquiry discovered that Paddy and two of his colleagues failed to disclose shares in which Paddy had invested, to the Assignee in Bankruptcy. These shares were held by Paddy in Rubber Plantation Trust and Base Metal Corporation and exceeded the value of £10.

The case opened on 7th July 1927 and concluded on 8th July 1927. Paddy was sentenced to six months in each of the five charges: and they were concurrent. The case against his two colleagues, Thomas Buckley and James Lothian were dismissed as the jury disagreed.

With the sale of the family residence in Mount Street on 18th August 1927 by order of Vincent Crowley the official receiver and the sale of the factory and yard in Mount St on 9th May 1930 it could be said that Paddy's fortunes had gone full circle; there was nothing left to salvage from his business or his family life.

The records show that Paddy left for America on 19th March 1929, he was fifty years old. He is believed to have met up with his mistress Miss Cribben in America. There are a number of stories as to the status of this relationship, but as none of these can be verified, no conclusions can be reached. Paddy got a job working on the railways in New York. An old associate of his recognized Paddy one day while he was going to work, they got talking about old times; his friend offered Paddy a job in his speak easy, which he took. Later Paddy moved to California, but eventually he returned to Ireland in the early 1930's

Chapter 4.

The Years of Peace

I know of no great man except those who have rendered great service to the human race (Voltaire 1694 – 1778)

On returning to Ireland Paddy found the real meaning of the saying-: you can count your real friends on the fingers of one hand. Many of those who had boasted of being in Paddy's company in the days of wine and roses were now prone to say that they knew not the man. Fortunately, there were a few who did not forget his kindness, his enlightening company, and his unstinting generosity.

There is a story told that Paddy on his return sought out a member of the clergy whose church had benefited greatly as a result of Paddy's generosity in the good years. The visit was twofold, to get a feel of how the land lay; and to ask for some help. Paddy failed to get beyond the hall door; he was informed in no uncertain terms that he was not welcome. So much for the old Irish saying, charity begins at home.

In the early years of his return, Paddy shared his time between Kinnegad, Mullingar and Longford. While in Longford he lived in Reynolds guesthouse in Bridge Street and went to M.J. Lyons Wool and Tannery works at Bridge Street, where he assisted with the work. Many of the people I spoke to in Longford remember him quite well as a kind and considerate man who allowed the children to play among the bales of wool. His usual routine when going in to work was to call into the Little Garden, a local shop which sold vegetable and flowers; he would buy a pink carnation and put in his lapel. In the summer evenings he could be seen taking a stroll down by the canal, and at times he could be observed bathing his feet in the water. Paddy was often heard to say, "Water clears your head and revives your spirit".

Although Paddy in his youth was a teetotaler, later in life he acquired a taste for port wine, his favourite being Dows. He could be seen some evenings in Gaffney's licensed premises having a glass of Dows and smoking a cigarette. On one such evening a local youth dropped into the premises on his way to the local greyhound stadium. On seeing Paddy, he asked him if he was going to the dogs. Paddy replied, "Son, I have been gone to them for the past twenty years and I'm just on my way back"

Every year at Christmas, Paddy received a Christmas card from the treasurer of the Bank of England. He was sitting in the bar one Christmas eve after having received the card in the post when the barman asked if the card was from one of his girlfriends; Paddy took from his pocket a one pound note, he said to the barman "Do you see the signature on this pound, well that's the same man who sent this card" while at the same time showing the barman the Christmas card.

During the years that Paddy stayed in Longford, he spent Christmas with the Lyons family in Lamagh, Newtown Forbes.

When in Mullingar, Paddy's port of call was usually McDermott's shop. The McDermott's and the Weymes's were first cousins. Mr McDermott would always treat him to a couple of packets of cigarettes and put a fiver in his top pocket. The greeting and conversation were cordial, but there was always an undercurrent of unease and regret. Those of his former workers, whom he met on his visits to Mullingar, were always delighted to meet him. They did what they could to support and help Paddy despite being poor themselves. They remembered, that in his good times he never failed to look after them.

There were few friends to greet him on his visits to Kinnegad; it seemed that many of the locals had short memories, the many and extensive good deed that Paddy performed for his hometown were long forgotten.

Samuel Drake once wrote—Because it is a truth, and a melancholy truth, that the good things that men do are often buried in the ground, while their evil deeds are stripped naked, and exposed to the world. It would seem that this was the case in Kinnegad.

In the mid 1960's Paddy made the decision to put a stop to his travels and arranged for to reside in the county home in Mullingar; a building he had helped to construct through his generous donation. There was nowhere he could call home and the years and toil had left their mark. Life there as in most such institutions was basic, but at least he a roof over his head, regular meals and comfortable bed.

On the 1st October 1966 Paddy said goodbye to this world and went to meet his maker; he was in his 87th year. He was buried in Coralstown cemetery near his hometown of Kinnegad on the following Monday. The heavens opened, a daylong downpour as if the gods were weeping at his passing. There is no tombstone to record his passing and no epitaph to his life. His good friend the late John Quinn once said; "Paddy remained a gentleman to the end – kind – courteous - charitable in word, thought, and deed. He held no grudges and took the world as it came". There was no eulogy spoken, and his grave bears no marker.

Chapter 5

The Next Generation

Your name you got from your father; it was all he had to give

When Paddy Weymes bade this life goodbye he left behind him a family who had established themselves in the new state and played no small part in its development.

Thomas Joseph was the first born to Paddy and Ethel. He was born in June 1905 and died in November 1962 and is buried in Coralstown Cemetery. He was a member of the Garda Siochana where he rose to the rank of Sergeant. Thomas was a Gaelic footballer of repute; and he was a member of the most successful Monaghan team during the period 1927 to 1930 when the county won the provincial championship and the McKenna cup. He later played for Cavan when he served in Kill Garda station. He was keenly interested in horses, and there are still some people in Clones, who regarded him as an expert in the equine world. Thomas and Margaret Weymes with their daughter Annette

Michael was the second son, he was born in February 1907, and he died in July 1937 being killed at the battle of Villa Franca in the Spanish war. Previous to that he had served in the Irish army and also the Garda. His brothers Andrew and Patrick also fought in the Spanish Civil war. In many quarter Michael would be regarded as a bit of a rebel and a bit like his father in his directness and attitude to life. To his comrades who fought with him in Spain he was a brave and gallant leader.

Andrew, the third son in the family was born in July 1908 and died in June 1960. Andrew is remembered as a daring character. He served in the British army during the 1939/1945 war. At the time of the D-day landings, he was on leave; on returning he was informed that his entire regiment was wiped out. He was married to an Austrian lady who he met during his army service. He lived out his life in Dunfermline, Scotland.

William was born in December 1909 and died in 1995. He was married and had three daughters and one son. He was employed by CIE.

Bridget Mary, the first daughter was born in March 1911 and died in February 1992 in St. Camillus nursing home Killucan and is buried in Coralstown. Bridget was an officer in the American army during the 1939/1945 war. She met her husband who was a refugee Slovakian doctor in 1951. She separated from him later in 1951. Bridget was a strong-willed lady who did not tolerate fools lightly.

Anne Mary was the second eldest daughter who was born in April 1912 ad she died in 1997 in Bray, Co. Wicklow. He family nickname was the Duchess after she had as an extra played that part in a film that was being shot at Ardmore Studios. She married John Forrestal; they had no family.

Joseph was born in May 1913 and died in December 2008.

PICTURES OF PATRICK JOSEPH WEYMES

Weymes Shop in Mullingar

PJ Weymes & Ms Cribben

COLCHESTER

WEMYS

According to Burks peerage Francis Wemys b.1777 (Wife Elizabeth Colchester) parents were Francis Wemyss b.abt 1750 and Miss **Agar** of Danesfort Kilkenny. His Uncle was Colonel Maurice Wemys d.1803 Emsworth. Maurice had 2 brothers Francis above and James who served together in the 58 Regiment of Foot. These three are mentioned in the Will of Francis William Wemyss 1782 as relatives.

The Wemyss married into the Agar family before in Mary Wemys b.1665, Parents Henry Wemyss and Elizabeth Blundell. She married abt. 1701 James Agar 1670 Gowran, Kilkenny, Ireland. *See chapter Wemys of Kildare.*

*Faulkner's Dublin Journal: Dublin, Ireland-Tues., 19 Mar 1765-Sat. 23 Mar **1765**-Died on Temple-bar, **Lieut. Henry WEMYS**, descended of a noble Family, and a near Relation of the **Right Hon. the Countess of Brandon.** NOTE: Father James Agar mother Mary Wemys. (This is Francis and Joyces Blundell son)*

Three brothers- Unknown Wemyss Parents

Finding their parents: The name Francis first appeared with the Wemys of Ireland with Francis Wemys of Kildare's Grandson of Sir Patrick b. 1670. So, it makes sense that they are from this line. The three brothers were born about 1740s so Dr Patrick would have been too young. Francis William line is accounted for. Reverend William only had one son William. That leaves Henry b. abt 1780 or James b.abt 1709. Finally, Stella Wyndham Alymer was born 1889 at Courtown Kilcock Kildare. The Aylmer family were settled at Lyons Kildare by the close of the 14th century. Francis Wemyss and Joyce came from Kilcock. Finally, The Colchester Wemyss show similar features to my Westmeath family.

James Wemyss b. 1744 Danesfort Kilkenny - Ensign 1754 promoted to Captain in 28 January 1758. LT James Wemys June 4th 1762, 58th Regiment of foot. Irish Army List 1757-72: LT James Wemys age 25 years b. Ireland 58th Regiment of foot reviewed at Charles Fort 14th June 1769. His brother Francis was in the same regiment at the same time in 1762.

Francis Wemyss b.abt 1743 Danesfort Kilkenny. He married Miss Agar abt 1776, Ireland. Their son was Francis Wemys b. 1777 d. 17 Apr 1848 Westbury Court, Gloucestershire.

West Indies: The 58th Regiment of Foot was first formed in 1755 during the Seven Years' War (1754-1763). The French and Indian War was fought between the colonies of Great Britain and New France, supported by American Indian allies on both sides.

Maurice Wemyss b abt 1742 Danesfort Kilkenny. Died 1803 Emsworth Hampshire England.

Both Maurice Weymes and his nephew Francis Wemyss of Colchester's were in the marines. Francis was the main beneficiary in his Uncle Maurice Wemys 1803 will Southamptonshire.
Maurice a bachelor married the widow Mary Danford at St George the Martyr in Southwark on 31 October 1795. Their witnesses were William & Dorothy Dawson. Maurice died 25 Nov 1803 in Warblington Mary also died the same and is buried in Warblington Hampshire in 1803.

Court Martial Major General Maurice Wemyss 1798

A military court martial confirmed the sentence Maurice Wemyss on 7th February 1798. The hearing had taken place between 4th & 22nd January 1798 at the Marine Barracks in Portsmouth. Major General Maurice Wemyss was the Colonel Commandant of the Portsmouth Division of the Marines. It seems that he was charged in relation to his intention to abolish the Divisional Fund and "perverting it to other uses other than those for which it was originally intended" and the charge was proved. It would seem that after the second day of the proceedings, he said that he would accept retirement and so avoid the trial, but the prosecutors refused to accept this. It was said that he intended to charge £52 that he had spent himself to the government under the heading of "barrack repairs." It was said that his conduct was "derogatory to his situation and rank.... and the trust reposed in him."

He was also accused of "gross and violent treatment towards Captain & Adjutant Lethem." This charge was also proved.

The Court was of the opinion "that Major General Maurice Wemyss, Colonel Commandant of Marines, from the irregularity of his conduct in the several instances before-mentioned, is not fit for the discharging the duties incumbent on the Commanding Officer; but in consideration of his the prisoner's long services, age, and infirmities, did therefore only adjudge him to be placed on half-pay."

He had over forty years' service.

WILL of Maurice Wemyss

Dept: Records of the Prerogative Court of Canterbury PROB 11/1401, P 389
Date: **29 November 1803:** Will of Maurice Wemyss of Emsworth, Hampshire.

Southampton Estate to nephew **Captain Francis Wemyss Marine Corps**

Emsworth this eight day of October one thousand eight hundred and three Being of sound Mind and understanding but of infirm state of Body knowing the uncertainty of human Life I do hereby declare this to be my last Will and testament I revoke all other Wills made by me at any time heretofore I give to **Despard Cronsdale Esquire** of Golden Square London and to
William Dawson Esquire of Hive House near Stanmore Middlesex five hundred pounds in the Irish five per Cents In Trust to pay to my faithful and attentive Servant **Hannah Commer** now living with me but on condition she shall remain in my Service till my death aner the said Stock of five pounds Irish 5 PCts I give to Jane the wife of John Midl annuity of twenty pounds a year by half yearly payments after the death of the said Hannah Commane of Bedhampton for ever for her sole use and benefit and in case she the said Jane should be deceased then to her child or children by the said John Midlane secondly I give and bequeath to the said Jane Midlane five hundred pound Irish five per cent stock for her sole and separate use and to be entirely at her own disposal I give and bequeath to Dispard Cronsdale and to William Dawson five Guineas each for a Ring which I request their acceptance of as a small Token of my regard The whole and Residue of my Estate and Effects I give and bequeath to my reputed Nephew Captain

Francis Wemyss of the Marine Corps I do hereby constitute and appoint the said Captain Francis Wemyss and John Mildane as above the Executors of this my Will but if it should so happen that he said Captain Francis Wemyss should die before me I then and in that case give and bequeath the said Residue of my Estate and Effects to Ann Eliza Arabella and Grace daughters of George Thompson of Portsea in the County of Southampton equally to be divided with Catherine Vivian the Daughter of John Vivian Purser in His Majesty's Navy share and share alike. Maurice Wemyss. Witness to signing D Dawson of Hive House Stanmore Edmund Padeson Emsworth

This Will was proved at London the twenty ninth day of November in the year of our Lord one thousand eight hundred and three before the Worshipful William Adams Doctor of Laws Surrogate of the Right Honorable Sir William Wynne Knight also Doctor of Laws Master Keeper or Commissary of the Prerogative Court of Canterbury lawfully constituted by the oath of Francis Wemysss Esquire one of the Executors named in the said Will to whom administration was granted of all and singular the Goods Chattels and Credits of the Decreased he having been first sworn duly to administer (power reserved of making the like Grant to John Midland the other Executor named in the said will when he shall apply for the same

Maurice Wemyss* Parish, County Emsworth, Hampshire. **Date Proven** 29 November 1803, **TNA Item and Image ID** 606236. *PCC Abstracts of Wills: Wills Proved at Prerogative Court of Canterbury. 29th November 1803. Source: UK Data Archive. LL ref:* **wills_1800_1810_2531955_606236.** *Unique Project ID* **2531955**

WESTBURY COURT

All that remains of Westbury Court is the gardens is now owned by the National Trust having been thoughtfully laid out by Maynard Colchester in the early 18th century and added to by successive generations. At the time of this painting, circa 1845, the original manor at Westbury Court had been demolished, as indeed had the later houses, resulting in the Colchester family residing at another home nearby. This picture taken about 1902 is the canal at Westbury Court built by Maynard Colchester the house which can be seen connected to the pavilion was built by Maynard Willoughby Colchester Wemyss in 1896 and eventually pulled down in the 1960s. When this picture was taken the Crown Prince of Siam stayed here. The Gardens were built by Maynard Colchester and many of the plants for it were supplied by "Cousin Richard Colchester the Gardener", whom we have not yet connected into the family tree.

COLCHESTER WEMYSS FAMILY

of Westbury Court and Wilderness Gloucestershire

FRANCIS WEMYSS *b1777* Son of Francis Wemys & Agar Ireland

Major Francis Wemyss was b.1777 at Danesfort Kilkenny Ireland and d. 17 April 1848 and was buried at Abenhall1 England. He was a major in the Royal Marines. Francis married Elizabeth **Colchester** 12 Nov 1808 in St Mary, Marylebone Rd, London. Elizabeth was descended from the marriage of Sir Duncombe Colchester and Eliz eldest daughter of Sergeant Maynard, marriage 1655. Elizabeth Colchester was b. 2 July, 1787, d. 3 Apr 1821 and was the third child of John Colchester who married Elizabeth. John's only son died aged 23. The family descends from Richard of Ilmington in about 1500. She did not own the estate, her sister Helena did. Helena married a Willoughby, who assumed the name Colchester to inherit Westbury Court. In turn, his son Maynard Willoughby assumed the surname Colchester-Wemyss so as to inherit another estate.

Francis Wemys Army *War-Office, June 7, 1814. His Royal Highness the Prince Regent has been pleased, in the name and on 'the behalf of His Majesty, to appoint the following Officers of the Royal Marines to take rank by Brevet as undermentioned the commissions to be dated June,4, 1814. Henry Cox, Edward Carter Hornby, Francis Wemyss, George Jones.*

Letter from Rear Admiral Sir Philip Charles Durham: **SIR, *Venerable, Saintes, August In, 1815....... This dispatch will be delivered by my Flag Lieutenant, Francis Wemyss, an intelligent and zealous officer, who will give their Lordships any further particulars; and I beg leave to recommend him to their Lordships' protection. 1 have the honour to be, & c. P. C. DURHAM, Rear-Admiral, Commander in Chief. '*

His Will was proved in 1848 at the Prerogative Court of Canterbury and instructed that his main home in Gloucester was sold and that together with all his other monies was to be invested. The interest was to be used for the benefit of his daughter Mary Elizabeth. The trustees were to be his son James Robert Wemyss and his son in law Charles Barton. It only mentions Mary Elizabeth, James Robert and Charles Barton. His sons, Francis, and John and daughter Dorothea, who married Charles Barton are not mentioned. Francis junior seems to have only died a few months later, so if he was already ill, that might explain why he wasn't included. However, Francis junior had a wife and children. Additionally, John died in 1863. The only explanation is that all the other children had been adequately provided for at an earlier date.

SOURCE: * Gazette Issue 16906 published on the 7 June 1814. Page 14 of 28, War-Office, June 7, 1814. **Gazette Issue 1762 published on the 18 September 1815. -Page 5 of 8-page 1013. Admiralty Office, September 18, 1815. COPY of a. letter from Rear Admiral Sir Philip Charles Durham, K. C.B. Commander in Chief of. His. Majesty's. ships at the Leeward islands, to John Wilson Croker, Esq.......... To John Hrilson Croker, Esq %oc. SfC. 8tc. * Acteon, Monsieur de Venancourt, Capitaine dc Fregate; Picture The sitter, a member of the Colchester family of Westbury Court, Gloucestershire.

Francis Wemyss b. 1812, d.27 Jun 1848. Captain Bombay Engineers married 1841 Eliza, daughter of Major General Dickinson, Bombay Engineers. He died two months after his father.

James Robert Wemyss HEIR b.1815 at Westbury Court, Gloucestershire. Died unmarried 12 Aug 1856 Abenhall Westbury Court, Gloucestershire. *No issue.*

John Maurice Wemyss b. 1820, .18 Mar 1863, Hampshire, United Kingdom

Doretha Maria Wemys* b. abt. 1814, d. 1899, Westbury Court, Gloucestershire. Married 30 Apr 1842 **Charles Burton**, Abenhall Church, Gloucestershire. Their children were Catherine Alice, Julia Dorothea, Charles Asgaugh b.1846. On the 21st, Charles Barton Esq of Wadham College, Oxford and the Inner Temple, London, only surviving son of the late Rev C Barton, DD dean of Bocking, Essex to Dorothea Maria, eldest daughter of Major F Wemyss of Gloucester.

Mary Elizabeth Wemys b. 1816 Westbury Court, Gloucestershire, d. 24 Nov 1910, Abenhall, Gloucestershire. Founded in 1869 'The Gloucester & West Gloucestershire Society for the Prevention of Cruelty to Animals', memorial plaque in Gloucester Cathedral. Unmarried, In Will of James Robert C Wemys.

Doretha Maria Wemys b. abt. 1814 at Westbury Court, Gloucestershire, d.1899. She **Married** 30 Apr 1842 Abenhall Church, Gloucestershire, **Charles Barton** of Wadham College, Oxford.

Doretha Wemyss & Charles Barton Children

Catherine Alice Barton b.1843 **Julia Dorothea Barton B. abt 1845, Charles Asgaugh Barton** B.1846 Died 1846.

Major Francis Wemyss b.1812 Cork Ireland. d. aged 36 years on 27 June 1848 at Westbury Court, Gloucestershire buried at Abenhall. Francis m**arried**** 23 Jan 1838 Elizabeth Dickinson, b. 1819 Bombay India, d.17 Jan 1863, Byculla, Christ Church Presidency Bombay India. She remarried in 1862 O'Connell and died on 17 Jan 1863.

Army*-Francis was a Lieutenant and later Major in the Bombay Engineers. He lived in Gloucester, also lived in Holles Street, Cavendish Square, London (Lord Byron born 1788 in Holles Street). Westbury Court, Gloucestershire.

In the British Newspaper Archive, Family Notices- Francis Wemyss Captain- Event Type: Obituary,**05 Jul 1848,** United Kingdom, age:36, Father's **Francis Wemyss** Major. He died 2 months after his father.

Elizabeth's Honeymoon Diary *She kept a journal for her courtship and marriage.*

Helena Michie Excerpt- Honeymoon

From Bombay to Malabar point where they borrowed the house of a wealthy friend, was one day longer than the bride wanted it to be. She wanted to go back to her mother's home after three days but was prevented from doing so by her mother's obligations. The honeymoon was a success as it was consummated. Though Elizabeth vowed never to return to Malabar again.

Extract from her diary *Although everything was arranged for our comfort and it was the place I rather would be at in the last few days than anywhere else. , yet is associated with a period altogether the most unpleasant of any girls life...I don't know what would have become of me with anyone else but David (her name for Francis)he has been very kind good and considerate.*

FRANCIS WEMYSS & ELIZABETH DICKINSON children

Francis Wemys-b.1845 and d. 03 Jul 1848 Westbury On Severn, Gloucestershire, England

Maynard Willoughby Colchester Wemyss-b.13 Aug 1846 Long Hope, Gloucestershire, England and d. 17 Jun 1930 The Bell House, Westbury-on-Severn. *See Chapter.*

Harriot Catherine Wemyss. b.22 Dec 1841 Poonah, India. d. 15 Aug 1929, Westbury, (Burkes peerage) aged 87 years, of Washwell House, Painswick, unmarried. Buried at Westbury Churchyard. Harriot was employed as Annuitant.

Alice Wemyss b.13 Sep 1848.d. unmarried 26 Feb 1928, Washwell House, Painswick.

SOURCE: *Burks landed gentry. ** Parish register transcripts from the Presidency of Bombay, 1709-1948, *** Victorian honeymoon in her diary -Cambridge University Press 978-0-521-86874-7 - Victorian Honeymoons: Journeys to the Conjugal

MAYNARD WILLOUGHBY COLCHESTER WEMYSS *b.1846*

The 2nd son of Francis Wemys and Elizabeth Dickinson

He started out as a Willoughby, who took the name Colchester to inherit the Colchester estate. Maynard Willoughby was b. 13 Aug 1846 Long Hope, Gloucestershire, England and d. 17 June 1930(age 83). The Bell House, Westbury-on-Severn, leaving issue. He held the office of Deputy Lieutenant (D.L.) of Gloucestershire. He was invested as a Commander, Order of the British Empire (C.B.E.). He graduated with a Doctor of Laws (L.L.D.).

Maynard married Mary Clare Dickenson of Deal, Sussex, England on 14 June 1871 St Saviours, Westbourne Grove, Middlesex, England. She was the daughter of Rev. Edward Newton Dickenson. Mary Clere d. 3 January 1908.

Maynard Willoughby Colchester Wemyss & Mary Clere Dickenson Children

Sir Maynard Francis Wemys (Edward) b. 12 Mar 1872 West Hoathly, Sussex. 28 Feb 1954, West Hoathly, Sussex. **Married** Maria Alice Disney Leith on 11 Oct 1898.They had two sons Patrick and Francis.

Lt.-Colonel John Maurice (Jock) Colchester-Wemyss b. 20 Mar 1881 Mitcheldean, d 29 Jan 1946 Wendover Cheltenham Gloucester. (Burke's Irish Family Records). Married-The 3 Mar 1909 Stella Wyndham M.B.E. Co. Organiser W.V.S only daughter of Major John Algernon Aylmer, 4th Dragoon Guards, of Courtown, Kilcock Co. Kildare. He died 25/1/1946 leaving issue- more presently.

Cecil Dorothea Colchester Wemyss('Dolly') b. 21 Apr 1876 West Hoathly, d. unmarried 15 Nov 1928 Westbury on Severn, Gloucestershire (national trust).

Margaret Alison Colchester Wemyss b. 12 Feb 1885 Gloucestershire, United Kingdom, d. 04 Jan 1935 Cheltenham Gloucester. Qualified in 1918 as a midwife. Died unmarried.

Geraldine Mimie Clere Wemyss b. 07 Jan 1874 London, Middlesex, England. Died 16 Feb 1948. **Married-**01 Jun 1898 Westbury, Robert **Bathurst,** (born 18 May 1875 and died 07 Mar 1929). His father was Charles Bathurst mother Mary Elizabeth Hay. Geraldine died 16 Feb 1948, **leaving issue. Daughter** Finetta Dorathea Bathurst born 06 Jun 1899 d. dec1970. *Married 6 April 1929 Henry Bristowe (son of Hubert Bristowe), they were divorced in 1940. She then legally changed her name by Deed Poll in 1940 to Finetta Dorethea Colchester. Her father in Law was Hubert Carpenter Bristowe lived at Wrington, Somerset, England.* He was registered as a Licentiate, Royal College of Physicians, London (L.R.C.P.). He graduated with a Doctor of Medicine (M.D.). They had one daughter.

CROWN PRINCE VAJIRAVUDH OF SIAM

In 1905 Maynard Colchester accepted the guardianship of three of the Crown Prince's younger brothers who were starting first years of Western education_____By 1912 had severe financial difficulties (death duties on the death of his wife 1908?), he moved to Bell House nearby and found tenants for Westbury Court. Crown Prince helped out with Estate mortgage for a few years but in 1918 Estate, excluding Westbury Court, had to be sold. Was presented in Feb 1918 with C.B.E. at Buckingham Palace. June 1918 was using a bicycle with 3-speed gears to get around (petrol rationing By Jan.1920 all of loan from King of Siam paid back with interest as well. June 1923 outbreak of cholera in Gloucestershire and a case of Small Pox in Westbury. Re-vaccinations carried out. Maynard Willoughby had bad reaction to his. 24/12/1924 "Dolly' and Margaret (both living with Maynard Willoughby at Bell House) had a wireless set, he had difficulty in understanding electricity. **Crown Prince Vajiravudh of Siam.** On the eve of Thursday 21st August 1902 large and elegant audience was invited by Mr & Mrs Colchester-Wemyss to Westbury Court for a performance organised by Crown Prince Vajiravudh whilst staying with them. The performance took place in the Iron Room suitably decorated. This was a superior out-house built behind the Court House and constructed in part of corrugated iron; it was sometimes used as an unofficial village hall. The triple bill was received with tremendous applause. after the plays, supper was served in a marquee on the lawn and the distinguished company, strolling around the gardens in the moonlight, were further fascinated by hundreds of coloured lights reflected in the water.

SOURCES: Information kindly given by the National Trust. Colchester. https://gloucestershirearchives.wordpress.com/2015/07/21/the-extraordinary-story-of-the-letters-between-maynard-willoughby-colchester-wemyss-and-king-rama-vi-of-siam/

SIR MAYNARD FRANCIS COLCHESTER WEMYSS *b.1872*

son of Maynard W Colchester Wemyss & Mary Dickinson

Sir Maynard Francis Colchester-Wemyss, K.B.E. (1920), formerly of Westbury Court, Glos. Lord of the Manors of Little dean, Mitcheldean, Glos. The Lea and Baysham, Herefordshire. D.L. (Doctor Law?) (1919) and J.P. (1906 -1949), High Sheriff 1919, Capt. in The Cameroonians (Scottish Rifles) (ret), President Croquet Association, member of Council of Wine and Food Society. Many years Chairman of Severn Board of Conservators (resigned 1929); served with the Cameroonians 1890 – 1903, in India and South Africa, member of Joint War Committee of B.R.C. during World War II, and Hon. Controller of Food in Auxiliary Hospitals in England and Wales. Member of B.R.C. Demobilization Board. Born 12 March 1872, educated at Eton and R.M.C., married 11 October 1891 **Maria Alice** (d.7/12/1940), 2nd **daughter of late Gen. Robert William Disney Leith**, C.B. of Glenkindie, and Westhall, Aberdeenshire, and sister of Lt-Col 5th Baron Burgh, Gordon Highrs.

NOTE: Colchester-Wemyss, Sir Francis A handbook on modern croquet. Pleasures of the Table, The London, James Nisbet.

SOURCE: Burks peerage-Landed Gentry 1952 King of Siam. By an extraordinary coincidence my aunt May Weymes who was a military Nurse in the 1930 was later a nurse to the king of Siam family.: *www.rootsweb.ancestry.com,A new order. - Honours for war work. The first list. Announced: - The Times | August 25, 1917, p. 7 & 8

Sir Maynard Francis & Maria Alice Disney Leith children

Francis Disney (Frank)Colchester Wemyss b.10 Aug 1899.d after 1954 **No Issue. Army** 25/10/1924 serving in Ashanti. *Francis Disney, Lieut the Cameroonians (c/o Barclays…Salisbury S Rhodesia; b 10 Aug 1899 educ Malvern, _____

Passenger Lists Leaving UK 1890-1960-Mr F D Colchester-Wemyss, Age -54. Birth year 1900, Occupation -Director, Departure 5/8/1954, Departure port -Southampton, Destination port -Cape -Country South Africa.

Colonel Patrick Maynard Colchester Wemyss* b. September 1905 Shropshire, d.07 Dec 1963 Derbyshire. Died no **issue.** Patrick Maynard gained the rank of Colonel in the service of the Royal Engineers (Territorial Army). He was decorated with the award of Territorial Decoration. **Married** 01 Mar 1934 **Alba Gladys Leith.**

Passenger Lists Leaving UK 1890-196: Patrick M Colchester-Wemyss-Age 26, Birth year 1905, Occupation -PLANTER, Departure year -1931, Departure day 23/12, Departure port -London, Destination port -Kingston Country -Jamaica-Jamaica direct fruit line Ltd.

LT-COLONEL JOHN MAURICE (Jock) COLCHESTER WEMYSS

Son of Maynard Willoughby Colchester Wemyss & Mary Clare Dickenson

John was b.20 Mar 1881 Mitcheldean.d.29 Jan 1946 Wendover Cheltenham Gloucester. **Married** 03 Mar 1909 Kilcock Kildare, **Stella Wyndham Alymer** born 16 Feb 1889. Died 27 May 1973. Only daughter of Major John Algernon (4th Dragoon Guards, of Courtown, Co. Kildare) & Blanche Wyndham Aylmer. She was a co-organizer of the Women's Voluntary Services (W.V.S.). She was invested as a Member, Order of the British Empire (M.B.E.). They had one child-Edward John Hugo Colchester.

Lt.-Colonel John Maurice ('Jock') Colchester-Wemyss Bought Westbury Court 1944 from his brother Sir Maynard Francis Colchester-Wemyss (1872-1954). Educated at Marlborough. 1914 sailed as Adjutant and Paymaster with sealed orders. 1915 Chief Intelligence Officer, wounded. 1916 on General Staff in East Africa. Feb. 1917 expected back at Westbury Court after 6 years abroad, India for four years, then East Africa for two years. April 1917 sent to Salonika as second-in-Command of Regiment. June 1917 invalided home from Salonika with malaria, July in hospital. Dec 1917 awaiting new Orders. April 1918 ordered to France as Major in Royal Scots. May 1918 now Lt-Colonel in Command of 6th Source Battn. Kings Own Scottish Borders. Oct 1919 ordered with Regiment to Burmah, Stella his wife to join him later. May 1920, he led a surveying expedition on Siamese/Burmah borders including River Pakchar. July 1920 ordered to Andaman Islands. March1922 given control of Army Detention camp at Colchester. He gained the rank of Lt.-Colonel in the service of the Cameronians (Scottish Rifles). He held the office of Justice of the Peace (J.P.) Glos. [1932]. He was invested as an Officer, Order of the British Empire (O.B.E.) [1918].

The gardens were sold in 1967 to National Trust. Stella sold Westbury Court to Property Speculators in 1996. It was made into residential home and retirement bungalows built.

SOURCE: National trust Gloucestershire. **Taken from Landed Gentry. Burks Landed Gentry. *Irish Marriages 1845-1958, John M Colchester-Wemyss Registration year 1909, Registration district Celbridge, County Dublin, Kildare, Meath, Country Ireland National Trust Colchester.*

EDWARD JOHN HUGO COLCHESTER WEMYSS

Last of male HEIR of the Colchester Wemys

Edward was b..16 Feb 1910 Wendover Cheltenham Gloucester's. 20 Feb 1974. **Married** 1938 Frances Elizabeth_____ 23 Nov 1919.d. 23 Dec 2004 Wendover Cheltenham Gloucester. Chief of police -Served in Jamaica, Superintendent, British Solomon Islands Pro- rectorate Police Force. Superintendent of Police Barbados. Educated Melvern. Edward was associated with The Marconi Company Limited-automotive Division, Mamable [?] House, Great Baddow. Edward John & Frances Elizabeth Children 2 daughters one died unmarried and the other had a daughter.

Passenger Lists Leaving UK 1890-1960 E J H Colchester-Wemyss, Age 42, Birth year 1910, Marital status M, Occupation, Departure port London, Destination port, Sydney. John Hugo Edward Colchester Wemyss departed Hawaii, United States, arrived Honolulu, 1900-1953 Immigration & Emigration.

Letter from Edward John Hugo Colchester Wemyss

Dear Mr Colchester

I return herewith the Colchester Saga. I am sorry that I have not done so before. I took it down to Gloucestershire and showed it to my mother, who was very interested in it. I went, whilst I was there, to see the Wilderness which was as you probably know the hunting lodge of Sir Duncombe Colchester, & was incidentally [where] my father was born. My Grandfather sold it when he rebuilt & went to live at Westbury Court. The Wilderness has now been turned into a college for further education & they propose to remake the original Gardens. From the point of view of the Colchester Saga. My grandfather, Maynard Colchester-Wemyss was probably the only person ever to have been chairman of the Gloucestershire County Council and Chief Constable of Gloucestershire at the same time. This was during the 1914-18 war, when he told the then Chief Constable who wanted to go back into the army, by all means do so, and that he would do his job for him, whilst he was away. We also have I think probably a record in the order of the British Empire: Grandfather Maynard CBE, Eldest son Francis Maynard KBE, Youngest son Maurice OBE, Grandson Hugo OBE, Daughter in law Stella Wyndham MBE, Grandson & wife MBE,

Again, very many thanks. I leave here on Monday for the Lincs Division, Yours sincerely Hugo Colchester Wemyss.

SOURCE: *Giles Colchester. *National trust Gloucestershire*

Tithe Survey. The earliest reference to the surname was in the Hearth, Money (Tax) Rolls of 1622—James Wemys (sic) townland of Danesfort.

DESCENDANTS OF ROBERT WEMYSS

Given by kind permission by Robert Wemys Thomastown, Kilkenny Research.

Birth ROBERT WEMYSS on 3rd August 1882, parents were Robert and Ellen, his baptism was on 6th August 1882. Marriage of ROBERT and ELLEN was noted in civil records from Thomastown District,6th February 1879. _____We sought death record of this Robert and noted it on 19th October 1907 from Thomastown District as follows: 19th October 1907, Robert Wemyss, married 50 years, labourer, Jerpoint Abbey. Death reported by Ellen Wemyss, who was present at death. *Source: Thomastown District Death Register, no.12. p58 Office of Co. Clinic Kilkenny.*

Civil Parish of Danesfort: The Census of Population 1901 returns included one ROBERT WIMS (sic) resident in Jerpoint Abbey townland, there were ten persons in his household.

Extracts of marriage and baptism from the Civil District of Thomastown, Co. Kilkenny

Robert Weymes Married: Ellen Kavanagh, Marriage date: 6th February 1879, Witnesses: John Kelly & Ellen Forrestal. Husbands Residence: Thomastown, Occupation: Civil Servant.

Roberts Father: **John Wemyss/gentleman,** Wife's Residence: Jerpoint, father: Thomas Kavanagh/Labourer. Note: (Ages given as full). Source: Thomastown District Register 4 page 110.

There was no ecclesiastical record of marriage noted but the following baptisms were noted to them:

JOHN: Birth date: 13th June 1881, Baptism date: l4th June 1881, Sponsors: John Cody & Ellen Forrestal, Residence: Jerpoint

ROBERT: Birth date: 3rd August 1882, Baptism date: 6th August 1882, Sponsors: Anne Byrne (Sp2 not recorded). Residence: Jerpoint

MARGARET: Baptism date: l8th May 1884 Sponsors: Patrick Cullen & Elizabeth Spellane, Residence: Jerpoint

JAMES: Birth date: 8th November 1886, Baptism date: 9th November 1886, Sponsors: Edward Walsh & Mary Walsh, Residence: Logan Street.

THOMAS: Birth date: 25th April 1893, Baptism date: 27th April 1893, Sponsors: John Byrne & Mary Anne Walsh, Residence: Jerpoint.

Source: Thomastown Catholic Parish Records/register 3 pages 284,289,295,306. Register 4 pages 12,39,49. *Kilkenny Archaeological Society . Note: Records are transcribed as they appear in the register, hence variation in the spelling.* SOURCE: Picture Kilfane Glen & Waterfall @KilfaneGlenWaterfall Park

ROBERT WEMYS

(Given by Bob Wemyss)

Generation No. 1

1. ROBERT1 WEMYSS was born 1847, and died 1907. He married ELLEN Kavanagh in 1879 Thomastown Kilkenny. She was born Abt. 1855 in Thomastown Kilkenny.

Children of **ROBERT WEMYSS and ELLEN** is:

2.   John1 b.13 Jun 1881
ii. ROBERT 2 WEMYSS, b. 03 Aug 1882. d. Thomastown Kilkenny*.
iii.   Margaret b. 18 May 1884
iv.   James b. 08 Nov 1886, Logan Street
v.   Ellen b. 16 Mar 1889, Logan Street
vi.   Catherine b. 18 Mar 1892 Maudlin Street
vii.   Thomas b. 25 Apr 1893 Jerpoint.

Source: Thomastown Catholic Parish Register/Records 3&4

Generation No. 2

2. ROBERT 2 WEMYSS (ROBERT1) was born 1882, and died in Thomastown Kilkenny. He married ANNIE MONOGUE 1. She was born Abt. 1880.

Children of **ROBERT WEMYSS and ANNIE MONOGUE** are:

i.   Robert 3 b.1912 d.1984
ii.   ANTHONY 3 WEMYSS, b. Abt. 1920; d. November 2, 1993, Ash rd. Kingsmeadow Kilkenny. Worked as a chief.
iii   PATRICK Francis WEMYSS. Died in England.
iv.   Joseph Wemyss served in UK forces during WW2
v.   Thomas Wemyss. Worked on the railways, served in UK forces during WW2
vi.   John2 Wemyss Worked as a farmer.

3 Robert3 Wemyss (Robert2) was born in 1912 and died in 1984. He married Mary Kelly; she was born in 1918. Children of Robert 3 and Mary had 4 boys and three girls.

NOTE TC: **OTHER HISTORY Wemyss** Thomastown.

Roberts family descended from **MARY NOLAN** b.abt 1830, d.1905 Patrick street Kilkenny unmarried. Mary had a son Robert Wemyss b. 1847 d. 19 Oct 1907 Thomastown Kilkenny. On the certificate it says father John Wemyss gentleman. By all account Mary lived an impoverished existence, on a census said a damaged roof of her house, her son Robert was present at her death.

Civil Service Evidences of Age Collection - CSEA - 192-0103.jpg

Mary Nolan of Knocktopher seamstress. Do solemnly declare that Robert Wemys now seeking to be a rural port messenger is my son and that he was born in Patrick street Kilkenny on the eight day of March 1847_____baptised by Reve Hamberry. Declaration 20th December 1867.

IRISH DEATH 1864- 1958: Robert Weyms age at death 50, Birth year 1857, Registered Oct - Dec 1907, Registration district, Thomastown Volume 4, Page 447 Kilkenny Ireland. SOURCE: record set: Ireland, 19th Century Directories, Title: Thom's Irish Almanac 1877, Copyright: Royal Irish Academy

THOMAS WEYMES & ANNE WHALEY Parents *unknown.*

Thomas Weymes b.abt. 1790 d.1827 Kingscourt Cavan. Thomas in *1808* is written as a parishioner in the Kingscourt, Cavan Church of Ireland. Thomas married Anne Whaley about 1810. Following Thomas death, she went to Kingston Canada with her five children, four boys and a girl, where she died the following September. Her children Margaret, Thomas, James, were members of the Wellington Street Methodist Church, of which James was one of the trustees.

Francis Weymes b. 1807 Kingscourt Cavan Ireland, d. 27 Dec 1866 Kingston Ontario Canada. Wife Elizabeth Peterson. Children Robert and Annie Elizabeth. **Robert Weymes** b.1811 d.25 Jan 1855 Ontario Canada.

James Weymes -The Lightning Flash. James b. May 16th, 1815, in Kingscourt, Cavan, Ireland, d.15 Dec 1889 in Brantford Ontario Canada. James was a Police Magistrate, and an old pioneer resident of Brantford. When James was twenty-one, he parted with his brother, who was a City Surveyor, and went west to Toronto, which was a smaller place than Kingston at that time, and taking a boat there to Hamilton, arrived in Brantford, August 30th, 1836. He once tossed a penny to see whether he would go to London or remain in Brantford, and he remained in Bradford and had only one dollar and fifty cents on his arrival here. He worked with the wealthiest man in Bradford Mr. A. Huntington, and received a good business education. James then entered into the sale and manufacture of boots and shoes near the Iron Bridge, and continued working at his trade about 1857.

Magistrate About 1860 he retired from active business and in 1858 was appointed Magistrate and Police Magistrate in 1865, holding that position for a number of years. He was councillor for two or three years, and also Reeve and Deputy Reeve, and subsequently Mayor for three terms. He was deeply involved in improving the city, and he built sixteen residences and one business block on Colborne Street.

Chief of the Six Nations Indians for twenty-two years he had been a chief of the Six Nations Indians, and was held in high esteem by them. They came to him for advice and counsel; and they had implicit confidence in his judgment. When a misunderstanding takes place between husband and wife, the woman would immediately apply to his worship. After admonishing both, setting forth the duty the one owes to the other, reconciliation would take place, and the results are many happy families on the reserve through his instrumentality. In 1860 he was called Rugystondya: by interpretation, The Lightning Flash.

Married -James Weymes was married in 1840 to Mary O'Neill, a native of Ireland. They had seven children; Mary died in August 1863. He married again in 1865 to Mary Gray, a native of Ireland, and two children were born of this union. His children were Charles, Mary, Thomas, James.

Meath Ireland Parish Records Parish of Ennis keen, County Meath Ireland 1802 1802 saw Bishop Thomas Lewis O'Beirne instruct his registrars to obtain from the clergy, accurate written lists of their parishioners, with particulars of the family members. **Thomas Weymes Kingscourt 1802.** SOURCE: https://sites.rootsweb.com/~irlmea2/Church/parish_of_enniskeen.htm

DONEGAL WEYMES

John Weymes b.1762, was a Donegal Fisherman. He was tried at Carrickfergus Co Antrim in 1823 and sentenced to deportation for life. He was put aboard the Castle Forbes, which berthed on 20th January 1824. He was sent to Windsor-source state records of New South Wales.

Transcribed from the Parish Registers- Transcribed from the Parish Registers as written. Variants spelling of the surname possibly these are all Scottish. There is no further record of any marriage or births for them in any records, and on checking with the Ulster Museum in Omagh who have records of emigrants to USA there is no reference to Wemyss, so they must have returned to Scotland, moved to another county or died out.

Clondavaddog COI -**Rachel Weyms**. Date of Christening 31 October 1796, Father: John Weyms Mother: Isabella McDonnel

Tullyaughnish COI -**Isabella Weymss**. Date of Christening 28 September 1810, Father: John Wemyss Mother: Isabella (surname not recorded)

Ramelton Third Presbyterian Church -**James Wamys** b.24 September 1840, Christening 24 January 1841, Father: **John Wamys** Mother: Sarah Russel

Letterkenny First Presbyterian Church- **Matilda Wemyss** b. 2 July 1849 Christening 5 March 1850, Father; **John Wemyss** Mother: Sarah Russel

Sarah Agnes Weymss b. 27 January 1851 Christening 25 June 1851, Father: **John Weymss** Mother: Sarah Russel

Ramelton Third Presbyterian Church- Robert Wayms Christening 7 November 1842, Father: John Wayms Mother: Sarah Stewart

Lower Sackville Street and the Pillar depicted by William Henry Bartlett in the early 1840s-*SOURCE: Wiki*

Wemys in Dublin Prisons: Weymes/Wemys who spent time as a guest of the state in the prisons of Mountjoy, Kilmainham and Grangegorman. The earliest record is that of a **John Weymes** a native of county Antrim who is shown as been registered in Kilmainham on 28th June 1823, he was 50 years of age and was to be deported. On the 20th November 1838 Elizabeth Wemes age 60 years was a guest in Grangegorman prison. **Patrick Weymes** *(see Offaly)* is registered as being admitted to Kilmainham on 12th April 1841, he was age 27. He was awaiting deportation; however, his sentence was reduced to 6 months on appeal. In 1921 a **Thomas Weymes** was sentenced for 15 years to Mountjoy for robbery.

Garda Síochána A number of Wemyss have served at various garda stations in Dublin since the foundation of the state, and from 1968 to 1972 the commissionaire of the force Michael Wymes was resident in headquarters in the Phoenix Park.

BMD CHURCH OF IRELAND DUBLIN 1700

St Paul Dublin COI) Burial of **HENRY WEMYS** of N/R on 25 February **1748**

THOMAS WEYMES Children – St Audoen's Dublin (COI)

*JAMES WEYMS of N/R (Father: Thomas), Baptism of 9 January **1791** St Werburg Dublin (COI)*

JAMES WEYMS of Essex St (Father: Thomas), N/R Baptism of October **1792**

JAMES & CATHERINE WEYMES Children

WILLIAM WYMES of (Father: James), St Catherine's Dublin (COI) Baptism of 29 September **1794**.

*JAMES WEYMS of Thomas St (Father: James), Baptism of 4 February **1797**.*

JAMES WEMYS of N/R (Father: James), Baptism 20 November **1798**.

BMD CHURCH OF IRELAND DUBLIN 1800

JOHN EDMOND WAMES of 2 SWIFTS ROW (Father: **John**), St Marys Dublin (COI) Baptism 8 October **1843**

MARY ELLEN WEYMES of 2 Camac place Dolphins Barn, St Catherine's Dublin (COI) Burial of 20 March **1879** (Age 8 Years).

Parish Donnybrook Dublin Burial Record **John Wim's** Date of Death: 13 May **1878**, Age: 75 Donnybrook Dublin (COI).

*HUGH EVELYN WEYMES of 6 Brandon Terrace Basin Lane. Burial St Catherine's Dublin (COI), 30 January **1880** (Age 7 Months).*

ANNA WEMS- Baptism 12 Jun **1767,** Father-Jacobi **(James)Wems**, Mother Marie Wems, Witnesses Andrew Cunaghan & Marie Dillion

CATHERA WEMYS of N/R, St Nicolas Dublin (RC) Baptism of 15 February **1767,** Father: **ELIAE (Elia)WEMYS**, Mother CATHEA, Sponsor GILBERTUS RELLY, MARIA DOWDAL

MARGT WYMES SS. Michael & John Dublin (RC) Baptism of **1788,** Father, **MICHAEL WYMES**, Mother MARY [WHYTE], Sponsors PAT GRIFFIN, CELIA WYMES (? Sligo tree)

BMD ROMAN CATHOLIC CHURCH 1800

JOSEPH ANTHONY WEYMAS of Holles St Hospital Dublin (Father: **William**) (Mother: Margaret Quinn), St Andrews Dublin (RC) Baptism of **1896,** Sponsors: John Burke Dillon/ Margaret Murphy

Dublin census of 1851: Thomas Wemys 3. Francis St Court St. Nicholas Without.

BMD GALWAY 1800

1008. **Luke Weyms**, Achonry Tuam Galway Baptism Jan 14, **1827**. (FHL film 256,560)

Michael Weyms, Mary Murphy b.abt. 1775 married 24 Sep 1800. St Pauls Dublin Arran Quay (RC)c

SOURCE: *Series description Crossle genealogical abstracts and miscellaneous military records, Extracts from Army Returns 7 Vols 1787, Archive National Archives of Ireland, Repository National Library of Ireland. Church Burial Record. Sackville St picture Wiki*

SLIGO WEMYS

This Chapter is Michael Weymes work and his tree has no connection to the Danesfort or Westmeath line.

Michael Weymes -My grandfather was born in Carrowgilpatrick near Skreen in Co. Sligo in 1868. He came as an RIC policeman to Co. Westmeath, and married and settled near Delvin.

My family tree is now complete and as a result of that great experience I have joined with my colleague and friend Theresa (we are not related except in spirit) to use this webpage to help, assist, and encourage all the Weymes and variants who may be contemplating writing up their family history. We have oceans of research filed if you don't find what you are looking for please contact us, we are happy to do look ups.

Picture Michael Weymes researcher

WEYMES EARLIEST RECORDS SLIGO

The earliest written reference to Weymes in Ireland is recorded in Volume two of the Calendar of Justiciary Rolls page 185-6. It concerns a **Ralphy Wymes** who had come before a baronial court in Nobber in Co. Meath in 1306. However, Co. Sligo can claim to be the home of the Weymes in Ireland. During the period 1897 to 1901 there were 340-recorded births and 140 marriages of variant Weymes in the county. Sligo is also unique in that more variants of the surname are recorded there than in any other county. Although there is no verifiable evidence as to where the Sligo Weymes came from it is most probable that they were originally working-class Scottish Protestant settlers who came in through Sligo port.

Home of the Wymes in Sligo

The 'home of the Wymes' in Sligo was and probably still is the area around Carns, Bunduff, Cliffoney and Moneygold where the name is usually spelled Wymbs or Wimbs and the families are sometimes referred to as the 'The Bunduff Wymbs'. There are still a number of Wymbs families in the area. In the Ballymote area the spelling of the surname is usually Wims. The main bases of the name in this area are Rathdooneymore.

The parish of Skreen/Dromard parish is the home parish of Michael Weymes (one of the authors) and his ancestors, however there are no family members in the area to day; the last one to live their Martin died in 1933.

Also born in Lisnarawer near Skreen in Co. Sligo was Michael Wymes the Commissioner of the Garda from 1968 to 1972. His father Michael together with two of his brother, John and Joseph joined the RIC and were posted respectively to Louth and Westmeath. The descendants of these three brothers are now to be found in many Irish counties, as well as the USA, England and Scotland.

Sligo Weymes abroad

Many of the Weymes recorded in other counties of Ireland and indeed across the world have ancestral roots in Sligo. Henry Wymbs who hosts a popular radio show each Sunday on Radio Oxford is also a Sligo native. Other well-known Sligo Weymes are the Wim's from the Rathdooney area of Ballymote. Many of these served the Catholic Church as priests and nuns both at home and abroad. In later articles we intend to write in more detail about many of the variant Weymes who made significant contributions to the world we live in.

The Sligo Wymes

From the years 1799 to 1901 County Sligo had the highest number of Wymes in Ireland. Records show that there were in excess of 350 births and 141 marriages of the surname during this period. The Tithe Applotment of 1823/1828 has 30 entries for the surname and the Griffith Valuation of 1858 has the name recorded 26 times. The main spellings of the surname in Sligo during this period are as follows. In the Ahamlish area it was Wems, Wims, Wymbs and Wimbs. In Drumcliff the surname was Wemyss and Wymbs. Skreen and Dromard has the name recorded as Wymes, Wyms and Wims, whereas in Easkey it was Wyms. Ballisodare used the Wims and Wimsey spelling.

Cloonacool and Curry used Weymes, Wimsey, and Wymsey. In Ballymote the spelling was Wims, and Emlafad and Kilmorgan used the Wimsey and Wymms version. In Sligo town it was Weymes and Wyms. Of course, it was not unusual to find the same families spelled in a different version that the one recorded on their birth certificate. Indeed, the rare instances where members of the same family are recorded under many variants of the spelling.

In the Shadow of Benbulben

There are a number of references to Wymbs in Joe McGowans book, 'In the Shadow of Benbulben'. There are also photographs that include Wymbs'. The father of the Garda Commissioner Michael Wymes (1968/1972) also named Michael was born in Lisnarawer, Skreen, Co. Sligo. Research continues in the Sligo Wymes to endeavour to establish when and where in Sligo it first became established.

Three interesting Stories on the Weymes of Sligo

On 3rd October 1811 the Alknomac departed from Sligo port with 79 passengers. Listed as a passenger is a James Wymbs. The ship ran aground at Martha?s Vineyard on the night of 13th December 1811. All of the crew and passengers were saved and stayed in the old town for nine days. The captain hired a sloop to take the passengers on to New York but it was driven ashore near Newport Rhode Island on 24th December 1811. Again, all were saved and they made the remainder of the journey by land to New York. They arrived there on 18th January 1812.

Listings of Sligo Wymes in shippings

There are many listings of Sligo Wymes in shipping's manifests and in Ellis Island records and also in the 1881 English Census. The following is an example: -On 26th April the ship Jefferson sailed from Sligo to New York and listed on the passenger manifest are Thomas Wymbs age 36 years and his brother Michael Wymbs age 30 years both dealers from Carns in Sligo.

Faulkner's Journal

Sligo 22nd March 1793; Wymms who had been confined in the jail for cow stealing and who had affected his escape by undermining the prison wall in company with Tunny, were retaken the following day, put on trial and found guilty. Sligo 26th March 1793: On Friday the assizes ended when the case of Wymms who was found guilty the previous day was brought up to receive the death

sentence. The grand jury recommended him as an object of mercy and the humane judge promised to recommend him as such on his return to Dublin.

County Sligo Weymes Records

Between 1797 and 1901 there were in excess of 340 births and 130 plus marriages recorded for the Weymes surname and its variants in Co. Sligo, Ireland. These records are presented in chronological form, and they should be of benefit to anybody researching the Weymes surname and its variants.

Later we intend to publish on this website all of the Griffith Valuation, Tithe Applotment, and 1901 Irish Census records that pertain to the variant Weymes who lived in County.

The Sligo Wymes

From the years 1799 to 1901 County Sligo had the highest number of Wymes in Ireland. Records show that there were in excess of 350 births and 141 marriages of the surname during this period. The Tithe Applotment of 1823/1828 has 30 entries for the surname and the Griffith Valuation of 1858 has the name recorded 26 times. The main spellings of the surname in Sligo during this period are as follows.

In the Ahamlish area it was Wems, Wims, Wymbs and Wimbs. In Drumcliff the surname was Wemyss and Wymbs. Skreen and Dromard has the name recorded as Wymes, Wyms and Wims, whereas in Easkey it was Wyms. Ballisodare used the Wims and Wimsey spelling. Cloonacool and Curry used Weymes, Wimsey, and Wymsey. In Ballymote the spelling was Wims, and Emlafad and Kilmorgan used the Wimsey and Wymms version. In Sligo town it was Weymes and Wyms.

Of course, it was not unusual to find the same families spelled in a different version that the one recorded on their birth certificate. Indeed, the rare instances where members of the same family are recorded under many variants of the spelling.

References to the Sligo Wymes

Here are a number of references to the Sligo Wymes that may be of interest. On 26th April the ship Jefferson sailed from Sligo to New York and listed on the passenger manifest are Thomas Wymbs age 36 years and his brother Michael Wymbs age 30 years both dealers from Carns in Sligo.On 3rd October 1811 the Alknomac departed from Sligo port with 79 passengers. Listed on the passenger is a James Wymbs. The ship ran aground at Martha's Vineyard on the night of 13th December 1811. All of the crew and passengers were saved and stayed in the old town for nine days. The captain hired a sloop to take the passengers on to New York but it was driven ashore near Newport Rhode Island on 24th December 1811. Again, all were saved and the made the remainder of the journey by land to New York. They arrived there on 18th January 1812.

Sligo Wymes' in shipping's manifests

There are many listings of Sligo Wymes' in shipping's manifests and in Ellis Island records and also in the1881 English Census. Again, some of these can be had by contacting the email address listed

above. There are a number of references to Wymbs in Joe McGowans book, 'In the Shadow of Benbulben'. There are also photographs that include Wymbs'. The father of the Garda Commissioner Michael Wymes (1968/1972) also named Michael was born in Lisnarawer, Skreen, Co. Sligo. Research continues in the Sligo Wymes to endeavour to establish when and where in Sligo it first became established. SOURCE: *Descendants of John WYMES -http://homepage.eircom.net/~wemyssr1/*

Thomas Weymes *Parents from Sligo -* Information taken from Ireland Census 1911

Thomas Weymes Born 1868 Sligo Died possibly 1944 Mullingar. **Married** June 1895 Kinnigad Westmeath, **Mary Reilly** Born 1875 Died unknown. Had 9 children 7 living.

Census 1901

In the 1901 Census Thomas Weymes was living in 3 Holihans lane as a carpenter not there in 1911 census. they are listed as WYMS. Also, Mary, James, Margaret, and Mary Reilly. (Mary Reilly born 1836 Westmeath Widow.)

Census 1902

Living in 3 Holihans lane as a carpenter

Picture Pat and Mary Weymes 1938

Census 1911

In the census returns of 1911, same family living in 38 Bishopgate St. They are listed as follows: Thomas (carpenter) Mary, John, Elizabeth, James, Margaret, Thomas, Anthony, Gerrard; also, William Plunkett and Mary Reilly.

Children All born at 38 Bishopgate St Mullingar, Westmeath

Census 1911 Living at 38 Bishopgate St. They are listed as follows: Thomas (carpenter) Mary, John, Elizabeth, James, Margaret, Thomas, Anthony, Gerard; also, William Plunkett and Mary Reilly.

Entitled to Vote List 1936 Weymes found in the list of Electors in the Mullingar Register for 1936/37 Thomas, Mary, John and Lizzie lived in Bishopgate Street.

Entitled to Vote List 1937 There were the following Weymes listed as being resident in Bishopgate St, Mullingar. Thomas, Mary, Anthony, John and Lizze.

Thomas Joseph Weymes & Mary Reilly Children

Margaret Weymes Born 1898 3 Holihans lane Westmeath

Married Patrick Kenny in 1919 still in Mullingar, they then moved to Dublin and then Liverpool in the 1920's - with all their children. Most of the family are still in the Liverpool area.

Mary Weymes (Taken from parish register Kinnegad) Born abt 1898 3 Holihans lane Westmeath. Died unknown.

Elizabeth Weymes 1908 Died unknown.

Thomas Weymes & Mary Reilly *children*

James Weymes 11 Nov 1896 3 Holihans lane Westmeath Died unknown.

(John) Thomas Weymes (Tommy)Born 1902

Gerrard Weymes 1910, 3 Holihans lane Westmeath. Died -Unknown

Anthony Weymes Born 1906 3 Holihans lane Westmeath Died 19 May 1951, Bishopgate Mullingar Westmeath

John Joseph Weymes Born about 1904, 3 Holihans lane Westmeath, Death unknown.

Church Baptism Record

Name: **James Weimes** Date of Baptism / Birth: 11/11/1896

Address: Not Recorded Parish / District: MULLINGAR, Denomination: Roman Catholic

John Thomas Weymes & Elizabeth Lily Briody

Married Elizabeth Briody born about 1910 Died 28th November 2007,

Patrick Joseph Weymes-Born 1925,38 Bishopgate St Mullingar

Jack (John) Weymes Born about 1927 38 Bishopgate St Mullingar

THE GREAT IRISH FAMINE IN SLIGO

Summary of Various Reports and Comments

Charles K. O'Hara was chairman of the Co. Sligo Board of guardians in 1846/47. Mr. Crichton, Somerton, Ballymote noted the crop failure in 1846 was not bad. 8/3/1846...Mr. Cooper of Markree saw a cloud fall over the land which gave notice of the impending corp failure.

Autumn of 1846: One landlord evicted 30 families affecting some 150 individuals. Feb. 8, 1847: Thousands die from starvation.

The Sligo workhouse had become a pesthouse, and was abandoned by the guardians, in terror. Dysentery was the main killer of the young. May 1847: Sligo is a plague spot; disease in every street. Sligo was one of the Indian corns out spots. Its port was used to receive the shipments of this grain directly from America. By May 1846, Co. Sligo had joined 17 other counties in request for public works projects. In 1845, Co. Sligo had only one fever hospital. At one point in 1846, some 100 individuals were reported to have marched through the streets of Sligo Town with loaves of bread fixed on poles.

When the local guardians promised to give them both work and increased wages, the crowd dispersed. In April 1846, Sir Robert Palmer, an absentee landlord, from Co. Sligo was attacked for his luxurious living, while people died of starvation on the hovels of his estate. In 1847, Sligo was listed with many other Poor Law Unions of the West as being, distressed.

This meant that the areas, so named, required external financial assistance to alleviate the suffering. The additional aid seems to have been insufficient as the Sligo Union, like many others in the West, was the scene of crowds gathering regularly at the meetings of the guardians and vice-guardians; and the troops had to regularly disperse these people. February 25, 1847-The Sligo Champion - The coroner is still busily engaged in this country; The people are still dying of hunger, while the stores of the Commissary General are full of corn, but political economy prohibits it being touched. The following inquests were held during the week on the bodies of:

Francis Kelley, Catherine Hoy, Maurice Conroy, John Caucurn, James Kilmartin, Michael Tighe,

Patrick Conolan, Michael Hare. The verdict in every instance was 'died of starvation'

October 30, 1846...Mr. Dobree a seasoned and unsentimental Commission officer, wrote that in spite of an order to stop giving out supplies; it was quite out of his power to shut his stores altogether against a little relief for the poor people, and he did not intend to do so, without a positive order to that effect. When told he must close, he retorted on November 3, that in spite of the most harassing applications he had screwed them down to 23 tons for his enormous district last week. He had extracted a solemn pledge from relief committees to distribute only to those who had absolutely no food of any kind.

Sligo was not a grain-growing country, and it was useless to tell the people to consume their own supplies. When a concoction called 'soup' was being used to feed the people. Mr. Dobree noted: it was 'no working food for people accustomed to 14 lbs. of potatoes daily'. By late January 1847, highly respected inhabitants, of Liverpool, England, were asking for relief from the influx of Irish paupers.

Thousands had left Ireland with the intention of seeking help in that English city. On February 3rd, a member of the House of Lords was reporting of the arrival of over 3000 since the 1st of that month; 701 from Co. Sligo. While it was expected that the soup kitchen scheme would alleviate some of the problem, boilers for making soup had not arrived in Sligo even as late as April of 1847.

On October 20, 1847, a Mr.T.N. Redington, a government official, notified his superior that the Poor Law rates would not, because they could not, be collected, in Co. Sligo. It was also noted by Lord Sligo that 'public funds must feed our poor or they must die, and how are these funds to be produced. August 1, 1847 found, outside of the fever hospital, three wretched creatures, who were groaning on mats on the other side of the road because they could not be taken in. As things worsened, the anger of the people turned to their landlords.

Many of the gentry left the country in fear. By December 1847, a sub-inspector of police had a list of at least 10 landlords in Leitrim and Sligo, who were marked men, their lives are not worth a sheet of paper. Mid-summer 1848 found the disease on the potato crop was still present. Throughout the west, including Co. Sligo, the blight was the same as in 1846. In October, the British government stopped relief supplies and the people who were still alive realised they had to emigrate to survive. These emigrants were farmers; of a good class; and the country needed them. In Sligo and Donegal, a Poor Law inspector reported that the better, more energetic farmers are selling up and going. As early as the autumn of 1845, blight was in Ireland.

The Sligo Champion noted the existence of the problem elsewhere; and noted on October 25th, it is with deepest regret we find ourselves compelled to confirm the rumour of the failure potato crop in this county, a decay in the chief, we may say the only article of food of the peasant. In November, chairman Major O'Hara of the Sligo workhouse Guardians, indicated that no one can say his crop is safe. In January 1846, O'Hara was planning public road projects and was to add many workers to his estate staff in the summer. An August issue of the Sligo Journal noted that O'Hara had employed over 300 men, daily, during the previous six months and had provided liberal amounts of oatmeal for them.

Indian meal arrived in Sligo in March 1846 but did not go on sale until May. While the 1845-46 famine was bad, some potatoes were saved for planting in the spring. By August 1st, the Champion was reporting blight and a week later O'Hara said 'last year was a season of plenty compared to what the present is likely to turn out'. In September, 20,000 pounds was granted for relief projects in the county.

However, by November, the workhouse had 1227 inmates and was closed. Between October and December 1846, over 3000 had emigrated to America from Sligo. Throughout black 1847 things were horrible as noted in the previous extracts.

This account deals mostly with local parish events for that period. The Sligo Champion also noted the emigration of another 3000 from Sligo Port between January and May of 1847.

A letter to the Journal in December 1847 praised O'Hara for distributing clothes, coats, trousers, petticoats, and blankets to more than two hundred families on his estate and supplying them with bread, beef and mutton.

In January 1848, the Champion noted, 'the condition of the poor in Sligo and neighbourhood is truly frightful'. The next month 'the misery which the people are now enduring beggars all description', and in March, 'many deaths will take place from absolute want'.

The Sligo workhouse, like all such facilities, was designed to be unattractive and the poor only entered as a last resort. Sligo's building was supposed to hold 1200 so, in 1847, additional sheds were built to handle 70 more. By April 1848, the place had to be extended to house the over flow and reached a capacity of 1700.

1849 found the worst was over and only about a third of the potato crop was hit by the blight. In 1850, a new Union was created out of Sligo's Poor Law Union and set up in Tobercurry. In that area, the O'Hara family was still aiding the poor as late as 1871, even though major Charles had died and his widow, Lady Anne Charlotte was looking after the family estate.